ATTENTION DEFICIT DISORDER

A GUIDE FOR PARENTS & EDUCATORS

Attention Deficit Disorder

Helpful, Practical Information

Elaine K. McEwan

Harold Shaw Publishers
Wheaton, Illinois

Acknowledgment is made to the following for permission to reprint copyrighted material on pp. 66–69:

> The Home Situations Questionnaire is reprinted with permission of the author and publisher from Russell A. Barkley, *Attention Deficit Hyperactivity Disorder: A Handout for Diagnosis and Treatment* (New York: Guilford Publications, 1990). Copyright Guilford Publications.
>
> The ADHD Rating Scale is reprinted with permission of the author, George J. DuPaul, and the publisher, Guilford Publications. Copyright Guilford Publications.
>
> Items from the ADD-H: Comprehensive Teacher's Rating Scale (ACTeRS) are copyright © 1986, 1988, 1991 by MetriTech, Inc., 4106 Fieldstone Rd., Champaign, IL (217/398-4868). Reproduced by permission of the copyright holder. Permission has been granted for this publication only and does not extend to reproduction made from publication.
>
> The School Situations Questionnaire is reprinted with permission of the author and publisher from Russell A. Barkley, *Attention Deficit Hyperactivity Disorder: A Handout for Diagnosis and Treatment* (New York: Guilford Publications, 1990). Copyright Guilford Publications.

ISBN 0-87788-056-5

Cover designed by David LaPlaca

Edited by Esther Waldrop and Joan Guest

Library of Congress Cataloging-in-Publication Data

McEwan, Elaine K., 1941-
    Attention deficit disorder / Elaine K. McEwan.
      p. cm.
    ISBN 0-87788-056-5 (paper)
    1. Attention-deficit hyperactivity disorder—Popular works. I. Title.
RJ506.H9M424 1995
616.85'89—dc20   95-18443
                                       CIP

02 01 00 99 98

10 9 8 7 6 5

Contents

INTRODUCTION:
The Author's Story

My mother didn't take me to the church nursery or send me to Sunday school when I was very small, because she was too embarrassed by my "wild" behavior. Rumor had it at church that I was "retarded," and my parents were keeping me in hiding. I drove the teacher in my one-room schoolhouse classroom to distraction with my constant interruptions and hyperactivity. But she always managed to couch her report-card comments positively. "Elaine needs a hobby to keep her occupied." "Elaine's energy needs to be channeled into positive interests." She stopped short of asking me to stop bugging her. I was always finished first, so she put me to work helping others, even if they were older. When I moved into upper-elementary grades, my energies were put to work in administrative tasks—answering the telephone, running the mimeograph machine, grading papers for the teacher, and straightening out storage closets. These were all excellent preparation for my later administrative career.

I talked and moved nonstop—often running wildly in circles in the kitchen, pretending to be a horse, until the day I ran smack into a corner and collapsed on the floor sobbing as blood gushed out of my head. My mother was always in tears over the things I ruined . . . her new refrigerator scarred by my ice skates, her glass hurricane lamps shattered by a falling table, my aunt's antique clock smashed to bits. I left a wake of havoc and ruin.

The bows and waistlines on my dresses were always ripped out, and I sliced my thumb on the day of the big piano recital. Clumsy did not begin to describe me. I tore moldings off the garage door as I learned to back out of the narrow opening. But somehow through all of this, my parents affirmed and encouraged me.

I started working for my father in his grocery store when I was six. I stocked shelves, put potatoes in ten-pound bags, and swept the front porch. My parents kept me busy every waking hour. When my father bought a department store, I began to work there at the age of twelve—marking merchandise, stocking shelves, and waiting on customers. My confidence grew as I learned to sell overalls to farmers and fit babies for their first shoes.

In school, I learned to sit in the front of the room, keep my mouth shut, and keep my hands busy taking copious notes. Classmates knew that I literally recorded everything the teacher said—even the jokes. I started studying and organizing for exams weeks in advance. I knew my weaknesses well and learned to compensate for them. Fortunately, I had a lot of love and reinforcement along the way. I believed that I could do or be anything I wanted to be. My home was organized and structured. Expectations were high and nonsense was not tolerated. Today, I might be diagnosed as having ADHD—Attention Deficit Hyperactivity Disorder (with hyperactivity only). But in the late 1940s I was simply a child with a lot of energy that needed to be channeled. I learned from personal experience what children with ADHD need.

As a fifth-grade teacher in the 1960s, I provided structure, organization, expectations, good home-school communication, and lots of hands-on learning for all of my students, many of them with ADHD. When one approach didn't work, we tried another. There was no child who couldn't behave and learn in my classroom. As an elementary-school principal in the 1980s, I continued to believe that all children could learn and succeed in school. And that is the philosophy I espouse in this book. Children with ADHD can succeed at home, in school, and in the community. They can manage their difficulties. They will grow up to be successful adults who can make a positive contribution to our society. Our obligation as parents, professionals, and educators is to accept, love, and understand them and then find ways to help them succeed.

There are three assumptions I have made in the writing of this book:

- Children with ADHD have the potential to be creative, useful, productive, and successful members of society.
- There is no stereotypical child with ADHD. Each child is unique, and each combination of symptoms will vary.
- ADHD is a biologically based condition that has life-long implications.
- Children with ADHD are at risk of failure in school, social rejection, and behavioral complications unless we all work together as a team.

Some authors and researchers refer to the "ADHD child." Although the phrase "a child with ADHD" is more cumbersome, I have chosen to use it almost exclusively because, to me, it communicates an important concept. Your child, who may happen to have ADHD, is first and foremost a child, a unique and special human being. Beware of permitting professionals, educators, or society in general to define your child by his or her disability. Although I personally have a hearing impairment, I do not think of myself as a hearing-impaired person, but rather a person who happens to have a hearing impairment (among many other distinguishing descriptions). I believe the same respect should be accorded to children with ADHD. That characteristic should not define who they are or what they are capable of doing.

As you read this book, you will meet a variety of real families. Each family has one or more children with ADHD, and in some cases, one or both parents also have ADHD. I have chosen to describe the disorder, its diagnostic methods, common treatments, strategies for school success, and techniques for home management through the stories and experiences of these "real people" because they provide rich examples of the unique challenges that each child with ADHD poses. They will also provide inspiration and motivation to you to use your own creativity and energy to bring out the best in your child. The children in these families range in age from seven to twenty-nine; there are twenty-three males and five females. Many of the parents who shared their stories with me can reflect with pride on the *adult* accomplishments of their children. Others have only recently received a diagnosis of ADHD and are beginning to develop treatment plans and cope with the implications of the disorder for their family lives. Some are still struggling with unsolved problems, and others are just beginning to ask the difficult questions. To protect the anonymity of each family, pseudonyms will be used. See Appendix A for a complete list of the families and a summary description of their stories.

In the chapters ahead you will find the information and inspiration you need to help your child with ADHD. Chapter One provides an overview of ADHD, describing the range of symptoms and answering the most commonly asked questions about the disorder. Chapter Two describes how ADHD is diagnosed, and Chapter Three introduces the many professionals who can help you develop a workable treatment plan for ADHD. Chapter Four discusses the use of medications in the treatment of ADHD and assists you in making a decision about whether to use this often-controversial tool.

Chapter Five contains a wealth of information about your child's schooling: special education laws and programs; the best teachers and schools for your child; your legal rights; and successful classroom strategies for helping children with ADHD succeed in the academic world. Chapter Six moves to the home front and will show you how to develop a behavior-management and discipline plan that can make life with your child more enjoyable and less hassled. Chapter Seven includes answers to the most commonly asked questions parents have about living with a child who has ADHD. Chapter Eight addresses the family structure and reminds you of the importance of keeping your marriage and family intact while dealing with the complexities of an ADHD diagnosis. Finally, Chapter Nine summarizes what the Bible has to say to families with ADHD and offers a positive and hopeful note for the future.

1

UNDERSTANDING ATTENTION DEFICIT DISORDER

Making sense of the complex issue of Attention Deficit/Hyperactivity Disorder (ADHD) is not an easy task, especially if you're trying to parent a child whom you suspect may have the disorder or one who has already been diagnosed. Loads of different and complicated words are used, making it difficult for the layperson to read and interpret research results. Promises of interventions and cure-alls are forthcoming from every quarter. Meanwhile, life with your child threatens to engulf you like a giant undertow. As you struggle for air against the crushing waves of emotional and physical overload, you want help, reassurance, empathy, practical information, and an action plan. You will find all of that in the pages of this book.

What Is ADHD?

Perhaps you suspect that your child has ADHD. Many parents with children who have ADHD knew their children were different from the moment they brought them home from the hospital. Karen Beacon describes her daughter, Jennifer, an attractive fourteen-year-old.

From the first night home from the hospital she slept no more than twenty minutes at a time. I used to turn on the vacuum cleaner next to her crib. This finally helped her to stop crying. It was diagnosed as colic. She still has the same problems falling asleep today.

Others begin to suspect their child is different as soon as he or she becomes mobile. Kandi Rollins describes her nine-year-old son, Christopher, as an infant.

He could crawl in and out of his crib easily by eight months. He was walking at eleven months, and he's been running ever since.

Although parents may suspect their child is different in some significant ways, a definitive diagnosis of ADHD is not usually made until a child enters school. The structure and expectations of the traditional classroom frequently pose a challenge to the child with ADHD that crystallizes the frustration, anger, depression, and failure that are often a constant part of life for the child with ADHD. Symptoms that were merely annoying or even nonexistent in the comfortable home setting often become debilitating at school. Kay and John Kingman had long suspected their six-year-old son, Brett, had a problem, but it was only when his teacher began sending home reports of problems with attention in school, combined with statements from Brett that "he wasn't a good person and couldn't do anything right," that they sought professional help.

> I think the psychologist expected me to cry or something when he told us that Brett had ADHD, but it came as a relief to have someone confirm my thinking that he really did have a problem. Sometimes people would tell me it was my imagination. But I knew.

For many parents, particularly those whose children do not exhibit hyperactivity and impulsivity, problems do not crystallize until children are well into their schooling careers. Jennifer Beacon, now fourteen, was not diagnosed until she was ten. Her mother, Karen, describes the problems that led to investigating the possibility of ADHD:

> She had a very high degree of depression and anger with no external causes. Her schoolwork and concentration did not match up with her capabilities. A long conversation with a learning disabilities teacher informed me for the first time of ADHD.

Matt Harris managed to make it all the way to high school before his parents suspected ADHD. A strapping and handsome nineteen-year-old, he is about to leave for college to study radio and television. His mother, Lori, tireless in her efforts to be an advocate for Matt, left no stone unturned to help him once she suspected a problem.

> The fact that Matt might have ADHD did not occur to us. When he was a sophomore in high school (first semester), we realized that if we did not look for professional help, he might not be eligible for college. Each semester Matt

would say he was not going to get behind and was going to make the grades we all knew he was capable of making. The pattern was that first quarter he would start to get behind and have a grade of D or maybe a very low C. Then second quarter he would work very hard and receive a high B that would bring his semester grade to a C that would go onto the transcript. This pattern had been repeated many times over the years. That year we got professional help.

For some parents and even grandparents, experiencing the symptoms of ADHD in their offspring is like watching reruns on the late show. Kara, a forty-one-year-old grandmother who is homeschooling her ADHD grandchild, Joey, has ADHD herself.

I have always known I was different, and as an adult I was told that I was hyperactive. Talking to someone in a crowded room is almost an impossible task, and sitting still in church with my mind on track is a challenge to say the least. I dropped out of high school in the tenth grade because learning was always difficult, and quite frankly I hated school. More than likely I have a processing disorder to complicate my ability to focus on information.

She empathizes with her grandson's problems more readily but still finds his nonstop talking and aggressive/destructive behavior difficult to handle.

When she began to research ADHD after Jennifer was diagnosed, Karen Beacon found a family history of ADHD that had somehow remained a mystery to her until that moment.

My daughter's grandfather and his sisters have ADHD very badly. Her great grandmother suffered terribly from it, too. This is all in the same family. The outcome was a tragic, loveless home filled with anger, abuse, and great sadness. These are giant chain links that can be traced, holding their victims prisoners through the generations, from both symptoms and the ongoing effects of dysfunction.

Children with symptoms of impulsivity and problems with concentration were originally labeled as brain injured, minimally brain damaged, hyperactive, and hyperkinetic. More recent and research-based terms include Attention Deficit Disorder, Attention Deficit Disorder with Hyperactivity, Attention Deficit Hyperactivity Disorder, and Undifferentiated Attention Deficit Disorder. Authors, physicians, educators, psychologists, and researchers often use the terms interchangeably, leaving the layperson confused and wondering just what the name of this disorder really is. But the symptoms that characterize the attention deficit disorders as a group—hyperactivity, impulsivity, and inattention—remain constant. Regardless of the current label, ADHD continues to baffle, intrigue, frustrate, and fascinate parents and professionals alike.

The validity of ADHD as a bonafide disorder has been subject to scrutiny, skepticism, and even hostility in the past two decades. A 1970 book by Schrag and Divorky, *The Myth of the Hyperactive Child,* painted a grim picture of children purported to have ADHD and the medications used to treat them. The Church of Scientology conducted a legal vendetta of sorts in the mid to late 1980s, suing school boards, physicians, the American Psychiatric Association, principals, and teachers to prevent the use of Ritalin as a medication to treat children with ADHD. Alfie Kohn, a respected education writer, questioned the existence of the disorder in a 1989 *Atlantic Monthly* article. ADHD has been called "the yuppie disease of the '90s" and "a highly debatable and pseudomedical concept." But for parents of children with ADHD, the problem is very real.

Weary of hearing surreptitious and snide comments about ADHD being a "cop-out for parents and kids who can't follow the rules" or a "racket for the medical profession," parents have joyously greeted the recent news of scientific investigations that give conclusive supporting evidence that ADHD is not a figment of some frantic parent's imagination, but a real disorder, the result of physiological differences in the neurochemistry of the brain. Children with ADHD are *unable* to inhibit or direct their behavior, through no fault of their own. They are in many ways not capable of personal management and directedness. The early and pervasive onset of this disorder clearly suggests that poor parenting, poor instruction, learning disabilities, and/or any other sociological or psychological process are not the causes of ADHD.

ADHD was first described in the middle 1800s, when children who were recovering from nervous-system diseases or injuries were observed to have ADHD-like symptoms. In the early twentieth century, a lecturer to the Royal College of Physicians described a group of youngsters who were aggressive, defiant, and resistant to discipline while also having problems with attention to tasks. In the 1940s, after an outbreak of encephalitis left children with symptoms similar to those of hyperactive children, it was hypothesized that hyperactive children were brain damaged. After further research determined that hyperactive children were not brain damaged, the label was changed to

Minimal Brain Dysfunction (MBD). It was not until 1965 that a diagnostic category, called Hyperkinetic Reaction of Childhood, was first established by the American Psychiatric Association. Hyperactivity was defined not as a biological problem, but as an environmental one. This set the stage for several years of "mommy bashing," in which ADHD-like behaviors were blamed on environmental conditions and poor parenting.

However, recognition that ADHD was a legitimate neurological disorder was affirmed when the American Psychiatric Association first established the diagnosis, "Attention Deficit Disorder With or Without Hyperactivity," in 1980. (This was described in the *Diagnostic and Statistical Manual of Mental Disorders—Third Edition*, known as *DSM-III*, the "bible" for professionals involved in the diagnosis and treatment of disorders.) Still in question, however, was the importance of hyperactivity as a symptom or defining criteria, often causing frustration and confusion for parents and educators. Initially, the symptom of hyperactivity was seen as a related characteristic, one that would create subtypes of the disorder based on its presence or absence. A child could have Attention Deficit Disorder whether he or she exhibited hyperactivity or not.

However, when the revised edition of the *DSM-III* was published in 1987, the disorder was relabeled Attention Deficit-Hyperactivity Disorder, and the subtyping of "without hyperactivity" was eliminated. Researchers were still unclear as to whether the "without hyperactivity" category was a subtype of Attention Deficit-Hyperactivity Disorder or a different category altogether. So, a category of Undifferentiated Attention Deficit Disorder was created for children who displayed marked inattention but did not have signs of impulsiveness and hyperactivity. The new edition of the *Diagnostic and Statistical Manual of Mental Disorders (DSM-IV)* now describes three types of the disorder:

1. Attention Deficit/Hyperactivity Disorder, combined type, which includes symptoms of both inattention and hyperactivity/impulsivity.
2. Attention Deficit/Hyperactivity Disorder, predominantly inattentive type, which includes symptoms of inattention only or primarily.
3. Attention Deficit/Hyperactivity Disorder, predominantly hyperactive-impulsive type, which primarily includes symptoms of hyperactivity and impulsivity.

The actual diagnosis as shown in the DSM-IV is as follows:

Attention-Deficit/Hyperactivity Disorder

A. Either (1) or (2):

(1) six (or more) of the following symptoms of **inattention** have persisted for at least six months to a degree that is maladaptive and inconsistent with developmental level:

Inattention
   (a) often fails to give close attention to details or makes careless mistakes in schoolwork, work, or other activities
   (b) often has difficulty sustaining attention in tasks or play activities
   (c) often does not seem to listen when spoken to directly

(d) often does not follow through on instructions and fails to finish schoolwork, chores, or duties in the workplace (not due to oppositional behavior or failure to understand instructions)

(e) often has difficulties organizing tasks and activities

(f) often avoids, dislikes, or is reluctant to engage in tasks that require sustained mental effort (such as schoolwork or homework)

(g) often loses things necessary for tasks or activities (e.g., toys, school assignments, pencils, books, or tools)

(h) is often easily distracted by extraneous stimuli

(i) is often forgetful in daily activities

(2) six (or more) of the following symptoms of **hyperactivity-impulsivity** have persisted for at least six months to a degree that is maladaptive and inconsistent with developmental level:

Hyperactivity

(a) often fidgets with hands or feet or squirms in seat

(b) often leaves seat in classroom or in other situations in which remaining seated is expected

(c) often runs about or climbs excessively in situations where it is inappropriate (in adolescents or adults, may be limited to subjective feelings of restlessness)

(d) often has difficulty playing or engaging in leisure activities quietly

(e) is often on the go or often acts as if driven by a motor

(f) often talks excessively

Impulsivity
- (g) often blurts out answers before questions have been completed
- (h) often has difficulty awaiting turn
- (i) often interrupts or intrudes on others (e.g., butts into conversations or games)

B. Some hyperactive-impulsive or inattentive symptoms that caused impairment were present before age 7 years.

C. Some impairment from the symptoms is present in two or more settings (e.g., at school [or work] and at home).

D. There must be clear evidence of clinically significant impairment in social, academic, or occupational functioning.

E. The symptoms do not occur exclusively during the course of [other serious mental illnesses or developmental disabilities]. . . .

Attention-deficit/Hyperactivity Disorder, Combined Type if both criteria A (1) and A (2) are met for the past 6 months. . . .

Attention-deficit/Hyperactivity Disorder, Predominantly Inattentive Type if criterion A (1) is met but not criterion A (2) for past 6 months. . . .

Attention-deficit/Hyperactivity Disorder, Predominantly Hyperactive-Impulsive Type: if criterion A (2) is met but not criterion A (1) for the past 6 months.[1]

This text of the *DSM-IV* is reproduced here so that parents and teachers can be aware of what professionals use as their basis for diagnosis. For purposes of clarity and brevity in this book, we will use the acronym *ADHD* to include all three Attention Deficit Disorders. Where appropriate, in referring to specific cases, we will differentiate between the three types mentioned above—the hyperactive and inattentive child, the primarily inattentive child, or the hyperactive child who has no attention problems. For example, Jennifer Beacon's diagnosis is Attention Deficit/Hyperactivity Disorder, predominantly inattentive type. She has no symptoms of hyperactivity. Neither does Matt Harris. His mother attributes his delayed diagnosis to this lack of hyperactivity.

> It probably kept his teachers from recognizing the diagnosis earlier. We all (including Matt) knew he was capable of doing better. I guess we were waiting for him to discover how to accomplish the task consistently.

Christopher Rollins and Brett Kingman have Attention Deficit/Hyperactivity Disorder, combined type. They are hyperactive and have related behavior problems of varying degrees. Their hyperactivity and challenging behaviors stand out more readily in classroom settings, whereas children with no symptoms of hyperactivity (like Jennifer and Matt) are usually labeled "underachievers," "daydreamers," or "lazy."

ADHD is a medical syndrome rather than a disease. A syndrome is more difficult for professionals to diagnose because it must be determined if a given collection of symptoms exhibited by an individual genuinely characterize the syndrome, are merely developmental delays that will disappear over time, or are symptoms of some other problem.

The developmental nature of ADHD means that a child does not suddenly acquire it nor does he or she ever really outgrow it.

The task of diagnosing ADHD is doubly difficult because most children will exhibit symptoms at one time or another in their developmental history. What child hasn't forgotten to take out the garbage without several reminders, interrupted constantly at the dinner table, or forgotten a homework assignment? The critical difference between a child with ADHD and a child who is immature or misbehaving is the number, severity, and constancy of the symptoms. Therefore, for diagnostic purposes, it is especially important to have an agreed-upon list of symptoms, a time frame during which those symptoms must be present, and a degree to which they must affect a child's functioning in social, academic, and family settings.

The disciplines that diagnose, treat, and prescribe for children with ADHD (medicine, psychology, psychiatry, and education) are constantly expanding and changing as further research and discoveries are made about what ADHD is, what its causes might be, and how best to help children and adults who have this disorder. Parents can try to stay abreast of information by buying books, subscribing to newsletters, joining organizations, and networking in their community.

Is ADHD a Common Disorder?

ADHD is the most common reason a child is referred to a psychologist or psychiatrist. Although figures vary slightly depending on the research study, the consensus is that ADHD occurs in 3 to 5 percent of the population. About one child in twenty will have ADHD. Although the ratio of males to females diagnosed with ADHD is about 6 to 1, females are probably underidentified. Researchers suspect that the ratio is closer to 3 to 1 in actuality. Girls are more likely to be identified with the type of ADHD that does not exhibit symptoms of hyperactivity and impulsivity. Unfortunately they may be labeled simply "daydreamers," "spacey," or "social butterflies," and their problem may go undetected and untreated.

In its overview of ADHD, CH.A.D.D. (Children and Adults with Attention Deficit Disorders) states that as many as 50 percent of children with ADHD are never properly diagnosed. Studies show that ADHD occurs almost as frequently in children in Europe, Africa, Australia, and South America as it does in the United States. More cases may be diagnosed in the United States because of the quality and quantity of research being conducted in this area.

Doesn't Labeling Children Do More Harm than Good?

Many critics have raised similar concerns about the use of labels. When specific diagnostic criteria for a disorder are printed in a volume such as the *Diagnostic and Statistical Manual for Mental Disorders* (e.g., the list cited earlier), there is the danger of relying too heavily on the medical model. This model, which clearly implies the problem is within the child, may overlook the environmental variables that can play a real part in causing or maintaining some of the problem behaviors. The use of a psychiatric label, particularly in the hands of the naive or uninformed, can sometimes result in the overidentification of children. Another potential problem with labeling children lies in the possible damage to a child's self-esteem as friends, family members, and teachers view him or her as having a disorder.

Parents must use great discretion in sharing information with children who have been diagnosed with ADHD and in educating siblings, extended family members, and teachers regarding the importance of sensitivity and understanding in the application of the label.

What Causes ADHD?

The causes of ADHD have been the subject of much scrutiny and study. The most current scientific consensus is that ADHD is primarily an inherited condition. Although brain injury can cause symptoms of inattention, hyperactivity, and impulsivity, fewer then 5 percent of children with ADHD whose records have been examined give evidence of brain injury. While environmental influences such as poor parental practices or family stress may increase the severity of the disorder or interfere with a successful treatment plan, they do not *cause* ADHD.

To the beleaguered parents who were castigated by critics for their poor parenting, to children who were labeled undisciplined and lazy, and to physicians who were accused of padding their caseloads to finance trips to the continent, a landmark study by Alan Zametkin and his colleagues at the National Institute of Health in 1990 provided the collective opportunity to say, "I told you so."

Using a scanning technique called positron emission tomography (PET scan), which allows study of the brain's use of glucose, the researchers described a significant difference between usage in individuals with a history of ADHD and those without such a history.[2] Adults with ADHD utilize glucose, the brain's main energy source, at a lesser rate than do adults without ADHD. This reduced brain metabolism rate was most evident in the portion of the brain that is important for attention, handwriting, motor control, and inhibition of responses. This study, along with others, has convinced researchers that ADHD is a neurological disorder.

What Doesn't Cause ADHD?

There are many misconceptions about the causes of ADHD. We will look at some of them here.

Poor parenting. Although it's been stated earlier, this statement bears repeating. *Poor parenting doesn't cause ADHD.* Reproduce this phrase in a counted cross-stitch sampler; have it framed and hung in a prominent place in your home. Mary Ellen Corcoran, a special education teacher and mother of nine-year-old Kevin, has put it very eloquently:

> I wish I had gotten some early advice on how to deal with criticism, both overt and perceived. Parents need to feel responsible for getting the proper help and for implementing appropriate behavioral measures. However, taking too personally the comments of family, friends, and strangers at the grocery store is counterproductive. It often feels like you can't win, because even when positive programming works and the child behaves, you get snide comments about bribery. "Why can't your child just be good?" they say. Maintaining a positive view of oneself as a parent is helpful in what is perhaps the central task of parenting an ADHD child: building self-esteem in a kid who gets into lots of trouble.

You probably need no reminders that parenting a child with ADHD takes an extraordinary amount of skill. Children without ADHD are far more forgiving, tolerant, and resistant to the parenting errors we all make. But children with ADHD need vigilance, energy, patience, tolerance, love, and acceptance in far greater quantities and with much greater consistency than kids without ADHD.

Food stuffs. Food coloring, additives, preservatives, and salicylates don't cause ADHD either. In 1973, Dr. Benjamin Feingold hypothesized that these omnipresent ingredients of junk food were the cause of hyperactivity. The theory drew a lot of popular press and struck a common-sense chord in parents. Most of us were looking for a good reason to ban junk food (even though we ate chocolate chip cookies in the closet after the kids went to bed). Although Feingold reported that the additive-free diet reduced ADHD symptoms, many carefully controlled studies by independent researchers have failed to replicate his findings. This is not to say that a healthy diet is not beneficial for your child. Some children with ADHD may have allergies related to food additives. But researchers looking for a causal link between ADHD and diet did not find one.

At this point, continuing claims that dietary substances are a major contributor to ADHD cannot be taken seriously, and the burden of proof that they do must rest with those who propose such etiologies.[3]

Other unproven causes of ADHD include the following:

Sugar. In the mid-1980s, refined sugar became the suspected culprit of ADHD symptoms. Studies at the National Institute of Mental Health, the University of Iowa, and the University of Kentucky were never able to demonstrate that sugar produced significant effects on children's behavior or learning. The current scientific consensus is that sugar does not produce large or clinically important effects on children's behavior and learning and certainly does not produce the clinical syndrome of ADHD.[4]

The under/overarousal theory. Developed by Zentall and Zentall in 1983, this theory suggests that mechanisms within the brain seek a certain level of stimulation and that children with ADHD have biochemical dysfunctions that result in underarousal. Therefore, to compensate for this low arousal, the theory maintains, children are predisposed to higher levels of stimulation from external stimuli.

Elevated lead levels. At present, there is evidence to show that body lead levels are associated only to a very small degree with hyperactivity and inattention in the general population of children. Body lead is therefore unlikely to be a major cause of ADHD in children.[5]

Smoking/alcohol consumption during pregnancy. Cigarette smoking and alcohol consumption during pregnancy is greater in mothers with children having ADHD. This biological link cannot be overlooked; however, the research shows no clear causality.

Lighting. In the mid 1970s, cool white florescent lights were hypothesized to cause ADHD. No relationship was found.

Are There Varying Degrees of ADHD?

Absolutely. While some generalizations can certainly be made regarding children with ADHD, each child is a unique case. Hence the need for an intelligent, thoughtful, and experienced diagnostician when determining whether your child has ADHD. The severity of a specific case of ADHD is determined by criteria based on the number of symptoms and the degree to which the impairment affects school and social functioning. A mild case will present few, if any, symptoms in excess of those required to make the diagnosis, and the impairment demonstrated in the school or social setting will be minimal. In contrast, a severe case of ADHD will present many more symptoms than the minimum required, and significant problems will be evident in functioning at home, school, and with peers.

What Else May Cause Symptoms Like ADHD?

It is not always easy to diagnose ADHD. Numerous emotional and physiological conditions mimic ADHD and serve to confuse parents, educators, and professionals. Beware of teachers, friends, and relatives who attempt to diagnose your child. Withhold all judgments until a comprehensive examination and evaluation has been completed by a psychiatrist (for emotional and mental disorders) or a physician (for medical conditions). Some of the problems which may look like ADHD are as follows.

Oppositional defiant disorder and conduct disorder. Children with these disorders are defiant and difficult to handle. They don't follow rules or do what they are told. But unlike the child with ADHD, who may also exhibit these symptoms because he or she attempts to comply and can't, the oppositional child simply refuses. Defiance in a child with these disorders is often directed toward the mother initially. The oppositional-defiant child's behavior may lack the impulsive, uninhibited nature of the child with ADHD. These disorders are more likely to be associated with poor parenting skills or a dysfunctional family system, while ADHD is not the result of either.

Anxiety/mood disorders. Anxiety disorders cause fretful and worrisome behaviors in children. Such restlessness is not the driven or hyperactive variety that is seen in children with ADHD. Children with anxiety disorders are not usually disruptive, but are more likely to be socially withdrawn. Children with anxiety and mood disorders do not have the preschool history of hyperactivity and impulsive behavior associated with the child with ADHD. When treated with stimulant medication that is prescribed for children with ADHD, these children often become teary and agitated.

Thought disorders. Children with thought disorders demonstrate unusual thinking patterns. They may fixate on strange ideas or objects and frequently have peculiar motor mannerisms. Children with ADHD do not typically present the odd fascinations and strange aversions seen in children with thought disorders.

Depression and anxiety. A depressed child may confuse the observer with a variety of behaviors, some that mimic ADHD without hyperactivity (sadness, lethargy, lack of motivation) or symptoms that are similar to ADHD with hyperactivity (acting out, inattentiveness).

Bipolar disorder. This disorder is a manic-depressive illness and is diagnosed much less frequently than depression or ADHD. Many children with bipolar disorder show periods of hyperactivity and are also likely to be aggressive and antisocial. Stimulant medication administered to children with bipolar disorder may result in a psychotic or manic episode. Lithium is usually prescribed for these children.

The following are medical conditions that may also produce symptoms similar to ADHD.

Hypo- and hyperthyroidism. The rapid heartbeat, irritability, and overactivity that are symptoms of hypo- and hyperthyroidism can be confused with ADHD. These symptoms will be intensified if treated with stimulant medication.

Side effects of medications. Some medications given to children for other medical problems may produce symptoms that mimic ADHD. Two antiseizure medications for epilepsy, phenobarbital and Dilantin, can produce symptoms of hyperactivity and irritability. A popular asthma medication, theophylline (sold under the popular names of Theo-dur and Slo-bid) can also cause ADHD-like symptoms.

Rare genetic disorders and gross neurological impairment. There are several rare genetic disorders that have ADHD symptoms as an associated problem. They include neurofibromatosis, Tourette Syndrome, and Fragile X syndrome. Children with these disorders will, however, have many associated physical problems as well as learning difficulties. Other impairments that may result in problems with attention, impulsivity, and hyperactivity are pituitary gland dysfunctions, Fetal Alcohol Syndrome, Williams Syndrome, injury to fetus from infection or trauma, hypoxia, and premature birth.

Narcolepsy. This disorder can produce symptoms of impaired attention, memory loss, and fluctuating levels of alertness.

Sleep apnea. Children who exhibit symptoms of hyperactivity, inattentiveness, forgetfulness, or irritability, or conversely are underactive, sluggish, and excessively drowsy, may have sleep apnea rather than ADHD. Treatment for sleep apnea includes removing enlarged tonsils and adenoids or part of the soft palate and dangling uvula at the back of the throat.

Seizure disorders. Children who have short absence seizures will stare off into space and lose total awareness of their surroundings for a brief period of time. Their lack of attention is not an attention deficit disorder. They will need to be treated with anti-convulsant medication.

Allergies and upper-respiratory illness. Allergies and upper-respiratory illnesses can certainly cause a child to be less attentive and on-task in school. Unfortunately, the treatment for allergies may result in side effects that do more harm than good. Both prescription and over-the-counter drugs cause either drowsiness or agitation, both of which make concentration difficult.

Hearing or vision problems. Children who have a history of chronic ear infections frequently have a difficult time paying attention in class. Even though they have passed the brief auditory screening at school, one cannot necessarily rule out hearing problems, particularly if the child has a history of frequent ear infections. Congestion in the middle ear can be treated with antihistamines.

Mental retardation. A child whose intelligence quotient is seventy or below may be identified in schools as mentally impaired. Problems of attention to task may be the result of mental retardation. However, a mentally impaired student may well have ADHD that is not the result of retardation.

Other. In addition to the aforementioned conditions, numerous family and social conditions may create symptoms in children that might appear to be those of ADHD. These include but are not limited to: poor parenting skills; alcoholism; domestic violence; sexual, emotional, or physical abuse; neglect; lack of adult supervision (latch-key kids); dysfunctional and chaotic home environment; split family (child alternates between living with parents who are divorced); parental separation/death; transient living (many moves and lack of stability); parental conflict and lack of agreement on key issues of discipline and child management; or overly high expectations and stress due to pressure to succeed.

These problems do not cause ADHD, but they can, of course, coexist with ADHD or create behaviors similar to ADHD. When present, these conditions will intensify and exacerbate ADHD symptoms.

What Problems Frequently Exist Along with ADHD?

Children with ADHD often have associated conditions and problems that do not warrant a separate diagnosis, but that certainly complicate the diagnosis and treatment. These conditions are either a result of the symptoms of ADHD (such as the social skills deficits that grow out of the intrusive/ aggressive behavior demonstrated by some children with ADHD), or they exist alongside ADHD (such as immature motor coordination or sleep disturbances). Let me caution you, however, as you read through this laundry list of problems associated with ADHD. You may be tempted to find your child in every description. Or you may jump to the erroneous conclusion that if your child has ADHD he or she will have all of the associated problems. This is not the case.

Academic performance problems. Forty to fifty percent of children will have learning disabilities diagnosed along with ADHD, while close to ninety percent will exhibit some type of underachievement in the school setting. Children with ADHD are typically on one day and off the next. They are consistently inconsistent. Not only do these swings in performance confuse teachers and parents, but they result in the child with ADHD missing a lot of information that other children in the classroom have learned. Over time, IQ scores of children with ADHD can drop seven to fifteen points because of inability to answer the test questions.

Many children with ADHD have a difficult time deciding which hand to use for writing, and they may continue to have difficulties with letter reversals and letter sequences into late first and second grade. This makes for difficulties in spelling, reading, and math. They will depend on finger counting and mnemonic aids longer than most children will. To further confound teachers and parents, however, many children with ADHD will be extremely artistic and skilled in mechanical or motor skills outside of formal academic requirements. Their preoccupation with fantasy, imagination, and creative activities may result in elaborate building, drawing, and playing with the superheroes who happen to populate the airwaves at any given point in time. Because children with ADHD have a difficult time learning to tell time and adapting their behavior within time limits, they frequently have problems with time in academic settings (don't finish work, can't make transitions, are unaware of the passage of time).

Learning disabilities. A learning disability (as defined by federal law) is a disorder in one or more of the basic psychological processes involved in understanding or using language, spoken or written. It may manifest itself in an imperfect ability to listen, think, speak, read, write, spell, or do mathematical calculations. The term does not include children who have learning problems that are primarily the result of visual, hearing, or motor handicaps; of mental retardation; of emotional disturbance; or of environmental, cultural, or economic disadvantage. In layman's language, a learning disability means there is a major discrepancy between a child's ability and performance. While children with ADHD often have a large discrepancy between ability and performance, the reasons for this discrepancy are different. Children who are distractible and inattentive will have a hard time learning. But if a child has a learning disability in addition to ADHD, merely getting them on task will not be sufficient. They will still have a problem with learning.

Speech and language disorders. Children with ADHD are more likely than children in the general population to have speech and language delays and disorders. Problems include delayed onset of talking, linguistic reversals (reversing words in sentences), articulation problems, and expressive inability. Expressive language delays result in limited vocabularies, word-finding difficulties, vague and tangential speech, and poor grammar.

Poor problem solving and organization. Children with ADHD tend to have difficulties with complex problem-solving strategies and organizational skills. They also are less efficient in their approach to tasks that require memorization. Their executive command centers seem to shut down when confronted with a large or complex task, and they use impulsive, poorly organized, and inefficient methods to complete a task.

Emotional reactivity. Children with ADHD often have short fuses. Because of their low frustration tolerance, they are quick to get angry, demonstrate excitement out of proportion to a situation, and overreact to what is happening around them. About fifty percent of children with ADHD exhibit some symptoms of emotional immaturity, and they are also at higher risk to develop depression as they reach adolescence.

Conduct problems. Oppositional defiant behavior, temper tantrums, stubbornness, verbal hostility, and angry outbursts characterize children with conduct problems associated with their ADHD. They may be verbally or physically aggressive, lie or steal, and in some cases may even exhibit antisocial and delinquent behavior. Children with ADHD who have associated conduct problems are a challenge to their parents and teachers and need structure and discipline in large doses from a very early age.

Developmental/medical problems. Children with ADHD may also exhibit a number of medical problems:

- Delay in gross motor skills (seen in 30-60 percent of children with ADHD)

- Delay in fine motor skills like handwriting (seen in 60 percent)
- Greater incidence of enuresis—bedwetting (seen in 45 percent)
- More difficulties with toilet training
- More likely to have accidents (46 percent are described as accident prone and up to 15 percent have had at least four or more serious accidents such as broken bones)
- Greater incidence of encopresis—soiling (seen in 10 percent)
- Frequent sleep disturbances (seen in 30 percent)

Social skills deficits. Half of the children with ADHD are likely to experience difficulty making and keeping friends. Because they are often selfish and self-centered they are rejected by their peers. Their lack of awareness of social cues results in immature play and social interests and little regard for the social consequences of their behavior.

How Does Having ADHD Affect Daily Life?

Reading about the symptoms and diagnostic criteria can't begin to tell the story of how having ADHD, particularly a severe case, will affect the life of a child or adolescent. John F. Taylor, in his book *Helping Your Hyperactive/ADHD Child,* has assembled a list of mental difficulties, physical challenges, and emotional upheavals that are part of life for and with someone with ADHD.[6]

Among the mental difficulties that Taylor describes are distractibility (e.g., Jennifer Beacon put a package of popcorn into the microwave, turned it to the wrong time and power and then was distracted), confusion, faulty abstract thinking (Matt Harris, nineteen, resents taking his medication because he wants to accomplish things "on his own,

without anyone's help"), inflexibility, poor verbal skills, aim-
lessness, perceptual difficulties (stumbling, running into
things, clumsiness, and awkwardness), and inattention to
body states (not feeling hunger, not feeling pain).

Physical challenges that confront the child or adolescent
with ADHD on a daily basis are constant movement, vari-
able rates of development, food cravings, allergies and sensitivities, sleep problems, and coordination problems.

The emotional challenges that are a part of an ADHD
diagnosis can keep both child and parent on a veritable
roller coaster. Self-centeredness, impatience, recklessness,
extreme emotionalism, and a weak conscience are all characteristics that may be observed.

The lives of children with ADHD often read like a page
from a suspense novel or a frame from a bad comedy. Mary
Ellen Corcoran describes life with Kevin, now nine, when
he was a toddler.

> I first suspected that Kevin had an attention deficit when
> he was eighteen months old. He moved constantly, run-
> ning from room to room, emptying tables and drawers.
> He also didn't progress very quickly in speech, but it
> struck me that he probably heard less speech than other
> toddlers because I couldn't easily run behind him yelling,
> "Kevin, look, it's a tree." Actually from his due date (he
> was a month early) until he learned to crawl, he was only
> happy when someone else was moving him, preferably
> very quickly in a car, stroller, or baby carrier.

Mary Ellen goes on to share the challenges of living with
Kevin now that he is older.

> Presently the only problem is that I'm afraid to leave the
> boys (Kevin is the oldest of three) alone with a baby-sitter.

Once we came home to sheets tacked to the wall in the front entryway so that the boys could swing out over the descending steps. However, we have worked pretty hard on the general atmosphere, and it has improved 100 percent.

How Can a Definitive Diagnosis Be Made?

A definitive diagnosis of ADHD can only be made by a highly skilled, trained, knowledgeable, and experienced professional. That individual might be a physician, a psychiatrist, or a psychologist. Often multidisciplinary teams work together to determine a diagnosis, each working in his or her own area of expertise. A teacher or principal cannot make a diagnosis. Grandparents are out, too. Even if your neighbor down the street has a child with ADHD, she isn't qualified to pass judgment on your child. Even you, as intimately involved as you are and have been in the development of your child, cannot make a diagnosis. But you can suspect, or have an idea, or harbor a concern or deep worry. If that is the case, determine who the best professional is in your area, and call for an appointment.

Is There a Cure for ADHD?

There is no cure for ADHD. There are no medications, behavior modification programs, or psychotherapy or counseling programs that will cure ADHD. The symptoms will always be a part of your child's life, although they may change or moderate as he or she gets older. But the symptoms must always be acknowledged and managed. Medication, behavior management programs, counseling, parent training, and school interventions will in many cases diminish the impact that ADHD can have on school success, social relationships, and achievement and satisfaction as an adult.

When Lori and John Harris sent Matt off to the college of his choice after his successful completion of high school, they thought their problems were behind them. They had spent two years of hard work developing a program for him that worked.

He did well when he had his support group (parents, counselors, etc.) around him, but the change to college took us back to the beginning. We were innocent of the maintenance necessary, even after success. It was almost as if we let our guard down and the "ADHD dragon" crept back in to haunt us. Matt stopped taking his medication because he forgot for a day or two, then decided he could make it on his own. His first year of college was a disaster.

What Factors Will Positively Affect the Future?

There are several important factors that will go a long way to ensuring that your child with ADHD "makes it." Everyone has a different definition of making it, but mine is simply this: "Achieving goals (in one or more areas), being happy with oneself, and having close and satisfying relationships with God, family, and peers." Here are some things to remember.

A child with ADHD is a person too. One of my children had a T-shirt that was a favorite of mine. It said in childish letters that looked like they'd been written in crayon, "I'm a person too." When parents and teachers recognize that a child has a bonafide disability and when they become advocates and supporters of the child instead of blamers and attackers, that child has an excellent chance of "making it." Taking this attitude does not mean condoning or accepting behavior, attitudes, or work that are substandard or holding the child with ADHD to lower expectations. It means working *with* the child, rather than as an adversary. Many parents whose children are diagnosed with ADHD speak of the release they find in the initial diagnosis. An enormous weight rolls off their shoulders as they realize their child isn't deliberately being bad. They aren't incompetent and irresponsible as parents. They begin to look at the problem as one in which parent, teacher, and child form a team to work against the mitigating effects of the disorder.

When asked about the best advice an adult (teacher, parent, doctor, counselor) can give a child with ADHD, nine-year-old Rachel Marshall penned these words in giant letters across the questionnaire she completed for me: "The thing that people have told me is that I CAN DO IT."

There are resources galore. Schools, communities, support groups, networks, and mental health agencies are available. Research shows that parents who seek out every available resource are more likely to have kids who "make it." Resourceful parents produce resourceful kids.

Mentors and confidants help. Children with ADHD who have a variety of supportive adults in their lives (teachers, employers, youth pastors, neighbors, grandparents, and other relatives) will be more likely to succeed. Your child will need as many supportive adults in his or her life as possible. He or she will be more likely to be better adjusted, with less risk of depression, when there are many people in which to confide other than parents. Karen Beacon has found such an individual for her daughter, Jennifer.

The most practical assistance is finally coming from a behaviorist/therapist/tutor who has ADHD and cannot

tolerate medication. Because she struggles (mostly successfully) herself, she can monitor, instruct, and empathize
with my daughter. She also is the very first successful
role model my daughter has ever had. She understands,
where my husband and I just cannot.

Parenting prowess is a plus. Some individuals can
pick up these skills on their own through reading or watching videotapes; others will need to attend parenting classes.
Developing a disciplinary system that is structured, consistent, and predictable is essential to maximizing success for
your child. Helen Brown, the mother of eighteen-year-old
Perry, reflects on the last six years.

Regarding discipline, we should have been more consistent. He responded well when I made sure I explained (or
asked him to explain) what the offense was, then told
him what the discipline was going to be, and then prayed
with him afterwards. He didn't even seem to like himself
until the discipline was handled. He would be much more
pleasant and free afterwards.

Flexible families flow. Although we've stressed the importance of structure and consistency, there is a strong
need for families with one or more children with ADHD to
be flexible enough to restructure their family environment
to meet the needs of the child(ren). Expectations that are
too rigid or unrealistic will not advance your child's progress.

Donna and Ryan Marshall (adults with ADHD who were
never diagnosed as children) are the parents of three children with ADHD—Sandra (age 7), Rachel (age 9), and Matthew (age 11). Donna shares how they have structured
their family life.

I guess I would say that ADHD has strengthened us. We all have a wonderful sense of humor, so we identify when it's just an ADHD thing. We probably need each other more than the average family does. We need each other's love and encouragement. We don't always get that from the outside world. We also need each other to complete tasks, to help explain things, and to remind us to conform to the rules of society.

A united front strengthens your child's chances. Your child's chances for success will be increased if you and your spouse seek help when you have personal or marital problems. Karen Beacon shares the view of many parents of children with ADHD.

We have to continually evaluate everything to keep the support systems going. I don't know how people do it without solid commitments and without the Lord. It takes a great deal of wisdom, patience, communication, and energy to keep things under control. How in the world do single parents deal with it?

Kandi Rollins, a single parent, has two children with ADHD (nine-year-old Christopher and five-year-old Cindy) and knows how difficult it can be. Divorced, she lives with her parents, both of whom suspect they may have ADHD as well. Kandi says, "Sometimes it feels like I have four or five kids."

What Should I Do if My Child Has Been Diagnosed with ADHD?

There are many actions, interventions, and programs that should be part of a comprehensive treatment plan for your child. Evaluate your family's progress with regard to these options listed below, and begin now to read, learn, grow, and change. Your goal is to provide the optimum home, school, and community. As you continue reading this book, you will find valuable information about each of these options to enable you to plan and make decisions:

- classroom modifications or special education placement
- teacher consultation/training about ADHD
- home behavior management plan
- parental counseling
- parental training in behavior management
- social skills training for the child
- counseling for the child

Will My Child Outgrow ADHD?

Although there is no cure for ADHD, some children do seem to outgrow it. However, the probability is not particularly high. At least seventy-five out of every one hundred children with ADHD will continue to have problems at school, with their families, and often with authorities as they get older. Therefore, it is very important to intervene early and to utilize every available resource to help your child.

What Does the Future Hold?

There are many reasons to be positive and hopeful about the future:

☐ We now know that ADHD is a biologically based disability, and we can stop blaming kids and parents for their behavior. Children with ADHD aren't intentionally disrespectful, naughty, and untamed. Their parents aren't incompetent, either.

☐ We now know that ADHD is a relatively permanent condition, so we won't be starting and stopping interventions and then wondering why kids aren't following through.

☐ There is much exciting research going on relative to how the brain works, and there are a number of exciting new theories about ADHD.

☐ We now know what kinds of homes and classrooms work best for children with ADHD, and we have many outstanding training programs for both parents and teachers.

☐ There are many networks, support groups, and national organizations that provide information to parents and educators.

☐ There are laws that protect the right of our children to an excellent educational environment.

◆ Endnotes

1. Reprinted with permission from the *Diagnostic and Statistical Manual of Mental Disorders,* Fourth Edition. Copyright 1994, American Psychiatric Association.

2. A. Zametkin, T. Nordahl, M. Gross, A. King, W. Semple, J. Rumsey, S. Hamburger, and S. Cohen, "Cerebral Glucose Metabolism in Adults with Hyperativity of Childhood Onset," *New England Journal of Medicine* 323:1361–66.

3. Russell A. Barkley, *Attention Deficit Hyperactivity Disorder: A Handbook for Diagnosis and Treatment* (New York: The Guilford Press, 1990), 99.

4. ———, *ADHD: What Can We Do?* Program Manual for Video (New York: Guilford Publications, 1992), 5.

5. ———, *Attention Deficit Hyperactivity Disorder: A Handbook for Diagnosis and Treatment* (New York: The Guilford Press, 1990), 100.

6. John F. Taylor, *Helping Your Hyperactive Child* (New York: Everest House, 1980), 15–27.

2

HOW CAN YOU KNOW IF YOUR CHILD HAS ADHD?

If you're living with a child in the "terrible twos" stage, you may find that the list of symptoms from the *DSM-IV* describes your child to perfection. So how can you know if your active toddler really has ADHD? Understanding what is "normal" from a developmental point of view may help you place your child's behavior in perspective.

How Early Can an Accurate Diagnosis of ADHD Be Made?

Although many parents readily identify symptoms of ADHD when their children are still toddlers and preschoolers (frequent conflicts, intense hyperactivity, short attention span, and oppositional and defiant behavior), most professionals are reluctant to make a diagnosis that early. For one thing, assessment instruments are not designed to measure ADHD in preschoolers, which makes drawing conclusions about one child's behavior in comparison to "normal" very difficult, if not impossible. Professionals are also reluctant to make a diagnosis based solely on behavior in unstructured settings. Further, parents are often the only identifiers at this stage in a child's development, yet corroboration by teachers is helpful in the diagnostic process.

Normally developing preschoolers exhibit all of the characteristics listed in the *Diagnostic and Statistical Manual's* description of ADHD. Laura Adams describes the process that finally resulted in a definitive diagnosis of her son Brian.

I suspected ADHD when he was two because of his hyperactivity and inability to sleep at night, even though I knew he was tired. He never *walked* down the hall; he literally *bounced* off the walls with his feet or did somersaults the whole way. Walking across the top of the swing set when he was two and riding his bike down the middle of the street without using his hands while standing on the seat when he was seven were also clues. I had him tested by a psychologist, a developmental pediatric neurologist, and the school district, and got three different reasons for his behavior. It was a frustrating time.

I finally had him tested again before second grade because of his constant remarks like "I'm stupid," and "I'm an idiot." Whenever I would tell him to do something or correct him he would say, "Just kill me." His symptoms were not evident to his teachers until the second grade.

I think my father had ADHD. He grew up on a Native American reservation in Nevada, and he was nicknamed "Little Johnny Everywhere."

What Are Some Early Indicators of ADHD?

There are a number of factors that seem to be associated with the occurrence of ADHD. Some are not well substantiated by research; but if taken as part of a much larger picture, they may help parents assemble the diagnostic pieces more completely.[1]

Early infancy indicators (birth–6 months)

- Inadequate sleep.
- Irritability.
- Excessive crying and colic.
- Feeding problems, such as difficulty nursing or accepting a formula, and differing appetite levels.
- Health problems such as allergies, colds, asthma, upper respiratory infections, and fluid in the ears.
- Poor bonding. The baby is not cuddly and responsive and is restless and difficult to manage during such routine activities as bathing, diaper changing, or feeding.

Late infancy indicators (6–18 months)

- Unusual crib behavior such as rocking and banging.
- Rapid or delayed motor development (such as crawling, walking, running).
- Rapid or delayed speech.
- Low adaptability to change.
- Sleep difficulties—including getting to sleep, staying asleep, obtaining restful sleep, and arising refreshed and pleasant in the morning.

Toddlerhood indicators (18–36 months)

- Aggressive: pushes, shoves, pinches, kicks, bites, and grabs toys and can't play cooperatively for a sustained period.
- Destructive: breaks, throws, and tears apart things, toys, and clothing because of anger, curiosity, or wear-and-tear from high activity level.
- Overactive: acts as if driven by a mainspring that is wound too tightly, resulting in nonstop movement and an inability to sit quietly for more than a few minutes.
- Incorrigible: underresponsive to parental correction, unconcerned when threatened with punishment, and requiring constant attention, reminding, and restraining.
- Reckless: accident prone, careless with common dangers such as traffic, and susceptible to accidental poisoning.

Preschool indicators (3–5 years)

- Stomach problems. By the time they are five years old, hyperactive children on the average have more serious gastrointestinal complaints resulting in contact with physicians than their peers.
- Lack of coordination in large or small muscle group activities. The child tends to produce sloppy and messy seatwork in preschool or kindergarten.
- Off-task behavior. These children wander away from their tables at school and do other than what the teacher is instructing the class to do, thus requiring an excessive amount of attention and supervision.
- Overactivity. They won't sit still and pay attention, won't sit for storytime, are out of their seats too often, talk out of turn, and make inappropriate and disrespectful comments to classmates and the teacher.

- Intrusiveness. Hyperactive children bother other children by talking to them, touching them, or intruding on their projects and play, as well as by inappropriately seeking attention, such as by clowning. This trend starts shortly after they learn to walk and begin interacting with other children.
- Aggressiveness. Children with ADHD are often aggressive toward classmates and cannot play cooperatively. They take their classmates' toys, hit them, kick them, and make them cry.
- Distractibility and short attention span when compared to other children of the same age.
- Parent-child conflict. Patterns of family disruption, such as nag-yell-spank cycles, become established. Parents often perceive the child as a negative influence on the family.

What Is Normal Attention in a Child?

Cooke and Williams outlined six levels of normal development of attention control based on Jean Reynell's research.[2] Awareness of these levels will keep you from jumping to erroneous conclusions about your child.

Level 1—Birth to One Year
Level 1 is characterized by extreme distractibility, in which the child's attention shifts from one object, person, or event to another. Any new event (such as someone walking by) will immediately distract the child.

Level 2—One to Two Years
Children in Level 2 can concentrate on a concrete task of their own choosing but will not tolerate any verbal or visual intervention from an adult. These children may appear

obstinate or willful, but in fact, their attention is single-channeled, and they must ignore all extraneous stimuli in order to concentrate upon the task at hand.

Level 3—Two to Three Years
Children's attention is still single-channeled in Level 3. They cannot attend to competing auditory and visual stimuli from different sources. For example, they cannot listen to an adult's directions while playing, but with the adult's help, they can shift their full attention to the speaker and then back to the game.

Level 4—Three to Four Years
The child in Level 4 must still alternate full attention (visual and auditory) between the speaker and the task, but now does this spontaneously without an adult needing to focus that attention.

Level 5—Four to Five Years
By Level 5, attention is two-channeled; that is, the child understands verbal instructions related to the task without interrupting the activity to look at the speaker. The child's concentration span may still be short, but group instruction is possible.

Level 6—Five to Six Years
In the final stage, auditory, visual, and manipulatory channels are fully integrated, and the child's attention is well established and sustained.

J. D. Call[3] presents the following guidelines as developmentally appropriate lengths of time for a sustained activity (like reading a story aloud or watching television):

Two Years—7 minutes
Three Years—9 minutes
Four Years—13 minutes
Five Years—15 minutes
Six Years—60 minutes

How Can I Be Certain of the Diagnosis?

Ideally, the professionals with whom you consult will be well read and conversant with the latest in diagnostic techniques, and will have available a wide range of assessment instruments. Many professionals use more conservative standards than those cited from the *Diagnostic and Statistical Manual of Mental Disorders,* taking care to avoid labeling children who may be borderline or simply developmentally delayed.

Parents who have already "diagnosed" their own child before consulting the professionals may be impatient with a lengthy evaluation, eager for the "answers" that will solve all of their problems. Don't fall into this trap, however. If you suspect your child may have ADHD, make sure that each of the following steps/criteria are met before you support the diagnosis of ADHD:

☐ Don't overlook the need for immediate interventions in the classroom and at home to handle your child's impulsivity or lack of rule-governed behavior. Don't wait for a diagnosis to take action.

☐ Make sure that your child's evaluation team includes medical personnel, your child's teacher, special services personnel in the school setting (e.g., school psychologist, behavior management specialist). You and your doctor cannot make the diagnosis alone.

☐ Make sure that the behavior exhibited by your child is not just antisocial, impulsive, and disruptive, but also includes a pattern of markedly inattentive and/or restless behavior noted by several observers through direct observation. Antisocial, impulsive, or disruptive behavior in the absence of other symptoms may indicate a conduct disorder rather than ADHD.

☐ Make sure that your child's scores on well standardized child behavior rating scales, completed by two or more members of the diagnostic team (parent, teacher, psychologist), are two standard deviations above the mean for same-age, same-sex normal children.

☐ Make sure that your child's symptoms are demonstrated across many situations (home, school, church, neighborhood, playground).

☐ Make sure that your child's symptoms began before the age of six and have lasted for at least six months, but optimally twelve.

☐ Make sure that your child's symptoms are not the result of significant language delays, sensory handicaps (e.g., deafness, blindness, etc.), or severe psychopathology (e.g., autism, childhood schizophrenia).

☐ Make sure that no other possible deficits (e.g., learning disabilities) or factors (e.g., teacher intolerance for active behavior) could account for the ADHD-like symptoms.

If you believe your child may have ADHD, don't hesitate to make an appointment with a professional immediately. Laura Adams has this advice for you:

My advice—get help! If you think there is something wrong, there probably is. Looking back, I should have trusted my gut feelings more. If I had, we all would have been a lot happier a lot sooner. Network with other parents of children with ADHD, and share ideas, frustrations, solutions, and knowledge. You will quickly find out which doctors, psychologists, schools, etc., in your area are best equipped to help your child.

Are There Different Degrees of ADHD?

Most definitely there are variances in ADHD. Taylor differentiates between borderline/mildly hyperactive children and those with more severe symptoms. This differentiation is done on the basis of scores on a screening checklist.[4] His research has shown that in general, the more severe the hyperactivity and the higher the score on his checklist, the more likely a child is to:

- consistently show symptoms of ADHD from setting to setting
- require high dosage levels of prescribed medication
- show sensitivities to many environmental irritants and chemicals
- be allergic to foods, pollens, animal dander, mold, dust, or medicines
- have noticeable symptoms before the age of two
- have increasing or consistent ADHD symptoms throughout childhood and adolescence
- experience little or no decrease in symptoms during adolescence
- have many symptoms as an adult
- have many cognitive impairments
- show severe behavior disturbance

- benefit little from counseling
- be aggressive toward others
- be enrolled in special education programs

The less severe the hyperactivity and the lower the score, the more likely the child is to:

- show variation in displayed ADHD symptoms from setting to setting
- respond to lower dosage levels of medication
- tolerate exposure to some environmental irritants and chemicals without showing ADHD symptoms
- have no allergies
- appear symptom-free until after the age of two
- show symptoms at a constant level or decreasingly from age three to adolescence
- experience a decrease in many symptoms during adolescence
- have few or no symptoms as an adult
- have few cognitive impairments
- show little behavior disturbance
- benefit from counseling
- get along well with other children
- remain in a regular classroom without special academic help

Your child may be at either end of the continuum suggested by Taylor or at some place in between.

Why Does My Child Exhibit Symptoms in One Setting and Not Another?

The variability with which children exhibit the symptoms of ADHD has often created confusion for both parents and professionals. This scenario frequently takes place: Parents describe Johnny as "bouncing off the wall." Doctor sees Johnny for a one-on-one interview and he is the model eight-year-old. Does Johnny have ADHD, or do his parents just need a different approach? Here is another more common scenario: Mother reports to Father that Samantha is "impossible to handle." Father takes the child out for ice cream, and they have a marvelous time. Is the problem Mother's or Samantha's? Five factors, identified by researchers, may help to explain these seeming contradictions:

1. The degree of structure in a given situation and/or the external demands made on the child to restrain his/her behavior will create variability in behavior.
2. The sex of the parent who is dealing with the child will affect behavior. Research has shown that fathers have fewer problems dealing with children with ADHD than mothers do.
3. The novelty or unfamiliarity of the situation will affect the child's attention level.
4. The nature of the task that children with ADHD are asked to complete as well as the complexity and frequency of instructions will have an impact on attention.
5. Whether the child is being rewarded or given consequences for paying attention will substantially affect the attention level.

Who Are the Professionals Who Might Be Involved in Diagnosis?

Depending on where the concerns have arisen regarding your child's behavior and/or academic performance, there may be many individuals who will play a part in a thorough diagnostic evaluation. In some straightforward cases, diagnosis is a fairly simple process involving the teacher, parents, and physician. In other cases that are more complex or less clear, other professionals may be involved. Each one will be able to reveal or uncover aspects of your child's behavior, social skills, personality, medical status, and academic skills. While you almost certainly *will not need to consult* all of these individuals, each one has an important role to play in both the diagnostic and treatment phases of your child's evaluation.

The parents' role in the diagnostic process is a crucial one. Since they have been observing and informally assessing their child since birth, they have quantities of information about their child's academic and behavioral strengths and weaknesses as well as the child's concerns about school and home. The parents' role will be one of coordination, and unless the evaluation is being conducted as part of a multidisciplinary case study at school, they will no doubt be the case managers. A case manager helps to coordinate all of the sources of information and keep the process moving forward.

The child may indeed be the primary catalyst for seeking professional help. Kay and John Kingman knew their son Brett was different, but his problems did not seem that serious. Although he always seemed to be in trouble with his two older siblings at home, that was chalked up to being the youngest. Even when he complained about nobody liking him because he was a brat, his parents didn't take his whining too seriously. But when he said that when he got older he was going to kill himself, he got their attention. They began to take seriously his problems with self-esteem at home and at school. They realized that he was crying out for help. They immediately made an appointment with a child psychologist for an evaluation. The diagnosis—ADHD.

Your child's teacher has a unique opportunity to observe the child in both academic and social settings. He or she knows the child's learning strengths and weaknesses and will have some suggestions about which behavior management and instructional techniques work best with the child.

The school social worker or counselor is a professional usually with a master's degree who concentrates on working with children in school. He or she may have information about the child, gained through counseling sessions, that is not available through any other professional. Children who are experiencing school adjustment problems are frequently referred to a social worker or counselor.

A child psychologist is a mental-health professional who has a doctorate in psychology and has passed a national or state licensing exam. Psychologists have training in psychological testing, diagnosis, and treatment. The school psychologist can provide consultation and support to the teacher, help the parents understand the school's strengths and limitations in meeting the needs of the child, and provide educational information to the teachers and parents. A school or private psychologist may also administer intellectual and academic performance testing or testing for emotional problems.

The family practitioner or pediatrician. A family practitioner is a physician who has had training in the care of individuals of all ages. A portion of his or her training has focused on children. A pediatrician is a physician whose training especially focuses on children. These physicians will often meet with parents alone to discuss concerns about their children and review information, obtain a thorough medical history, review the developmental and school history, and examine the child's medical, learning, and attending problems. The physician might also meet with the child alone (depending on age) to obtain his or her views of problems at home and school. During this time the physician might also informally assess the child's social and emotional status. A thorough physical exam will then be administered if this has not already been done. This may include a vision and hearing screening, blood tests for a chemical profile, and thyroid functioning test (to rule out any medical reasons for symptoms).

Other medical specialists (physicians with additional training in various fields) may be involved if necessary. These might include: a neurologist (to rule out seizure disorders), ophthalmologist (to check for visual or depth perception problems), ear/nose/throat specialist (if there have been chronic ear infections), allergist (to find and treat any allergies or asthma), and family therapist or social worker (for supportive intervention in family stress).

A child psychiatrist is an M.D. with additional training in childhood psychiatric (mental/emotional) problems. This physician may assist other professionals in distinguishing the diagnosis of ADHD from other psychiatric disorders, such as oppositional defiant disorder, conduct disorder, depression, bipolar disorder, and thought disorder. The child psychiatrist might treat for severe emotional problems that coexist with the attention disorders. The child psychiatrist will become involved if hospitalization is necessary should a child become unmanageable.

What Is a Diagnostic Evaluation?

A thorough diagnostic evaluation contains three major components.

The screening. The first aspect of the evaluation process is the screening, in which one or more adults in the life of a child (e.g., teacher, parent) identify signs within the home or classroom of ADHD-like symptoms. Teachers may note an inability to remain seated at appropriate times or displays of impulsivity and disruptive behaviors that differ sharply from other students in the classroom. Parents may note difficulties in following through with chores, careless errors in judgment based on impulsive acts, or total disorganization with possessions and materials. Teachers and parents may be asked to complete behavior ratings scales to determine whether a full-scale evaluation is necessary.

The assessment. This will contain several, if not all, of the following:

Parent interview. The interviewer will obtain from the parents information about the frequency and severity of behavioral problems; health history including complications before, during, and after birth; the child's developmental history related to the onset of the problem; history of other significant medical problems; any other environmental factors (i.e. family disruptions); other psychological factors (i.e. anxiety, depression); parent/family history; genetic factors (e.g., father also exhibiting signs of ADHD); parental disciplinary strategies; and a review of educational progress and placements.

Teacher interview. The interviewer will obtain the following information from the teacher: frequency and severity of behavioral problems, the areas of difficulty for the student in both academic and social situations, the areas of success for the student in both academic and social situations, the most effective means of instruction for the student, the student's current academic schedule, the most effective methods of discipline for the student, and the level of peer interaction and relationships.

Student interview. The interviewer will obtain the following information from the student: the student's perception regarding his or her behavior, the areas in which he or she has the most difficulty, the areas in which the student is most successful, the student's methods of coping with the pressures associated with home and school activities, and the student's perceptions of how he or she gets along with peers in social situations. Although there are structured interview questions that are standardized, diagnosis should not be made solely on the basis of an interview, particularly with a child.

Review of school records. By examining school records, the evaluator can obtain information concerning the onset of difficulties in school, comments made by past teachers, the trend of success or failure in school, areas of strength and weakness, and the level of peer and social interaction.

Parent questionnaires and rating scales. There are two types of parent rating scales: those which report on the child and those which are completed by the parents regarding their own practices. Some examples of child rating scales include the Child Behavior Checklist, Conners Parent Rating Scale-Revised, ADHD Rating Scale, Home Situations Questionnaire—Revised, and the Attention Deficit Disorders Evaluation Scale, Home Version. Russell Barkley believes that parent self-report scales are almost as important in the evaluation of children with ADHD as those completed by parents and teachers about the children. The Locke-Wallace Marital Adjustment Test (MAT) is a commonly used brief rating scale of marital satisfaction. Marital difficulties may affect a couple's ability to cope with behavior problems at home and their willingness to receive training. Two additional instruments used to gather information about parents are the Parenting Stress Index and the Parenting Practices Scale. See Figures 1 and 2 at the end of the chapter for an example of a parent questionnaire.

Teacher questionnaires and rating scales. The teachers who have worked with a student for a long period of time should be the ones to fill out a questionnaire as the information will be more reliable. Teachers may be asked to rate students in areas of behavior, social skills, and academic performance. Some examples of behavior ratings are ADHD-H Comprehensive Teacher's Rating Scale (ACTeRS), School Situations Questionnaire—Revised, and Attention Deficit Disorders Evaluation Scale, School Version. Some examples of social skill ratings are Social Skill Rating System and Walker-McConnell Scale of Social Competence and School Adjustment. An example of an academic scale is the Academic Performance Rating Scale. See Figures 3 and 4 at the end of the chapter for examples of these scales.

Direct observation of behavior across settings. While assessment instruments can provide a wealth of information, there is no substitute for observing the child in his or her natural setting. Children with ADHD may well be model students in unique or one-on-one situations, so observing these children in a natural setting is especially important. Among the pieces of information that will be noted are:

- the position of the student's desk
- the amount of contact with the teacher
- the length of the assignments
- the instructional mode (e.g., lecture, small group work)
- possible auditory and visual distractors
- degree and frequency of peer interaction
- child's response to behavioral management program
- severity of problems
- child's method of organization of materials and activities
- the child's ability to transition from one activity to another
- the methods used by the teacher to inform the child about his/her daily routine and schedule

- the amount of work completed by the child as compared to peers
- the degree of difficulties in structured classroom settings versus nonstructured settings like lunchroom or recess

If a child is not yet enrolled in school, a structured observation can be held by giving the child a predetermined time interval in which to work, and then observing his or her behavior through a one-way mirror. The observation period can be divided into time segments, and the child is noted to be either on-task or off-task during each segment.

Academic classroom performance data. The evaluator should have access to samples of the child's work to determine areas of strength and weakness, the ability of the child to organize his or her thoughts and put them in a final form, and the frequency of careless errors.

Psychoeducational assessment. Intelligence tests and achievement tests cannot directly evaluate the possibility of ADHD. They can assist only in identifying areas of strength and weakness. They may well, however, identify the possibility of coexisting areas of disability, such as a learning disability or a speech and language disorder.

Medical examination. The medical examination is crucial to rule out any underlying medical factors that may be causing the child to exhibit symptoms of ADHD. Further, in cases where ADHD has been diagnosed, the child may benefit from medication to assist him or her in sustaining attention and controlling impulsivity. There are no medical tests that can be used to confirm a diagnosis of ADHD. There are two tests that have been used solely for research purposes: Magnetic Resonance Imaging (an X-ray depicting the brain's anatomy) and Positron Emission Tomography (scans which measure the brain's metabolism). An EEG

(Electroencephalogram), which measures the brain's electrical activity, is used when there is evidence of epilepsy or other conditions. There are no laboratory tests of blood or urine that can be used for the diagnosis of ADHD, although blood tests may well be used after medication has been prescribed and used.

The interpretation of results. Following the preliminary screening and a full multimethod assessment, the results must be carefully interpreted. Since ADHD is difficult to diagnose and can often be confused with other disorders, care must be taken to remain focused on several key variables. Return to these questions frequently during the discussion and decision-making process.

- What is the frequency of ADHD symptoms?
- What was the age of onset?
- How often do the behaviors occur in a variety of settings?
- How do the symptoms interfere with the child's ability to function?
- What other factors might account for the ADHD-like symptoms?

Following a diagnosis of ADHD, a comprehensive intervention plan must be developed that includes all aspects of a child's life—-home, school, and extra-curricular activities.

How Can I Be Sure I Have the Right Doctor?

Finding the right doctor (physician, psychiatrist, psychologist) is essential for your peace of mind. Russell Barkley, one of the most competent and professional practitioners in the field of ADHD, says that professional style in the assessment and diagnosis process is crucial: Each case must be served and evaluated humanely, diplomatically, sensitively, and compassionately. If your doctor is judgmental, or if you are not comfortable with the diagnosis or the style and manner of the diagnostician, seek out another opinion. That's what Laura and Lyle Adams did, and now they have found help and support.

Brian has a fourteen-year-old brother and an eight-year-old sister. They struggle with his impulsiveness, inability to get along, and need for immediate gratification of his needs. I'm sure they wish he wasn't around. This is why I feel medication is needed just as much if not more at home than at school. Why are doctors so stubborn about insisting they go off medication during weekends, vacations, etc.? Aren't family relationships just as important as schoolwork? I struggled with this issue and had to interview several pediatricians before I found one that would be flexible.

Karen Beacon points out the frustration that can occur when parents need to put all of the puzzle pieces together on their own.

ADHD crosses neurological, medical, and psychological fields. Unfortunately, the people in these fields don't interact very well. The parent is left to put the whole picture together alone. Thank goodness associative teams are beginning to be formed so parents don't have to constantly link the professionals. Parents needs to be firm in insisting that these different area experts (psychologist, physician, audiologist, neurologist, allergist, and counselor) talk to each other. Only *together* do they accurately complete the puzzle which is that precious child.

Evaluation Scales and Questionnaires

The following are examples of the questionnaires that may be used in assessment.

Figure 1. Home Situations Questionnaire.[5]

Child's Name _____ Date _____

Name of Person Completing This Form _____

Does this child present any behavior problems in any of these situations? If so, indicate how severe they are.

Yes/No If yes, how severe?

Situation	(Circle one)		Mild (Circle one) Severe
While playing alone	Yes	No	1 2 3 4 5 6 7 8 9
While playing with other children	Yes	No	1 2 3 4 5 6 7 8 9
Mealtime	Yes	No	1 2 3 4 5 6 7 8 9
Getting dressed	Yes	No	1 2 3 4 5 6 7 8 9
Washing/bathing	Yes	No	1 2 3 4 5 6 7 8 9
While you are on the telephone	Yes	No	1 2 3 4 5 6 7 8 9
While watching TV	Yes	No	1 2 3 4 5 6 7 8 9
When visitors are in your home	Yes	No	1 2 3 4 5 6 7 8 9
When you are visiting someone else	Yes	No	1 2 3 4 5 6 7 8 9
In supermarkets, stores, church, restaurants, or other public places	Yes	No	1 2 3 4 5 6 7 8 9
When asked to do chores at home	Yes	No	1 2 3 4 5 6 7 8 9
At bedtime	Yes	No	1 2 3 4 5 6 7 8 9
While in the car	Yes	No	1 2 3 4 5 6 7 8 9

Figure 2. ADHD Rating Scale[6]

Child's name _____ Age _____ Grade_____

Completed by _____

Rate each of the following items.

	Not at All	Just a Little	Pretty Much	Very Much
1. Often fidgets or squirms in seat	0	1	2	3
2. Has difficulty remaining seated	0	1	2	3
3. Is easily distracted	0	1	2	3
4. Has difficulty awaiting turn in groups	0	1	2	3
5. Often blurts out answers to questions	0	1	2	3
6. Has difficulty following instructions	0	1	2	3
7. Has difficulty sustaining attention to tasks	0	1	2	3
8. Often shifts from one uncompleted activity to another	0	1	2	3
9. Has difficulty playing quietly	0	1	2	3
10. Often talks excessively	0	1	2	3
11. Often interrupts or intrudes on others	0	1	2	3
12. Often does not seem to listen	0	1	2	3
13. Often loses things necessary for tasks	0	1	2	3
14. Often engages in physically dangerous activities without considering consequences	0	1	2	3

Figure 3. ADHD-H Comprehensive Teacher's Rating Scale (ACTeRS).[7]

Child's Name _____ Date _____

Teacher's Name _____

Below are descriptions of children's behavior. Please read each item and compare this child's behavior with that of his/her classmates. Circle the numeral that most closely corresponds with your evaluation.

Behavior Item	Almost Never				Almost Always
Attention					
1. Works well independently	1	2	3	4	5
2. Persists with task for reasonable amount of time	1	2	3	4	5
Hyperactivity					
3. Extremely overactive (out of seat, on the go)	1	2	3	4	5
4. Fidgety (hands always busy)	1	2	3	4	5
5. Completes assigned task satisfactorily with little additional assistance	1	2	3	4	5
Social Skills					
6. Behaves positively with peers/classmates	1	2	3	4	5
7. Skillful at making new friends	1	2	3	4	5
Oppositional					
8. Tries to get others into trouble	1	2	3	4	5
9. Mean and cruel to other children	1	2	3	4	5

Figure 4. School Situations Questionnaire[8]

Child's Name_____Date _____

Teacher's Name _____

Does this child present any behavior problems for you in any of these situations? If so, indicate how severe they are.

Yes/No If Yes, how severe?

Situation	(Circle one)		(Circle one) Mild ... Severe
While arriving at school	Yes	No	1 2 3 4 5 6 7 8 9
During individual desk work	Yes	No	1 2 3 4 5 6 7 8 9
During small group activities	Yes	No	1 2 3 4 5 6 7 8 9
During free-play time in class	Yes	No	1 2 3 4 5 6 7 8 9
During lectures to the class	Yes	No	1 2 3 4 5 6 7 8 9
At recess	Yes	No	1 2 3 4 5 6 7 8 9
At lunch	Yes	No	1 2 3 4 5 6 7 8 9
In the hallway	Yes	No	1 2 3 4 5 6 7 8 9
On field trips	Yes	No	1 2 3 4 5 6 7 8 9
During special assemblies	Yes	No	1 2 3 4 5 6 7 8 9
On the bus	Yes	No	1 2 3 4 5 6 7 8 9

♦ Endnotes

1. John F. Taylor, *Helping Your Hyperactive/Attention Deficit Child* (Rocklin, Calif.: Prima Publishing and Communications, 1994), 27–31.

2. J. Cooke and D. Williams, *Working with Children's Language* (Tucson, Ariz.: Communication Skill Builders, 1987).

3. J. D. Call, *Practice of Pediatrics* (Philadelphia, Pa.: Harper and Row, 1985).

4. John F. Taylor, *Helping Your Hyperactive / Attention Deficit Child* (Rocklin, Calif.: Prima Publishing and Communications, 1994), 44–45.

5. The Home Situations Questionnaire is reprinted with permission of the author and publisher from Russell A. Barkley, *Attention Deficit Hyperactivity Disorder: A Handout for Diagnosis and Treatment* (New York: Guilford Publications, 1990). Copyright Guilford Publications.

6. The ADHD Rating Scale is reprinted with permission of the author, George J. DuPaul, and the publisher, Guilford Publications. Copyright Guilford Publications.

7. Items from the ADD-H: Comprehensive Teacher's Rating Scale (ACTeRS) are copyright © 1986, 1988, 1991 by MetriTech, Inc., 4106 Fieldstone Rd., Champaign, IL (217/398-4868). Reproduced by permission of the copyright holder. Permission has been granted for this publication only and does not extend to reproduction made from publication.

8. The School Situations Questionnaire is reprinted with permission of the author and publisher from Russell A. Barkley, *Attention Deficit Hyperactivity Disorder: A Handout for Diagnosis and Treatment* (New York: Guilford Publications, 1990). Copyright Guilford Publications.

3

TREATING ADHD
Working Together
As a Team

"**H**yperactivity with ADD, without treatment, often results in school failure, rejection, family turmoil, all of which can lead to developmental delays and psychiatric complications stemming from low self-esteem and frustration," says Jerry M. Weiner, M.D., president of the American Academy of Child and Adolescent Psychiatry.[1] But it doesn't have to! There's a lot parents and educators can do to work together on behalf of the child.

Who Will Provide Treatment for My Child?

There are many professionals who might be involved with the parents in providing treatment for the child. They should work well together, sharing information and supporting one another in common goals.

The medical team will consist of your pediatrician or family practitioner and possibly a psychiatrist or neurologist. You may choose to use your physician as the first individual you consult for questions about ADHD. The family practitioner or pediatrician was probably involved in the diagnosis and will be involved if medication is used or if there are any questions about developmental delays. A psychiatrist may be part of the treatment team if there are additional mental illnesses, complicated family situations, or severe behavioral problems, or if a child has not responded to treatment from other mental-health professionals. If neurological problems are discovered (e.g. seizures), then the child will be referred to a neurologist, another specialized physician.

The mental-health team is made up of mental-health professionals such as a psychologist, a social worker or a family therapist. They might be involved with the family through the school or privately. These people can provide family education or parenting classes or groups within the school to focus on things like self-esteem and social skills. If family therapy is recommended, the therapist will help the family to change or avoid dysfunctional ways of behaving that grow out of the difficulties of raising a child with ADHD. A therapist can also help parents design effective behavior-management programs. If further testing is ordered, a psychologist would administer it.

The educational team might include any of the above mental-health professionals along with specialists in education. These are the folks who will focus on how the child can be most successful in school. They will identify and work on any learning disabilities or other impediments to education.

The **school nurse** or **health aide** is often an unsung hero in the treatment of ADHD. He or she will be responsible for setting up an effective, organized method of dispensing your child's medication (if prescribed), and the nurse's attitude and demeanor will go a long way toward encouraging your child to be consistent. There are many ways he or she can help, such as:

- offering a private place where your child can take medication
- keeping lunch tickets or passes in his or her office if your child takes medication and then proceeds directly to the lunchroom
- offering a friendly and encouraging word of positive reinforcement for your child's consistency in remembering to take the medication
- keeping careful records of the dosage and time of administration

Another educator who might get involved is the **speech-language pathologist.** Studies indicate that a higher than average percentage of preschoolers with ADHD also have speech and language problems. The speech-language pathologist is not only skilled at assessing and diagnosing speech and language difficulties but also at designing a program of treatment. Typical of the problems they might treat in children with ADHD are listening skills and communication control.

Children with ADHD do not attend to relevant stimuli, and their lack of selective attention contributes to poor listening habits. They switch topics abruptly and lose eye contact.

Many children with ADHD also need help in the area of communication control. They are frequently unable to

predict the consequences of their words and may say inappropriate things or speak at the wrong time. They often fail
to recognize conversational cues, and their narrative dis-
course is disorganized. They have trouble taking the perspective of the listener in order to determine what
communication will please, what will offend, and what
will create conflict.

How Can We Develop a Treatment Plan?

Once a diagnosis has been made, an intervention plan must
be developed. Each child's plan will be different, depending
on his or her degree of ADHD, coexisting conditions that
need treatment, and parental/family needs. But everyone
who will be involved in the implementation of the plan
should be involved in its formulation at some point. You will
be fortunate if you can locate a clinic setting in which all of
the professionals with whom you consult can work and plan
together in the same physical location. If this is not the
case, then you or one of the professionals will have to assume the role of case manager and keep everything coordi-
nated.

   If your child has been referred for an evaluation in the
school setting, the process will be somewhat different than
if you have taken your child to a physician or psychologist
for the initial evaluation. In the school setting, one individual (frequently the school psychologist) will make sure that
everyone fulfills his or her responsibilities with regard to
evaluation, will facilitate information sharing between all
of the professionals who have seen your child, and will
chair the multidisciplinary staffing at which decisions about
special services for your child will be made. Having many

professionals working at cross purposes or in isolation is almost as unfortunate as having no treatment at all. Unfortunately, you are the only person who will have the "big picture" with regard to your child's needs.

Chapters 4 through 8 will give a more in-depth description of each of the components of treatment, along with many specific ideas for implementation. Chapter 4 will discuss the use of medications in the treatment of ADHD. Chapter 5 will describe how to best work with the public schools to maximize your child's potential. Dozens of practical suggestions will be given for how to work with teachers and administrators. In chapters 6 and 7 we will examine the home front and look at how to manage your child's behavior, and in chapter 8 we will look at the family unit and what is needed to keep the marriage and family strong in the face of the challenges of ADHD.

Developing an intervention plan for your child should begin with a complete picture of your child. Only when everyone involved has a comprehensive understanding of your child can a meaningful set of interventions be developed. The MAPS (Map Action Planning System) process, developed at McGill University,[2] can be used to elicit important information that is relevant to the development of a more global plan to treat your child. The process takes from thirty to forty-five minutes, and the only materials required are chart paper and colored markers. Here are the directions for the process:

1. On a large piece of chart paper, write the MAP questions. On a second piece of chart paper, draw the circular flow chart in which to record the answers to each question.
2. Go through each of the six key questions:

The MAP Questions

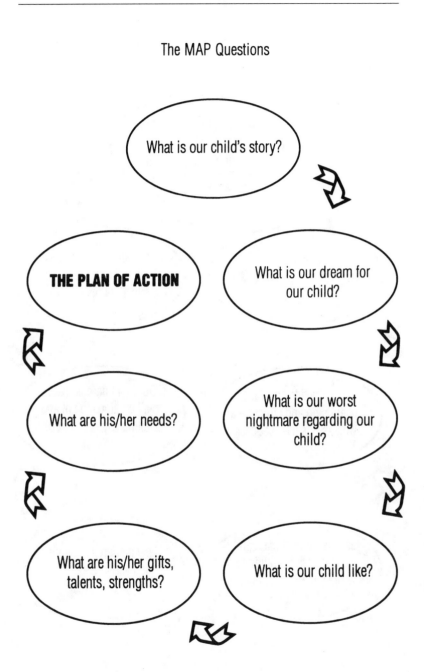

Sample MAP

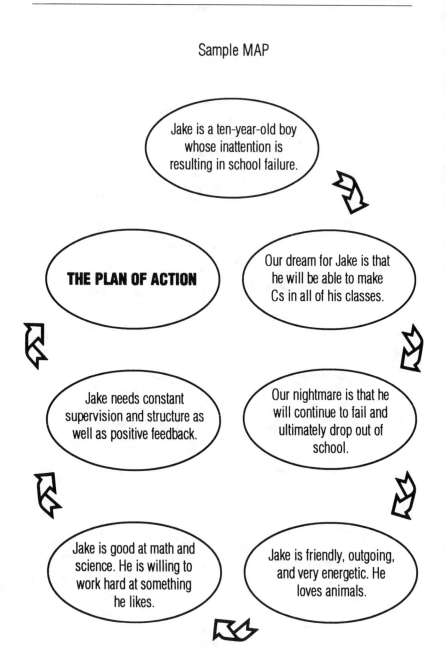

Jake is a ten-year-old boy whose inattention is resulting in school failure.

Our dream for Jake is that he will be able to make Cs in all of his classes.

Our nightmare is that he will continue to fail and ultimately drop out of school.

Jake is friendly, outgoing, and very energetic. He loves animals.

Jake is good at math and science. He is willing to work hard at something he likes.

Jake needs constant supervision and structure as well as positive feedback.

THE PLAN OF ACTION

The MAP questions are:

☐ What is our child's story?

☐ What is our dream for our child?

☐ What is our worst nightmare regarding our child?

☐ Who is she or he? What is she or he like as an individual?

☐ What are our child's gifts, strengths, talents?

☐ What are his or her needs?

3. Using the information collected, develop an action plan.

Identifying your child's strengths and weaknesses is particularly important when developing a plan. Focusing on the "islands of success" will increase self-esteem and generate other successes. This process can be used on many occasions over time to evaluate what has happened and indicate new goals for which to aim.

What Are the Components of a Treatment Plan?

The treatment of ADHD is comprehensive and multifaceted. There are usually four components to the plan: educational services, family education and training, counseling, and medical therapy.

Educational services. Your child will spend a significant portion of his or her waking hours in the school environment. Any treatment plan must include a school component.

Chapter 5 will provide more detailed descriptions of the interventions that will maximize your child's potential. The plan might include:

- alternate placement in a special education program
- assignment to a teacher specially trained or well suited to working with children with ADHD
- modifications to the school environment (e.g., preferential seating or alternate instructional styles)
- modified academic expectations (e.g., decreased work load, oral rather than written exams, permission to use computer for written assignments)
- modified behavioral expectations (permission to move about the room or leave seat more frequently)
- behavioral interventions (personal behavior management plan to include frequent reinforcers and consequences)
- administration of medication
- counseling services

Family education. A treatment plan might include family education and counseling. Education for the family is important for two reasons. First, it serves to take the spotlight off a misbehaving child and shifts it to a child who has a medical problem that needs to be managed. Second, it sets the stage for altered expectations and treatment for the child. Understanding all aspects of ADHD will help the family deal with the variety of reactions they may have to the diagnosis. Denial, relief, anger, and grief are all natural stages that families may pass through on their way to a healthy acceptance and proactive stance regarding the diagnosis of ADHD.

Joan Griswold has gone through several stages, not all of them expected.

My first response to the diagnosis was relief to know that there was an explanation for what was happening at school and for her behaviors at home (e.g., low tolerance for frustration, emotional instability, and extreme messiness). But now I have begun to deal with the grief, realizing that our daughter is going to struggle with this for a long time and that her options in life might be more limited because of it. The grief took me somewhat by surprise, I must admit. Also, after the initial start on medication, the positive effects of it lessened, so it wasn't quite the same cure-all.

Family training. It's critically important that parents be trained in parenting skills and child behavior management. Without training in behavior management and behavior modification, many parents will have a difficult time structuring the home environment, something that is essential for every family member's physical and mental health. Russell Barkley and his staff at the University of Massachusetts have identified eight general principles in the daily behavior management of children with ADHD.[3]

1. They require more immediate feedback or consequences for their behavior and activities than other children do.
2. They require these types of behavioral consequences more frequently than other children do.
3. They require more salient or substantial consequences to motivate them to do work.

4. It is critical that parents avoid the all-too-common tactic of trying punishment first to suppress unwanted behavior. Children with ADHD need positives before negatives.
5. Consistency is of critical importance to the management of children with ADHD—consistency over time and in different places and settings.
6. Parents of children with ADHD must try to anticipate problem situations.
7. Keeping the right perspective on the behavior problems that may arise is essential.
8. Parents should practice forgiveness.

When these principles are not part of the average parent's repertoire of parenting behaviors, training can help. Mary Ellen Corcoran uses the 1-2-3 Magic system, which she picked up in a parent training session with Dr. Thomas Phelan (see Bibliography for books and video tapes):

> An important element of this program is that there is no hitting or yelling. We paired it with a positive, problem solving approach.

Chapters 6 and 7 will provide a comprehensive plan for surviving at home, including how to develop your own behavior management program.

Counseling. A child with a disability can have a debilitating effect on even the strongest marriage and family. In addition to the individual counseling that might be prescribed for the child, parents may find it helpful to work with a counselor either by themselves or as a family. Karen and Sonny Beacon found their own resources wearing thin.

Our own tools for coping just didn't work anymore. We needed someone to give us a new set. We also needed hope and authorities in the field to affirm who our child is and to remind us that God doesn't make broken stuff.

Medical therapy. There are three classes of behavior-modifying drugs that are successfully used in the treatment of ADHD symptoms: stimulants, antidepressants, and the antihypertensive clonidine. Chapter 4 will provide detailed information on these drugs and important steps you should take before making the decision about drugs.

How Can I Make Sure the Plan Is Carried Out?

You must be prepared to be your child's advocate. While all parents serve as their children's advocates, your role as the parent of a child with ADHD is of monumental importance. No one else will have as thorough an understanding of your child's disorder and how it affects him or her. No one else will be aware of all of the aspects of the treatment plan and how they interact. No one else will have talked with all of the professionals involved. This will take time, energy, knowledge, organization, and communication skills. Here are some helpful hints:

☐ Don't be afraid to ask your doctors lots of questions. Ask them to explain words and terms you don't understand.

☐ Don't discuss your child in front of other people (e.g., doctors, friends, family members, teachers). Ask for a separate appointment, and attend without your child.

☐ Focus on the positive. Always ask the professionals what, if any, positive progress has been made. Mention to the professionals any progress that you have noticed.

☐ Communicate frequently with your child's teacher. Don't wait for the phone to ring. Ask questions, and above all, offer support.

☐ Have a complete and thorough understanding of the laws and the protection they give your child educationally.

☐ Ask lots of questions. No question is stupid or foolish—but be concise, and have your questions planned well in advance of meetings. Take notes during diagnostic conferences.

☐ Take a friend or advocate with you to diagnostic conferences and meetings. You will often be too emotionally involved to hear and process everything that is said.

☐ Be organized. Keep samples of your child's work (with and without medication if applicable).

☐ Save copies of all correspondence with the school (e.g., progress reports, notes, report cards).

☐ Make notes of all important telephone conversations with doctors, nurses, office staff, teachers, principals, etc.

☐ Keep track of the questions that arise between appointments and conferences, put them in writing before you attend, leave space after each question, and take notes as you receive information.

☐ Keep a log or a journal of your child's behavior to chart patterns that may be helpful in modifying medication or changing educational placements.

☐ Get involved in obtaining the best possible school placement for your child. Look for matches in your child's learning style and the teacher's teaching style. More on the best kinds of teachers for kids with ADHD will follow in Chapter Five.

☐ Whenever your child enters a new school or classroom, take lots of time to prepare him or her. Walk the child through everything, rehearse schedules, and discuss changes.

☐ Make a list of your child's questions. Encourage him or her to talk about ADHD and learn as much about it as possible (consistent with his or her developmental level).

☐ Be persistent, but be polite. Maintaining a positive and cooperative attitude will result in better outcomes for your child.

☐ Don't be afraid to ask for change if a plan isn't working. You can change doctors, counselors, even schools, but first use a problem-solving approach.

What Obstacles Might We Encounter?

Edward M. Hallowell and John J. Ratey, in their wonderful book, *Driven to Distraction,* point out some common problems you might encounter as you begin to implement your treatment plan.[4]

Certain people do not accept the diagnosis. Sometimes key individuals (e.g., teacher, parent, relative), caring and loving though they be, believe that ADHD is just an excuse for laziness, undisciplined behavior, and poor parenting. These folk will need a healthy dose of education. Their behavior may reflect anger and disappointment at the behavior of someone they love, which is certainly understandable, but these feelings do not invalidate the diagnosis. Take the attitude Mary Ellen Corcoran and her husband have adopted:

> Don't listen to busybodies who question the responsible treatment decisions you have made. You've agonized over the problem, while they are generally uninformed.

After an initial burst of improvement, progress slows. In the beginning, there may be a great deal of progress because medication is effective and all the parties involved are consistently carrying out their aspects of the treatment plan. Then someone is tired, someone gets sick, the dog dies, or some other domestic upset occurs, and everything falls apart. Lori Harris shares her insight when reflecting on the treatment of her son Matt.

> We were innocent of the fact that "treatment" and maintenance were worlds apart. Old habits formed over the years are hard to break. Even though medication was essential in Matt's success at overcoming the symptoms of ADHD, old habits of how to approach a task took much more effort and time to change.

Mary Ellen Corcoran points out a common pitfall that many parents experience.

I was optimistic that psychostimulant therapy would solve all the problems. As time went on it became apparent that there would be a series of challenges.

The person with ADHD does not want to try medication or is inconsistent with it. Young children may be resistant to taking pills or medicine, not because they object to the drug per se, but because they hate medicine generally. Older children may resent the idea of having to rely on medication. Matt Harris, now nineteen, falls into that category.

Our greatest struggle is to help Matt stay on his medication. Because he is nineteen years old, there is sometimes resentment. The need to accomplish things "on his own" without any help (including medication) is strong, so he sometimes conveniently forgets to stay on his daily dose.

No medication seems to work. It can take many months to find the right medication or combination of medications and the appropriate dosage. Work with your doctor.

You feel all alone. Sometimes it seems there's no one else who knows what you and your family are going through. Locate a support group right away, and begin to share the burden with others. Vivian Martinelli sings the praises of C.H.A.D.D. (Children and Adults with Attention Deficit Disorder).

C.H.A.D.D. has been a wonderful support group. We have a terrific group in our area, and I am very active in their monthly meetings. I have also attended one national conference and found it to be terrifically helpful. The feeling of being part of a group facing the same challenges gives me an enormous boost, which carries me through longer than a counseling session will. By attending C.H.A.D.D. meetings and sharing experiences with people, I am also reminded of the progress we've made and the problems we've actually conquered.

You can't find the right doctor. This individual is very important and worth spending a little extra on, even if it means going outside of your HMO or PPO.

Attempts at structuring keep falling apart. This will be a lifelong struggle. Just pick up the pieces, regroup, and restructure.

♦ Endnotes

1. Quoted in "Attention Deficit Disorders: A Guide for Teachers," published by C.H.A.D.D. (Children and Adults with Attention Deficit Disorder).

2. Marsha Forest and Evelyn Lusthaus, "Everyone Belongs," *Teaching Exceptional Children* 22 (Winter 1990): 32–35.

3. Russell A. Barkley, *ADHD: What Can We Do?* Program Manual to accompany video (New York: Guilford Press, n.d.), 11–17.

4. Edward M. Hallowell and John J. Ratey, *Driven to Distraction* (New York: Pantheon, 1994), 262–268.

4

MEDICATIONS
What You Need to Know

Whether to use medication may be one of the most difficult decisions facing parents of children with ADHD. While parents would never refuse insulin for a diabetic child, they often feel differently about medication for ADHD. Making the decision can be even more difficult when parents disagree or when a child is uncooperative. The best advice of the experts is to become informed before you make your decision. Consult the experts and read books or even original research studies. Don't make your decision based on "old wives tales," personal preference, or just one expert's recommendation.

How Can Medication Help a Child with ADHD?

There is a popular misconception that medications prescribed for ADHD act as tranquilizers on children. Nothing could be further from the truth. These medications permit children (or at least about 75 percent of those studied) to function in a more normal fashion. Researchers and physicians are not absolutely certain about the way in which Ritalin™, the drug most often prescribed for treatment of ADHD, works. It was once thought that Ritalin™ had exactly the opposite effect on children with ADHD than it did on children without ADHD. Hyperactive children would be calmed, and non-hyperactive children would be stimulated. But researchers have since determined that stimulants work for non-ADHD individuals in exactly the same way they do for individuals with ADHD. Stimulants increase alertness and on-task behavior while decreasing impulsivity and distractibility in most adults and children, with or without ADHD. For the child with ADHD, the improvements can seem dramatic (especially when combined with other interventions). Improved attention and concentration, decreased distractibility, decreased activity level, and improved school performance can be some of the results.

Will Any Medication Cure My Child?

Since ADHD is a syndrome and not a disease, there is no cure. Medication alone will not be the answer to your child's symptoms of ADHD. "ADHD is a chronic problem, which the child will have throughout life. You just don't write a prescription for medication without making changes in the child's school and home situation. Besides, without the right kind of support, the medication probably won't work."[1] The medications work best and are most helpful in an optimal environment: one that is free from stress and provides appropriate educational practices, good nutrition, structure and discipline, and many opportunities for achievement and building self-esteem.

Many parents report dramatic changes in their children's behavior after they take Ritalin™. Marilyn Byrne's son Bret

advanced three reading levels after he started taking Ri-
talin™ in second grade. Karen Beacon says, "The positive
effects are radical," when describing Jennifer's response to
Ritalin™. Janet Dixon refused to try medication for Jacob,
diagnosed at age seven, until he was nine:

> My concerns were that my friends and family said Ri-
> talin™ would turn Jacob into a zombie or stunt his growth
> [old wives' tales]. I took him off sugar and preservatives,
> and it didn't change his behavior at all. On medication,
> however, his hyperactivity is reduced.

Linda Adams tried every disciplinary program in the books—
marbles in jars, charts, time out, pulling cards, reality discipline, and finally in exasperation an occasional spanking
or two. She reports that "in all honesty, nothing worked
until we started the medication."

Danny Kingston is not considered hyperactive. He is very
energetic, however, according to his mother, and can sometimes be fidgety. But most of the time he quietly sits and
lets his mind do the wandering. He also "doodles" on his
papers a lot. The neurologist told his parents that because
he didn't have major learning disabilities or psychological
problems, he would probably respond well to a low dose of
Ritalin™ for his attention deficit. He now takes 10 mg. each
morning. His parents didn't tell the teacher so she
wouldn't have any preconceived ideas. Danny was skeptical. "These little ding-a-lings are supposed to keep me on
task?" When Danny came home from school that night,
he reported that his teacher's parting words had been,
"Danny, whatever you had for breakfast today, have it
again tomorrow!"

Donna and Ryan Marshall have three children with
ADHD. Ritalin™ has made a difference for each of them.

The medicine has worked wonderfully. There is a night-and-day difference with Rachel. She likes school again this year. She can hear what is being taught and see the writing on the chalkboard. Her school tests are almost normal. The medication has helped Matthew with his behavior problems at school. He seems to be able to think through the consequences better. Ritalin™ has made a difference in Sandra's loudness and the control of her body movements.

Is Medication Absolutely Necessary?

Many parents manage the symptoms of ADHD without medication, particularly when their children's symptoms are not very serious. Helen Brown's son Perry took the medication for about a month when he was first diagnosed at age twelve. He said the medication made him feel "weird," and his parents didn't pursue the issue with him. Behavior modification, training, and structure are enough for some children. But for many children the problems are severe, and medication will be essential in order for them to see results with other interventions.

Joan Griswold, a licensed clinical social worker and parent of a daughter with ADHD, hopes that parents will at least be open-minded to the possibility of medication.

Some parents have a suspicion regarding psychology and tend to struggle with both the diagnosis and the treatment of ADHD more than other parents. They may be particularly reluctant to try medication, hoping for a solution from diet, prayer, or some other alternative. I've run into so many parents who condemn their children to lives of constant negative feedback from others (due to their

disruptive and destructive behaviors) because they won't
even try medication.

Many parents are reluctant to place their children on a
medication that is still on the list of controlled substances
for which the U.S. Drug Enforcement Administration sets
annual production quotas. But recently several medical
groups, including the American Academy of Child and Adolescent Psychiatry, and Children and Adults with Attention
Deficit Disorders, filed a petition with the agency asking
that Ritalin™ be removed from the controlled substance list
since it has not been found to be addictive, given the typical
dosages prescribed.

What Medications Are Known to Be Most Helpful?

There are two types of medications used most often.

Psychostimulants. The medications most commonly
used for children with ADHD are the psychostimulants
Ritalin™, Dexedrine™, and Cylert™. (Note that the first
name below is a brand name for the drug and the name
following is the generic name.) These stimulants are usually the first choice of physicians and are effective for attentional problems, impulsivity, aggression, endurance on tasks,
and hyperactivity. Ritalin™ is most often prescribed for
children six years of age and older, while in children ages
three to five Dexedrine™ is more widely used.

Ritalin™ (methylphenidate hydrochloride) has been used
for more than fifty years and is the most widely studied
medicine given to children. It seldom results in serious side
effects and has a well documented history of results for
boys, girls, and adolescents with childhood histories of
ADHD.[2] Because it is a short-acting medicine, the ADHD

symptoms reappear when the dose wears off. Danny Kingston's medication has worn off by the time he comes home from school. His mother reports that evenings can be tense.

> If homework isn't done by dinner, he is shot for the day. He absolutely can't concentrate past a certain time in the evening, and that's when the "wailing and gnashing of teeth" occur. Even though we understand his "handicap," we sometimes get pretty emotional. We're working harder lately to get him to bed on time, even if schoolwork has to go undone.

Ritalin™ is not recommended if the following conditions exist: high generalized anxiety, motor tics or a family history of Tourette's Syndrome, thought disturbances, parents who might abuse the drug (children do not), age under six, depression, agitation, hypertension, glaucoma.

Ritalin™ requires a written prescription from a physician every thirty days. It cannot be called in over the phone to a pharmacy. One month's supply of Ritalin™ is, on average (obviously it varies with dosage), seventy dollars. Although the generic form is less than half the cost, it is sometimes not as effective as Ritalin™.

Dexedrine™ (dextroamphetamine sulfate) is the preferred stimulant for children under six. It can be used with a child as young as three years old. If Ritalin™ has not proved effective with older children, Dexedrine™ is the preferred second choice. More than 70 percent of those children who take Dexedrine™ respond positively. Dexedrine™ is not recommended if the following conditions exist: cardiovascular disease, hypertension, hyperthyroidism, glaucoma, hypersensitivity, agitation, history of drug abuse, motor tics, or a family history of Tourette's Syndrome. Dexedrine™ may seriously compound the effects of anxiety, bipolar disorder, thought disorders, hyperthroidism, and hypertension, so it is not recommended when these conditions are present.

Cylert™ (magnesium pemoline) builds up in the bloodstream and is taken only once per day. It is generally recommended after both Ritalin™ and Dexedrine™ have been tried unsucessfully. Careful monitoring of the liver function is necessary, however, since this drug can affect the liver. Cylert™ is not recommended for a child with liver damage or disease, one whose family has a history of hepatic disorders, motor tics, Tourette's Syndrome, or seizure disorders. It can be used, however, with hypertension, since it does not affect heart rate or blood pressure.

Antidepressants. A second group of drugs, the antidepressants, might be considered when psychostimulants create side effects such as motor tic disorders or when they do not work. This category includes Tofranil™ (imipramine hydrochloride), Norpramine™ (desipramine hydrochloride) Catapres™ (clonidine), Prozac™ (fluoxetine) and Wellbutrin™ (bupropion).

Frequently, finding the right dosage and combination of drugs will take time. The doctor prescribed 5 mg. of Ritalin™ twice a day for Brian Adams. It helped a little, but only lasted about an hour and a half, and he had a slight rebound effect. (A rebound is when the symptoms of hyperactivity, distractibility, and impulsivity come "bounding back" vigorously, along with some hostility and overreaction, after the medication wears off.) Then the doctor prescribed Tofranil™. This helped Brian's sleeping habits and mood swings but not his hyperactivity. Now he's on both Tofranil™ (100 mg.) and Ritalin™ (10 mg). The combination works well.

Kevin Corcoran was diagnosed with anxiety at the age of five. After behavioral interventions were recommended by a psychologist and implemented by the family, they returned to a psychiatrist when Kevin was six for a further evaluation. Imipramine was prescribed for anxiety. This seemed to help his behavior, but not his inattention. At the age of seven, he was shifted to Ritalin™ to improve his behavior and attention. Teachers reported better behavior and attention, but the quality of Kevin's work was still poor. His dosage was increased to 10 mg. twice a day. His on-task behavior and work completion have improved, but teachers still report that he is anxious. The situation is one of constant monitoring and communication between teachers and parents.

> When we see the psychiatrist the next time, we'll probably try a combination of Ritalin™ and Tofranil™. In terms of whether it works, it's been a balancing act with no total solutions. But it's definitely been a help.

Tofranil™, which is also used to treat enuresis, is often used with children who are anxious or have sleep problems, disturbed moods, a family history of depression or bipolar disorder, and those who have extreme anger and aggressiveness. This drug produces no rebound effect and must be given on weekends. Norpramine™ is not approved for children under age twelve. It is often used for those with anxiety and depression that may coexist with ADHD.

Catapres™ (clonidine) is often used to treat high blood pressure in adults but has been shown to produce improvements in hyperactive and impulsive behavior while decreasing aggressive behavior and outbursts in children with ADHD. This drug is recommended for highly aroused, overactive chidren who respond poorly to stimulants or who have had persistent side effects from stimulants. It can also be used with children who have motor tics or Tourette's

Syndrome. One to two months of treatment are needed to see any effects, however.

Prozac™ is one of the newer antidepressant drugs, which do not appear to be addictive or result in withdrawal symptoms. In addition to depression, it is frequently used to treat anxiety, addictive disorders, bulimia, and obsessive/compulsive disorders. This drug is very expensive, costing twenty times as much as some of the generic antidepressants, and its usefulness with ADHD is limited.

When all other psychostimulants and antidepressants have not proven effective, Wellbutrin™, another of the new antidepressants, has been suggested. The research on the use of this medication is new, and much of it has not yet been published. Consult pharamaceutical literature for possible side effects.

Other medications. Five unique medications are used for very specific diagnoses. Tegretol™ (carbamazepine), an anticonvulsant, can be used for children with ADHD who also have seizure disorders, especially complex partial seizures, which result in outbursts of aggressive behavior. Mellaril™ (thioridazine), Thorazine™ (phenothiazine), Haldol™ (haloperidol) and other major tranquilizers (neuroleptics) are used to treat severe psychiatric disorders or children with severe anxiety that may mimic the symptoms of ADHD.

How Do the Medications Work?

Medications for ADHD are believed to work in a fashion similar to the way insulin works with diabetics. Just as a diabetic's pancreas doesn't produce enough insulin, the brain of a person with ADHD is not producing enough of the neurotransmitter chemicals dopamine and norepinephrine.

Ritalin™ and the other drugs used to treat ADHD are known to produce dopamine and norepinephrine in the brain—both of which increase the blood flow in the areas of the brain that control alertness and attention. With the brain's increased functioning comes an improved ability to attend, control impulses, become more cooperative, and be aware of social cues. While the drug decreases the activity level of an ADHD child with hyperactivity, in ADHD children without hyperactivity, the drug increases alertness.

Contrary to the misinformation, rumors, and innuendo that circulated in the press a number of years ago, the drugs do not change a child's basic personality or values. They don't exert some sinister control over a child's behavior, and the child has total freedom to choose how he or she wants to behave. By taking the drugs, children with ADHD can choose to exercise self-control, pay attention to tasks, be persistent and thoughtful, and function more normally in school and at home. Researchers report improved peer relations, student-teacher relations, and family interactions as a result of medication. Even sports, music, and other nonacademic activities are positively affected. Use of stimulants does not lead to aggressive or assaultive behavior. Research has also shown that using stimulants does not lead to a greater risk of substance abuse or addictive behavior later in life.[3]

What Side Effects Are Sometimes Seen?

No major side effects are reported for Ritalin™, in use since the early 1950s, or Dexedrine™, in use even longer; nor is there a correlation between reliance on these drugs and later drug abuse. While you are certainly encouraged to check out the descriptions and possible side effects of any medication your child may be prescribed, take time to read the entry on aspirin as well. Any medication, prescribed or over-the-counter, must be used with discretion and in accordance with a doctor's orders, warning labels, and common sense. You must make the decision whether the side effects of the medicine are less disturbing than the disorder. Whenever any drug is improperly used, either through misdiagnosis or overdose, there is certainly room for questioning its usage.

Short-term side effects that occur frequently but are not usually severe (and often disappear altogether after several days of usage) are as follows: appetite disturbances (not being hungry and/or some mild sense of stomach upset), sleep disturbances such as insomnia, rebound hyperactivity, and increased irritability or mood change. Reported long-term effects are of greater concern to parents. At one time, children who took Ritalin™ were thought to be at risk for decreased growth. However, research has not substantiated any signficant differences in growth curves between children on or off the medication when followed through adolescence. Nevertheless, most physicians monitor height and weight as well as obtaining an annual CBC and chemical profile. Stimulants are, of course, discontinued if any problems are noted. The occurrence of motor tics is of more serious concern (muscle twitches or abnormal motor movements). Any nervous tic that occurs in association with Ritalin™ should be reported to your doctor immediately.

Among the most common side effects of antidepressants in children are nervousness, sleep disturbances, fatigue, or mild gastrointestinal upsets. These problems are usually short-term in nature and can often be eliminated by reducing the dosage. The side effects of clonidine include drowsiness and hypotension.

Frequently reported side effects for any of the above drugs are lethargy, depression, or becoming a "glassy-eyed zombie." Rather than being side effects of the medication, these are symptoms that the dosage of the medication is too high, the child is on the wrong medication, or the diagnosis is incorrect.

How Will the Doctor Find the Correct Dosage?

Physicians consider two variables when determining the correct dosage for your child—body size and the severity of your child's symptoms. If Ritalin™ (or another psychostimulant) has been prescribed for your child, your child will often begin at a dosage of one pill (five milligrams) twice a day, approximately four hours apart, usually in the morning and before lunch. If a child takes the pill before lunch, the dosage will be effective by the time he or she returns to the classroom after lunch. The doctor will ask parents and teachers to watch carefully for behavior changes, and if none are noted, the dosage can be raised by two-and-a-half to five milligram increments every three or four days until gradual improvement is noted. If side effects are noticed and do not go away, the dosage will have to be moderated. Younger children may start with a smaller dosage and have it raised more gradually. Those children with severe rebound hyperactivity may need a third dosage.

Some doctors will administer a stimulant medication trial including use of a placebo. These physicians may prefer that neither the teacher nor the child know when they are taking the drug and when they are taking the placebo so that the behavior monitoring will be completely objective. Others feel there is no need for a placebo versus drug trial because the changes in behavior observed when children take psychostimulants are so dramatic.

Time-released versions of the short-acting stimulants Ritalin™ and Dexedrine™ are now available—Ritalin SR™ and Dexedrine Spansule™. They have the advantage of lasting up to eight hours rather than just two to four. Having to take only one pill is a big advantage for children who are forgetful or who are embarrassed to be seen taking medication in front of their friends. The time-release forms do, however, have their disadvantages. The medication takes much longer to reach its peak effect and sometimes never achieves as strong an effect as the child needs at critical times.

Will Medication Help Every Child with ADHD?

More than 70 percent of the children diagnosed with ADHD respond positively to psychostimulants. Among those who do not, other medications may prove helpful. If the student's academic achievement is well below his or her potential, if behavioral control is a significant problem, or if the child has social skills deficits, treatment with a psychostimulant in conjunction with a behavioral management plan may be very helpful.

What Should I Know before Deciding about Drugs?

Knowing and trusting your doctor is critically important. Talk to others whose children have used medication. The majority of parents who completed questionnaires for this book were positive about what medication had done for their child (in conjunction with other interventions). Read about the drug being prescribed by your physician so that you can monitor your child for side effects. Begin now to monitor and observe your child so that you will have baseline information to use in comparing his or her pre-medication and post-medication behavior.

What Should I Tell My Family and Friends?

Family and friends may be critical of your decision to use medication. They may make insensitive comments like "Your child just needs more discipline," or "If you give your child drugs, he will become a drug abuser." Be armed with information, and then make up your mind to ignore ignorance. You're not drugging your child to make up for your ineptitude as a parent, and you're certainly not sacrificing your child to make life better at home. The medications used in the treatment of ADHD simply restore the abnormal biology of your child's body to a more normal state. The medicine does not control or stupefy your child; it facilitates his or her ability to focus.

What Should I Tell My Child about the Drugs?

You should be straightforward and honest with your child about what he or she is taking and the reasons. Be wary, however, of placing the responsibility for your child's behavior on the pill. Your child should not get the idea that the pill, rather than he or she, is in control of behavior. Avoid statements like "You're having a great day. Must be those pills you're taking."

What about Medication after School and on Holidays?

Generally, children on medicine for ADHD are put on medication for the school day alone, not after school and not during holidays or summer vacation if the child is not in summer school. For many parents and professionals, a strong case can be made for sometimes administering medication after school and on school holidays. If a child is having difficulties outside of school, why not? Family and friends are as important to a child (particularly a child with ADHD) as school performance. Positive success in school can quickly be negated by conflict, stress, and struggles at home. Ask the question: When does the child need it? Then work with your physician to develop a program that best meets the needs of your child. And always remain flexible to respond to the changing circumstances in which all children live.

What if I Choose Not to Use Medication?

Whether or not to use medications for the treatment of ADHD is your decision. Your doctor can recommend it, but ADHD is not a life-threatening disease, which if left untreated will result in death. There are many families who do not medicate and manage the symptoms of ADHD just fine. But do your homework before making the decision. Be sure you are not making the decision out of pride ("*My* kid doesn't need drugs!"), for unfounded reasons ("Those drugs will stunt his growth . . . make him a zombie . . . make him a drug addict"), or because of pressure from family members who don't really understand your situation. There are many cases of divorced spouses using a medication decision to punish each other (most often the noncustodial parent refuses to allow the custodial parent to try a child on Ritalin™.) Be sure that your decision whether to use medication is made with the best interests of your child in mind.

What about Alternative Treatments?

Some parents put off using medication because they want to try alternate treatments first. Yet many of these are either unproven or proven to be ineffective. Here are some of the more common alternative therapies:

Megavitamin therapy. During the past decades, interest in megadosing children with vitamins (orthomolecular therapy) gained some popularity. Large amounts of niacin, ascorbic acid, pyridoxine, and calcium were purported to cause improvements in children with learning and attention disabilities. The American Academy of Pediatrics Committee on Nutrition reported in 1976 that there was no objective evidence to support such an approach. While vitamin supplements are sometimes recommended by pediatricians, some of the vitamins recommended for this therapy can have toxic effects when given over a long period of time in large doses. There is a risk for young children, whose liver functions might not be able to break down and eliminate such substances from their bodies. Niacin can cause flushing, itching, decreased blood pressure, and excessive sleepiness as well.

Sensory integration training. This treatment was developed out of the field of occupational therapy by Dr. Jean Ayres, an occupational therapist based in California. Treatment involves working with a physical therapist to practice exercises believed to be important in developing better visual-motor coordination. Dr. Ayres hypothesized that the vestibular system (organs of balance in the inner ear) played a critical role in learning disabilities and attention disorders. Scientific studies have found little or no benefit from these exercises, and while they are natural and certainly not harmful, they are not recommended for the treatment of ADHD.

Play therapy. This type of therapy is really intended for children who have suffered severe emotional distress growing out of trauma or dysfunctional parenting. Unless there is a serious, documented emotional disorder coexisting with the ADHD, there is no valid reason for treating ADHD with play therapy.

Chiropractic treatment. Based on the idea that brain tissue was lodged or pinched between the bony plates of the skull, chiropractic treatment put forceful pressure on these plates, ostensibly to release the tissues and tension. This treatment has no scientific basis and may in fact be painful if not harmful.

Osteopathic treatment. Osteopaths assume that things that go wrong with the human body are the result of pressure of displaced bones on nerves and are curable by physical manipulation. While osteopaths concur with current thinking when they claim that children with learning and attention problems have documented difficulties that are related to the central nervous system's functioning, they erroneously link these problems to malfunctions in the musculoskeletal system. Current research indicates that ADHD has its origins in the malfunctioning of neurotransmitters in the brain rather than abnormalities within the central nervous system itself.

Irlen Lenses. Psychologist Helen Irlen has hypothesized that learning disabilities and attention disorders are caused by a neurological condition labeled Scotopic Sensitivity Syndrome (SSS). This condition causes perceptual problems related to light source, light intensity, wavelength, and color contrast.[4] She claims that 50 percent of individuals who are reading disabled actually suffer from SSS and can be helped with specially tinted lenses known as Irlen lenses or Irlen filters. Although there is no evidence to support her theory or the effectiveness of her treatment, glowing testimonials from satisfied customers keep her theory alive. If your child has vision problems, he or she should be evaluated by an optometrist or an ophthalmologist. Using Irlen lenses, which do nothing, may result in a treatable visual problem going without appropriate treatment.

Ocular-motor training. This proposal for treating not only ADHD but also reading disorders and learning disabilities with eye exercises has no research to support its effectiveness. The eye movement exercises proposed by some optometrists were thought to overcome patterns of abnormal eye movements in children with these disorders. The group of optometrists who offer treatment in ocular-motor training are called behavioral optometrists, and they target specific skills in their training program, like tracking, fixation, binocularity, and focus change. ADHD does not arise out of problems with the eye muscles or their movements. In 1984 the American Academy of Pediatrics, in conjunction with the American Association for Pediatric Ophthalmology and Strabismus and the American Academy of Ophthalmology issued a policy statement which included these conclusions:

> There is no peripheral eye defect that produces dyslexia and associated learning disabilities. Eye defects do not cause reversal of letters, words or numbers. . . . [N]o known scientific evidence supports the claims for improving the academic abilities of dyslexic or learning-disabled children with treatment based on visual training, including muscle exercises, ocularpursuit or tracking exercises, or glasses (with or without bifocals or prisms).[5]

Biofeedback. Biofeedback combines the use of relaxation exercises with electronic monitoring of muscle tension, which is then fed back to the person through displays of light on a panel or TV monitor or through different pitches of tones. This treatment is believed to relax muscle tension in various muscle groups of the body, thereby creating a calming effect for hyperactivity.

A variation of this treatment, EEG feedback or neuro-feedback, was developed by Dr. Joel Lubar of the University of Tennessee. The finding that children with ADHD seem to have less brain electrical activity, especially in the frontal lobes of the brain, encouraged Dr. Lubar to believe that if this electrical activity could be measured and converted to a color or sound monitor of some type, children with ADHD could be taught ways to monitor and increase this electrical activity. While the proponents make grandiose claims for the treatments, in studies using double-blind controls, the evidence is nonexistent as to its effectiveness in improving the symptoms of ADHD. The cost of the treatment is substantial (three thousand to six thousand dollars), and the trappings are impressive (equipment, wires, treatment rooms), so reports of success may be tied to the kind of expense and effort that parents have expended to participate. The treatment is certainly not a proven, nonpharmacological treatment for Attention Deficit Disorder, as advertised.

When evaluating alternative treatment methods that may sound appealing because of claims and testimonials, keep in mind the following questions suggested by Ingersoll:[6]

1. Is this theory consistent with existing knowledge in related fields such as anatomy, medicine, psychiatry, psychology, and education?
2. Is the theory consistent with what is specifically known about ADHD and learning disabilities?

3. What is the quality of the scientific evidence which indicates that the treatment is effective?
4. What are the costs involved, and what, if any, are the dangers associated with this treatment?

◆ Endnotes

1. Bennett Shaywitz, quoted in *Maybe You Know My Kid: A Parent's Guide to Identifying, Understanding, and Helping Your Child with Attention-Deficit Hyperactivity Disorder* (Secaucus, N.J.: Birch Lane Press, 1990), p. 108.

2. See the following studies cited in the bibliography for further documentation: Coons. Klorman, and Borgstedt; Pelham; Pelham, Bender, Caddell et al.; and Safer and Allen.

3. Virginia Department of Education, Health Professions, Mental Health and Mental Retardation and Substance Abuse Services, "The Effects of the Use of Methlphenidate: Report of the Task Force on the Use of Methlphenidate in the Treatment of Attention Deficit Hyperactivity Disorder Diagnosed Children," House Document No. 28 (Richmond: General Assembly of Virginia).

4. B. Ingersoll, *Your Hyperactive Child: A Parent's Guide to Coping with Attention Deficit Disorder* (New York: Doubleday, 1988), 202.

5. Ingersoll, 198.

6. Ingersoll, 86.

5

PUBLIC SCHOOL
Maximizing Your Child's Potential

Nowhere do the symptoms of ADHD affect a child's life more than in school. Even if the ADHD had gone unnoticed at home, a child's enrollment in kindergarten will often signal the end of peaceful oblivion.

About one-third of the children with ADHD have problems achieving at the level predicted by their IQ scores. One has only to read comments on the report cards of children with ADHD, and the sad tale is told. "Mary isn't working up to her potential." "I know that Sam could do better if only he tried harder." "Sally is a classic underachiever. She is very bright, but she isn't studying." These are the students who, without ADHD, would be honor roll material, but instead they are making Cs and Ds. A large percentage of students with ADHD (between 30 and 70 percent) have failed at least one year of school, and dropping out of school is a real risk for these children. The picture is not a pretty one. But read on. There is hope. The

pages ahead contain strategies, interventions, and suggestions for how you can work with your child at home and
work with the teachers at school to maximize your child's
potential.

What Are the Typical Problems?

The catalog of problems that children with ADHD have in
school (without treatment) makes for very depressing reading. These eager cherubs come bouncing (sometimes literally off the walls) into kindergarten at the age of five or six,
and immediately their excessive activity and vocalization
put the teacher on notice that here is a child who won't be
ignored for long. They can't sit still during story time; they
grab toys during playtime; they push and shove when they're
waiting in line for drinks or the bathroom; and they may
throw a temper tantrum or two just to show the teacher
who's in charge. Their enthusiasm for any task lasts only
as long as it takes the teacher to look in another direction,
and their "cubbies" soon resemble giant garbage heaps of
school newsletters that never made it home, forgotten belongings, and broken crayons.

They interrupt when the teacher is giving instructions,
and they want to talk about irrelevant topics when the
class is learning about seashells. Their classmates soon
shun them, and before the year is ended their enthusiasm
for school has turned sour. The parents are devastated; the
teacher is frustrated; and the poor child is launched on a
downward spiral of bad feelings. "I'm bad," "I'm dumb," and
"Nobody likes me" are frequently repeated phrases from
the lips of early elementary children with ADHD.

The problems will grow as the child gets older. Lowered
self-esteem and frustration at not being able to measure
up to the teachers' and parents' expectations will create

behavior problems and possibly even depression. That's the bad news.

The good news is that more and more is being discovered about how to create schools and classrooms that are conducive to meeting the needs of children with ADHD. Teachers and specialists are receiving training and developing empathy and understanding for their young charges. There has never been a more hopeful time for children with ADHD in schools.

How Can I Promote a Good School Experience for My Child?

No matter what the age of your child or the severity of the problems, you can make a difference in the quality of his or her education. *Start now* and resolve to adopt a positive, problem-solving approach and become a strong and eloquent advocate for your child.

Read and learn. Become informed about a variety of topics: your legal rights, the best medication therapies, the most recent research on learning theory, and the most effective interventions for home and classroom. Become an expert who is respected for possessing a wide range of knowledge.

Be visible and involved. As an elementary-school principal, I delighted in working with Lauren. Her two children with ADHD were challenging, but she was always proactive rather than reactive. Although she worked full time, she always had time to bring a treat for the teachers or volunteer for a weekend fun fair. She was highly visible and never afraid to interact with faculty. She didn't defend her children when they were definitely in the wrong, but neither did she apologize for their exuberant and sometimes boisterous approach to life. Faculty members at all grade levels knew her, not because her children were a problem, but because she was an asset to the school. Other parents run for PTO or school board or volunteer in classrooms. They are known as active, supportive, and involved parents.

Engage in problem solving, not problem making. If something happens at school that creates a problem for your child, learn to approach teachers and administrators with a can-do attitude. That doesn't mean you won't be asking for things for your child or pointing out where policies need to improve. But you will be willing to roll up your sleeves and work with school personnel to solve the problems, not sit on the sidelines and complain.

Use diplomacy and assertiveness, not aggression. You will soon become known as a troublemaker if you are aggressive, hostile, angry, or defensive. Of course, school staff are there to serve your children—that's what they're paid for. But they aren't paid enough to take abuse from parents. You'll accomplish more with honey than with vinegar, as the old saying goes.

Learn to listen. This is difficult for parents with an agenda in mind for their child. But you will be surprised at how readily school staff relate to you if you take time to listen to what they have to say.

Get to know your teachers and administrators. I'm not suggesting that you become a "school groupie," but become well informed about the most effective teachers, the communication style of your principal, and what the secretary likes with her coffee. This is information that can help you make things happen for your child.

What Can I Do if the Teacher Won't Listen?

Thankfully, there aren't many of these bad apples in schools, but only one can ruin a year for your child. I'm talking about the terrible teacher. This pathetic soul is overburdened or overworked and can reel off more excuses for why he or she can't meet your child's needs than words your child missed on the last spelling test. Below are just a few of the litany of excuses that will pour forth from his or her mouth whenever you question why your child can't be served. But if you've done your homework, you can have a ready response. Just remember the real reason behind this teacher's wall of resistance—fear. He or she is afraid of not being able to teach or manage your child. Your child is threatening the teacher's self-esteem and confidence. With a little coaching and help (from you and the principal), this teacher can usually be turned around.

Blowing smoke. This response serves to change the subject from your child's specific needs to the needs of all the children in the world. But *they* are not the subject of your concern. You just want your child to learn to read, or to stop getting kicked out of class during mathematics, or to have assignments modified to a reasonable level. "I believe in well-behaved students," she will say with a smug smile. Who can argue with that? "I believe that all children should be able to learn in a classroom." The hidden message is, of course, that if you would make your child behave and learn, she could do her job.

Your Reply: "I believe in well-behaved students and learning for all, as strongly as you do. That's why I want to support you in creating an environment in your class that will accomplish that for my child. Right now we have one misbehaving student who isn't learning. What can we do together to change that?"

Inadequate supplies and materials. This is a favorite excuse of a teacher who doesn't want to meet the needs of a child. He mistakenly assumes that special materials are needed to teach ADHD students.

Your Reply: "What supplies and materials do you need to do the job? I'll see that you get them." (If this is a genuine need, there is always money to buy materials. It's usually just an excuse, however, and your response will quickly remove that as an obstacle.)

Rigid standards. More traditional and established teachers frequently have a problem here. They are often well-intentioned and effective teachers but feel that changing their grading method or assignment criteria to meet your child's needs is somehow breaking the rules.

Your Reply: "I agree with you, Mrs. Smith, that changing your grading system might be perceived as giving my son special treatment. Would you agree, however, that our goal is for Johnny to learn?" (Hopefully she'll answer in the affirmative.) "If that's the case, then your grading system may be standing in the way of that. He will never be motivated or encouraged to learn (with his disability) under your present system. Could we just try a brief experiment to see if he might be more motivated if a different standard of measurement were instituted for a time?"

Ignorance. The teacher pleads ignorance. "I've never had a student like this before. I haven't had the training yet."

Your Reply: "I have some excellent reading material that might help you understand Johnny. I've spoken to the principal, and he has promised to get you into the first available training spot. I also have some motivating video tapes on ADHD and educational interventions that work. When would you like to borrow them?"

Personality clash. "I just can't work with your child. We can't get along."

Your Reply: "I know how difficult he can be at times. But he really likes you a lot. He talks about the great science experiments you do in class [or something else positive if you can think of it]. How about coming over to our house next week to get better acquainted with Johnny?"

Blaming the child. "Johnny is just going to have to get his act together. He's not going to make it through fifth grade if he doesn't start coming to class on time [or turning in his assignments, or stop talking to his friends]."

Your Reply: "I agree that Johnny must be responsible and accountable for his behavior. But a child with ADHD needs more structure and firmer rules and consequences than other children do. What can we do to tighten the communication between home and school? Would you be willing to complete assignment sheets that he will bring home every day?"

Passing the buck. "The school psychologist is really trained to work with children like this. Maybe Johnny could use some counseling. There's really nothing I can do."

Your Reply: "I'm pleased to hear that there's someone with expertise in the building. When could we meet with the principal and the psychologist (or counselor) to put together a plan for Johnny?"

Overburdened and overworked. "There are only so many hours in the day, and I've got thirty students. I'm working on my master's degree this year, too."

Your Reply: "I know how hard teachers work, and I'm really appreciative of all you do. How about a little bargain? If you'd be willing to implement this behavior management plan with Johnny, I'll help you out for the next two months in whatever way I can—making photocopies, cleaning and organizing, whatever you need."

Blaming the parent. "I must say, Mr. Jones, in my thirty years of teaching I've never encountered a ruder child than Johnny. Have you taught him any manners? Perhaps you should consider some parenting classes."

Your Reply: "Parenting a child with ADHD is one of the most challenging assignments I've ever taken on. I don't pretend to know all of the answers, but I do know that poor parenting is not one of the accepted causes of ADHD. We're working on his behaviors at home, and if my child knew that you and I were working together, too, it would definitely increase the chances of our both being successful. Would you be willing to try developing a plan together?"

This is strictly a medical problem. The teacher who responds in this way believes that treating your child with Ritalin™ will cure ADHD. He or she doesn't understand that medication is only the first step and that appropriate educational interventions are still needed to help your child achieve his or her potential.

How Will the Ideal Teacher Respond?

Teaching is a stressful and demanding responsibility, requiring strong emotional, psychological, and physical health, as well as effective instructional methods. Teachers who can effectively meet the needs of children with ADHD must be peak performers.

John Taylor, in *Helping Your Hyperactive / Attention Deficit Child,* has identified six key areas in which every teacher who works with ADHD children must excel:[1]

Guarding a child's self-esteem. Your child's self-esteem is very fragile, and a skilled teacher will do everything in his or her power to protect it and build it up. Brian Adams had a temporary setback when he transferred to a new school in third grade and encountered a teacher who shattered his self-esteem. The teacher screamed at Brian in front of the class and a visiting parent, telling him that if he couldn't sit down and shut up, she didn't want to see him at school on Monday. Needless to say, he wasn't there. Now, in another setting, he's thriving. His current teacher is understanding of his needs, and his mother reports that "everyone seems to really love Brian, even though he can be difficult."

Building on a child's strengths. Critical to your child's success in school is the identification of those things he or she does well. The skilled teacher will help to find those strengths and then affirm and encourage your child so that he or she feels special.

Pacing work. Children with ADHD demonstrate what is known as a *production deficit* when they encounter the demands of written work in the classroom. Children with ADHD do not have the motivation and persistence that keeps other children churning through mountains of seat-work, and the child with ADHD will be buried under piles of homework unless a sensitive teacher decreases the work-load to fit the child's capacities. This can be accomplished by sensitively monitoring assignments and determining more accurately when a concept or skill has been mastered. If reducing the workload isn't possible, then breaking the assignment into smaller pieces will serve the same pur-pose. Skilled teachers will weigh the issue of accuracy ver-sus productivity and work on the latter before addressing the former.

Modifying grading systems. The skilled teacher is able to answer the question, *What is the purpose of schooling?* Having answered that question correctly (to help students know how to study and learn), he or she will judiciously modify grading systems to avoid destroying the self-esteem and self-confidence of a child with ADHD.

Helping a child socially. The students in your child's classroom will react to your child based on cues they re-ceive from the adult role model in that classroom—the teacher. If the teacher includes your child in the group;

takes a preventive, proactive approach to behavior rather than a punitive, reactive approach; and uses humane and sensible disciplinary methods, your child will have the ideal social setting in which to grow and mature.

Using effective educational methods. This is the final and extremely important assignment of the classroom teacher: teaching critical skills and concepts to your child on a daily basis. Does the teacher have a clear idea of the outcomes for this grade level? Is your child's teacher skilled at modifying curriculum and presenting material to meet the needs of different learning styles? Is the classroom well organized and structured? Teachers at the elementary school level often receive more training and are more willing to "teach the child" rather than "teaching the subject." Appendices D and F contain a variety of helpful suggestions to modify classroom instruction. For students beyond elementary school, the Michigan Department of Education has provided an excellent set of strategies and techniques to enhance high-school instruction for students with ADHD. These can be found in Appendix E. These strategies would also be helpful for middle-school or junior-high school instruction.

What Does the Teacher Need?

Teachers are mere mortals who, when faced with a classroom of thirty-plus students, many of whom have special learning needs, often seem short-tempered and frustrated. Your child with ADHD is one of several students who will require curricular modifications and behavioral management plans, so be ready and willing to do some empathizing with the teacher before you make your specific requests. Above all, do not overlook the needs of your child's teacher. If those needs are not being met, work with administrators and district personnel to bring about change.

A report of the Michigan Department of Education ADHD Task Force identified twelve specific areas in which teachers need support regarding students with ADHD.[2]

1. Training in the nature of the handicapping condition, strategies and interventions, medication effects and side effects, classroom management, and other pertinent information
2. Participation in educational planning
3. Speedy and appropriate evaluation on students referred for ADHD evaluations
4. Assistance and support from school administration
5. Support-staff assistance, including at least one individual in each building designated and trained to act as a resource person
6. Adequate resources to meet the needs of students with ADHD
7. Adequate time for planning, coordination, and collaboration
8. A collaborative exchange of information
9. Some considerations given to class-size reduction when students with severe ADHD are assigned to a class
10. Clear, district-level written policy or guidelines
11. Flexible curriculum which allows for the needs of all students
12. Adequate parent information, such as books, videos, handouts, and/or parent workshops

What Is the School's Legal Responsibility?

Every public school has the responsibility to educate every student, but special rules and regulations govern the education of students with disabilities. Clearly, if your child has been diagnosed with ADHD by a professional, he or she has a disability. However, your child's *eligibility* for special services as a student with disabilities is subject to special rules and regulations. (See Appendix G for a case study evaluation flow chart.) Enlightened school districts provide training for staff regarding symptoms of ADHD, classroom modifications, and instructional techniques. But that will not always be the case, so forewarned is forearmed.

You may find that your district tries to play "the money game." This game is characterized by phrases such as "Our budget doesn't permit us to offer special help," or "We don't have the money to help every child with a problem." Or they may play on your sense of fair play with statements like, "If we offer help to your child, we'll have every parent wanting the same thing." Perhaps the classroom teacher has already provided some modifications to the curriculum and you're asking for more. "We've already done more for you than for anyone else. You should be thankful for what you're getting." These approaches, while not acceptable, do not carry the emotional sting that blaming your child or intimidating you brings. If your child has a difficult behavior problem and the teacher is unable to manage him or her in the classroom, your child can become the victim, and unless you take care you will find yourself on the defensive.

In reality the school system should be on the defensive, because they are not providing adequate help for your child. The final two approaches that might be taken by a school administrator include the "jargon approach" and the "expert approach." If you are perceived to be inexpert or unknowledgeable about education and ADHD, you may be subjected to condescending lectures laced with jargon or pompous statements from a so-called expert. Your approach to any or all of the above stances by your local school district should be one of firm, quiet, calm, but assertive statements that emphasize only one thing: You are an advocate for your child, and you want appropriate help for his or her needs.

When Is a Child Eligible for Special Education Services?

The Individuals with Disabilities Act (IDEA, PL 101-476), formerly the Education of the Handicapped Act, authorizes and funds special educational services.

In 1990, when Congress was considering the reauthorization of IDEA, they debated including ADHD as a separate disability category. This would have made students with ADHD eligible for special services solely on the basis of their ADHD. However, Congress decided, upon the recommendation of the U. S. Education Department, that since many students with ADHD were already eligible for special services by virtue of coexisting disabilities, they would not create a separate category. At the time of this decision, Congress directed the Education Department to solicit comment regarding how children with ADHD were served in the public schools. The department received more than two thousand responses regarding this issue, and on September 16, 1991, they issued a Policy Memorandum expressly recognizing children with ADHD as eligible for special education and related services under federal law. The Policy makes clear that children with ADHD qualify solely on the basis of ADHD when the ADHD itself impairs educational performance or learning, under both (1) Public Law 94-142, Individuals with Disabilities Act (IDEA) Part B, "other health impaired statutes and regulations"; and (2) Section 504 of the 1973 Rehabilitation Act plus its implementing regulations. This departmental policy statement did not define ADHD as a new disability category, but rather confirmed and elaborated that ADHD was a disability already covered by existing law.[3]

Therefore, to receive special education services, a student must undergo an evaluation conducted by the school district and be found to have:

- one or more of the thirteen disabilities specified in the IDEA;
- impaired educational performance or learning under IDEA Part B—"other health impaired statutes and regulations"; or
- impaired educational performance or learning under Section 504 of the 1973 Rehabilitation Act plus its implementing regulations.

Two categories among the thirteen specified in the IDEA into which many children with ADHD fall are learning disabilities and serious emotional disturbances. Children with ADHD have a higher rate of learning disabilities than children without ADHD.

The Federal definition of a learning disability is as follows:

A disorder in one or more of the basic psychological processes involved in understanding or in using language, spoken or written, that may manifest itself in an imperfect ability to listen, think, read, write, spell, or do mathematical calculations. The term (learning disabilities) includes such conditions as perceptual disabilities, brain injury, minimal brain dysfunction, dyslexia, and developmental aphasia. The term does not apply to children who have learning problems that are primarily the result of visual, hearing, or motor disabilities, of mental retardation, of emotional disturbance, or of environmental, cultural, or economic disadvantage.[4]

Practically speaking, your child will be labeled as learning disabled only if he or she has the ability to perform but does not perform in school on a level with peers in the areas of oral expression, listening comprehension, written expression, reading comprehension, mathematical reasoning, and mathematical calculation.

A second disability category (of the thirteen listed in IDEA) through which many children with ADHD are qualified to receive special education services is "emotionally disturbed." An emotional disturbance is defined by the Federal Government as follows:

1. An inability to learn which cannot be explained by intellectual, sensory, or health factors;
2. An inability to build or maintain satisfactory interpersonal relationships with peers and teachers;
3. Inappropriate types of behavior or feelings under normal circumstances;
4. A general pervasive mood of unhappiness or depression; and
5. A tendency to develop physical symptoms or fears associated with personal or school problems.
   The term includes schizophrenia. The term does not apply to children who are socially maladjusted, unless it is determined that they have a serious emotional disturbance.[5]

One other disability of the thirteen listed in IDEA, and cited above as the second way to access special education services, is the "other health impaired" category.

This category includes all chronic (longstanding) or acute (recent onset) impairments that result in limited alertness that adversely affects educational performance. Under this category, a child with ADHD may be eligible for special education services without having any other disability (such as a learning disability or an emotional disturbance).

Even if your child does not qualify for special education services because of a specific disability or a health impairment, there may be other alternatives. In some cases, children will be eligible for services under Section 504 (of the Rehabilitation Act of 1973), which is a non-special education method of providing services to students with disabilities. Section 504 is a civil rights law rather than a funding law (which requires every recipient of federal aid operating a public elementary or secondary education program to address the needs of children with disabilities). As defined in Section 504 regulation, a "person with a disability" is any person who has a physical or mental impairment that substantially limits a major life activity (such as learning), who has a record of such an impairment, or who is regarded as having such an impairment.

The choice about whether your child will receive special education services (if eligible) is *always* up to you. Many children with ADHD do not need to be labeled or to receive special education services if they are receiving medication and handling the academic and social demands of school with the help of regular classroom teachers and parents. This "least restrictive" approach to meeting your child's needs is, of course, to be preferred. Labeling your child serves no purpose if he or she is being well served without any labels. However, if your child is not succeeding in school and is having severe academic and social problems, you may want your child to be evaluated, and, if found eligible, to be serviced. Remember that the diagnosis of

ADHD alone does not guarantee or ensure special education eligibility. A school district cannot, however, refuse to evaluate your child because he or she has already received a medical diagnosis of ADHD.

A formal individualized education plan—a document required if your child receives special education services under IDEA—is not mandated under Section 504, but developing an IEP and offering special education services *would* be one way of meeting the free appropriate public education requirement of Section 504. The September 16, 1991, memo issued by the Education Department suggests that the guidelines could be met by:

- providing a structured learning environment
- repeating and simplifying instructions about in-class and homework assignments
- supplementing verbal instructions with visual instructions
- using behavioral management techniques
- adjusting class schedules
- modifying test delivery
- using tape recorders
- using computer-aided instruction and other audio-visual equipment
- selecting modified textbooks or workbooks
- tailoring homework assignments

Other modifications suggested by the federal government include:

- consultation services
- reduction of class size
- use of one-on-one tutorials, classroom aides, and note-takers

- a "service coordinator" to oversee implementation of special programs and services
- possible modifications of nonacademic times such as lunchroom, recess, and physical education.

Wherever possible, these interventions should occur in the regular classroom environment. (See Appendix F for a classroom intervention checklist.)

What Educational Options Are Available?

Following are a wide range of options to be considered, from least restrictive to most restrictive. Least restrictive, in educational terms, means the option provides all services within the regular classroom setting. A most-restrictive environment would remove your child from the regular education classroom, possibly even to another school.

Each option comes with its own set of advantages and disadvantages. The decision about how best to meet the needs of your child in the public-school setting will often be made by a multidisciplinary team (school psychologist, social worker, nurse, special education teachers, regular education teachers, and principal) at the school your child attends. If your child has been recommended for a case-study evaluation to determine eligibility for special services, this will always occur. This team may also be consulted to develop a program for your child, even if he or she has not been deemed eligible for special services under the options referred to earlier.

You will always (as required by law) be a part of any discussions and decisions involving your child. You, of course, also have the option of considering private or home-school alternatives as well. The following list is illustrative of all the options. Of course, some options will *only* be available if your child is deemed eligible under IDEA or Section 504 of the Rehabilitation Act.

Child not identified. If your child has not been identified as needing special-education services under IDEA or services under Section 504 of the Rehabilitation Act of 1973 through a formal case-study evaluation, following are several options that are available, along with a few advantages and disadvantages.

Option #1: Keep your child in the regular public school classroom.

Advantages
- No label has been attached to child.
- No special education records are developed.
- Child will not leave the classroom and be separated from his or her peer group.

Disadvantages
- Continuity of services depends on the skill and cooperation of regular education teachers.
- Plan is informal and will need extensive monitoring and support from parents.
- Level of service may be insufficient to keep child from experiencing failure in many academic subjects.

Option #2: Enroll your child in a private or parochial school.

Advantages
- No label has been attached to child
- No special education records are developed.

- Child will not leave the classroom and be separated from his or her peer group.
- Teacher-pupil ratios may be better.
- Teaching staff may be more compassionate and understanding.

Disadvantages
- Teachers may lack techniques and expertise to meet needs of child.
- Private school budgets don't always permit the extra staff training that is needed to work successfully with children who have ADHD.
- Support staff to train and advise teachers is often minimal or nonexistent.
- Parents of other children may apply pressure to teachers and the administrator when your child "diverts" teacher time from their children.
- Cost to parents may be substantial.
- Teacher-pupil ratios may be worse.

Option #3: Enroll your child in a parent-funded special school for children with ADHD.

Advantages
- Teacher-pupil ratios may be better.
- School may be connected to a university or hospital where up-to-date research and methodology are available.

Disadvantages
- Although your child may not be officially labeled by the public school, the label will be inherent because he or she attends a special school.

- Services may not be as complete as in public settings since funding is often completely dependent on tuition and endowments.
- Cost to parents may be substantial.

Option #4: Enroll your child in a parent-funded military or structured boarding school.

Advantages
- Structure, with expectations and consequences, is provided.
- Predictable daily routine.
- Tight external controls help some children control their antisocial tendencies.

Disadvantages
- Costly to parents.
- Rigid rules and inflexibility may exacerbate your child's inability to sustain attention on long tasks.
- Children who have conduct or oppositional problems may have conflict with authority.

Option #5: Home school your child.

Advantages
- Individual attention can be provided.
- Home vs. school friction can be eliminated.
- Learning program can be tailored to child's learning style.

Disadvantages
- Dual role of teacher/parent can be exhausting when working with children with ADHD.

- Parent may lack the skill needed to modify curriculum.
- Child who needs social skills training and opportunities will have few options in the home-school setting and may risk long-term social problems.

Child eligible for services in regular classroom. If your child has been determined to be eligible for services under Section 504 of the Rehabilitation Act of 1973, services can be provided in the regular public school classroom.

Advantages
- Child is labeled ADHD, but no special education label has been placed on the child.
- An IEP (individualized education plan) may or may not be developed for the child, but no special education records are kept, and no labels are entered into the child's school records.
- Services are provided for the child as needed.

Disadvantages
- Teachers and administrators may need special training to implement these services successfully.
- Teachers and administrators may not understand their legal obligation and may need encouragement to voluntarily and willingly implement this policy.
- The level of services may not be adequate to meet the needs of your child.

Child eligible for special education in the regular classroom. If your child has been determined to be eligible for services under IDEA and has been labeled as learning disabled, emotionally disturbed, or otherwise health impaired, and is offered services in the regular classroom, the following are a few options, along with advantages and disadvantages. This program, known as inclusive education, is being implemented in many school districts across the country and includes even children with very severe disabilities. More information will be provided on inclusive education in the next section.

Advantages
- An individualized education plan is developed.
- Clearly defined legal rights for you and your child are spelled out.
- All services are provided within the context of the regular classroom. Depending on the needs of the child, a resource teacher, one-to-one aide, or other personnel will assist the regular classroom teacher in modifying the curriculum and assignments.
- Students are not pulled out of their regular classroom and are not placed exclusively in a self-contained classroom where they will interact only with students who have disabilities similar to theirs.

Disadvantages
- Child has label and special education records.

Child identified for special education and services provided in regular class and resource room. Your child will be served by a regular classroom teacher and a special education resource teacher.

Advantages
- An individualized education plan is developed.
- Clearly defined legal rights for you and your child are spelled out.

- Child spends most of the day in the regular classroom and has the benefit of peer role models and social opportunities.
- Child receives special help that is geared to his or her needs.

Disadvantages
- Child is "pulled out" to receive support services of a resource teacher or other personnel. Although the special help is very beneficial, the child is clearly labeled as "different" and misses activities in the regular classroom whenever he or she leaves.
- Child is labeled.

Child identified for special education and services provided in a self-contained classroom. Your child could be "mainstreamed"—integrated into the regular classroom for his grade level—for some subjects, but he or she would spend the majority of the day in the self-contained classroom with students who have similar disabilities.

Advantages
- Teacher-student ratio is optimal.
- Special programming, such as the use of token economies or assigning points for acceptable behavior, can take place.
- The pace and organization of the classroom provides for as few interruptions and transitions as possible, maximizing learning time and minimizing opportunities for off-task behavior.
- Students work with the same teachers and can develop a routine.

Disadvantages
- Costly method for school district.
- No suitable peer role models for students.
- Very restrictive environment for students.

Child identified for special education and services provided in a self-contained special education school (possibly residential). These schools may be public or private schools whose tuition is paid for by the district. Decisions to place children in these settings are made based on the severity of the disability.

Advantage
- Offers children who would be incapable of receiving an education elsewhere an educational option.

Disadvantages
- Severely restrictive.
- Very costly.
- No suitable peer role models for students.

What Can I Do if I Am Not Satisfied?

There are several things that you as a parent can do if you are not happy with your child's educational program.[6] If your child with ADHD is having difficulty in school, you may:

☐ Request a psychoeducational evaluation to determine whether your child qualifies for special education under IDEA

☐ Submit a copy of any documentation supporting a diagnosis of ADHD

☐ Request that the evaluation also consider eligibility under Section 504 if your child is not eligible under IDEA

☐ If the school district does not agree to evaluate for eligibility under Section 504, contact the district's compliance officer and discuss your concerns

☐ If the district ultimately refuses to evaluate for eligibility under Section 504, then you may file a complaint with the United States Office for Civil Rights (see Appendix B)

If your child with ADHD is receiving special education services but the IEP (individualized educational plan) doesn't address his or her needs related to ADHD, you can:

☐ Request a staffing (multidisciplinary conference) to review the IEP and request specific changes necessary to address the ADHD (e.g., counseling or modified assignments)

☐ If changes cannot be agreed upon, write your disagreement on the IEP and sign it

☐ Contact the district's compliance officer and discuss your concerns about the educational needs related to ADHD

☐ Request mediation (voluntary), a due process hearing, or file a complaint with the United States Office for Civil Rights (see Appendix B)

If your child has been diagnosed with ADHD and is determined to not be eligible for special education, but is eligible under Section 504, you may:

☐ Request that a written plan be developed which will include the appropriate program to be provided by the district

☐ Urge the district to include the following components in the written plan as are found in the IEP: a statement of the present level of educational performance; annual goals and short-term instructional objectives; specific special education, if any, and related services; objective criteria for measuring educational progress; and academic modifications

☐ If the district refuses to include necessary academic modifications, related services or other necessary programs, indicate the disagreement in writing

☐ Request a copy of the school's procedural safeguards under Section 504

If your child with ADHD qualified for special education and has an IEP that outlines an appropriate program, but it is not being followed by the school district, file a complaint with the United States Office for Civil Rights.

If your child with ADHD has a written plan under Section 504 which you feel is appropriate, but it is not being followed by the school district, file a complaint with the United State Office for Civil Rights.

What Is Inclusive Education?

We have come a long way since 1975, when Public Law 94-142, the Education for All Handicapped Children Act, was passed. However, including students with disabilities in the regular classroom, with support help for both students and teachers, is still not a widespread reality. The exclusionary policies that were common before the passage of 94-142 resulted in more than a million children and young people with disabilities being totally excluded from the public schools of the United States. And while those inequalities have been addressed for the most part, educational practices have largely focused on creating special self-contained classes or pull-out tutorial services. Although the student is receiving educational services, he or she is separated and isolated from peers and the mainstream of school life. Public Law 94-142 gave rights to children with disabilities and their parents or guardians. These rights are worth rereading as you consider the equity implied in the isolation of students with disabilities. PL 94-142 gives the following rights:

☐ The right to a free appropriate public education, with all necessary supportive services, for all young people between the ages of five and twenty-one, no matter what their disability. *All children will be served.*

☐ The right to be fairly tested and evaluated by a team of professionals. The law requires that schools and other agencies give tests to children that show both their strengths and weaknesses. All tests must be given in the child's own language and in such a way that his or her abilities and disabilities are accurately displayed.

☐ The right to receive this education in the least restrictive environment (LRE) possible for each child, to discourage both the practice of segregating children with disabilities from others (because it's better for them) and the perception of educating the disability rather than the child.

Students are to be educated in a separate classroom or school only when the nature and severity of their disability makes it impossible to meet their educational needs in a less restrictive environment. ,

☐ The right to an Individualized Education Program (IEP) for each child, listing specific educational goals and objectives along with a timetable for them, with a proviso that the IEP be reviewed at least once a year. Parent participation in the evolution of the children's IEP has been termed the core element of the law. Your child has a right to a full range of educational services, which may include such related services as special transportation, speech/language therapy, counseling, occupational or physical therapy, or other services necessary to enable your child to benefit from special education.

☐ The right, in the case of parent dissatisfaction with the school's implementation of the law, to an impartial due process, a series of steps available for parents to appeal against evaluations, placement decisions, or programs with which they disagree, or (what turned out to be the most frequent source of action) against failure by the school to provide related services necessary for the child to benefit from the other rights.

What if My District Does Not Support Inclusive Education?

The story I am about to relate is a true one. The names have been changed to protect the anonymity of the family involved. Kevin is currently in seventh grade. He is a child with severe learning disabilities, and in many school districts across the country he would be in a self-contained

learning disabilities class. His classmates would all be severely learning disabled like him. He might be mainstreamed
for physical education or art, but the students in his classes
would be strangers; he would have no friends from elementary school with whom to share games or art activities.

Kevin's mother became involved in Kevin's education from
the moment he was placed in a self-contained early childhood class. She often disagreed with decisions made at
staffings and went head to head with the director of special
education on many occasions. She became a tireless advocate for special education causes and in the process learned
a great deal about school politics and funding. She ran for
the school board and was elected. Kevin moved through the
elementary grades, but his mother was not satisfied with
his placement in a self-contained class. He had no neighborhood friends and never was invited to birthday parties
in the neighborhood.

When she heard about an inclusive education program in
Canada, she convinced the superintendent and her fellow
board members to send a delegation to observe the program
in action. Today, Sally's district is a model of inclusive education, and Kevin attends middle school with his peers.
Support teachers work with Kevin in the regular classroom
and offer assistance to the regular classroom teacher in
modifying curriculum and assignments to meet Kevin's
needs.

How Can I Become my Child's Advocate?

Becoming an advocate for your child takes time, energy,
and emotional stamina. Most parents have discovered that
problems can be resolved by taking one step at a time
through the maze of hierarchy and bureaucracy. But it
takes patience and persistence. Solutions do not always

come without pain. Marilyn Bryne found that most of her problems were with individual teachers, not the system. She advises:

> Don't meet with a single teacher, especially if there's a big complaint. Rally the library lady, the gym teacher, the principal, teacher aides . . . whoever you can find, and have them all meet together with you. The more opinions, the better. You often learn the overriding truth, as opposed to one teacher's lack of patience.

Karen and Sonny Beacon struggled with Jennifer's progress through elementary and middle schools:

> Until this year, the schools and teachers have made life hell for us. We have encountered stubborn ignorance and very unprofessional attitudes. Teachers have exacerbated the problem to the point of our despair. The first and most necessary element is effective, honest, and ongoing communication. If a teacher or administrator won't even come up with that, there's not much hope.

Now that Jennifer has reached high school, her parents have found a receptive administrator who in turn motivates and encourages teachers to help each individual student.

The Marshalls have three children with ADHD. None receive special education, but Sandra is receiving special help in reading. Donna describes school as a "nightmare."

> The teachers are not taught what ADHD is. A child with ADHD is not "behind" or "stupid or "out-of-order." I fight for my kids, but I do become exhausted and give up for moments.

The O'Briens recommend relying on your own good judgment. Their son John has just entered high school, and they are not finding the understanding that the Beacons have encountered.

> Don't accept that the school knows best. It's in the school's best interest to refuse to address the needs of your child. It's not in your child's best interest for this to occur. Keep everyone informed all the time. Maintain open communication with the school. Don't let the school pass the ball back to you. Force them, with repeated contact, to deal with the issue. Do not let labeling stop you. It's in your child's best interest to find out if there is anything wrong and do all you can together to help him.

There are several key components to effective advocacy:

☐ Be informed and aware. Vivian Martinelli recommends joining the local C.H.A.D.D. chapter in your area and then reading everything you can get your hands on.

☐ Share information and resources with teachers and administrators.

☐ Communicate often with teachers and administrators. Don't let small problems become major crises. Know as many details about your child's school day as possible. Be aware of particular situations, times of day, school activities, and subjects that are difficult for your child. Offer support to your child as well as to his or her teachers.

☐ Know your rights, and exercise them with good judgment and clear thinking.

☐ Give generously of your time and energy in volunteer efforts at your school. Even if you work full-time, you can find ways to let teachers know that you care.

☐ Seek evaluations from professionals. Use community resources such as hospitals, pediatricians, psychologists, family physicians, child psychiatrists, community mental health agencies, or other family service agencies to determine their level of interest and expertise in evaluating and treating ADHD.

☐ Keep careful records of all of your child's work, copies of all correspondence with the school, and a log or journal of conversations with all professionals.

☐ Be persistent in your efforts. Think of advocacy as a process that is ongoing throughout your child's schooling experience.

What Kind of School Is Best?

There are five important characteristics that, if present in a school, will enhance your child's chances of school success. These characteristics are as follows: a learning success philosophy, clear rules and expectations, consistent implementation of consequences, structure and organization, and rich motivational programs with incentives. If these beliefs and behaviors do not pervade the school and are not practiced by all of the staff members (including secretaries, custodians, classroom aides, and lunchroom supervisors, etc.), your child may have a difficult time adjusting to different expectations from the librarian, gym teacher, music teacher, lunchroom supervisor, and classroom teacher.

Everyone can learn. The administration and staff members must believe that all children can learn. I was an elementary school principal for eight years. The motto of our school was "All can learn." These words were painted in a prominent place in the school hallway, where every student and teacher saw them each day. The philosophy that all children can learn means that expectations are high, but that teachers do whatever it takes to bring a child to mastery of important skills and concepts. Whether it takes more time, different materials, or another instructional approach, the teacher has a responsibility to find a way.

Clear rules and expectations. The behavioral expectations in the school must be clearly stated and consistently applied in all classrooms and learning areas. There is nothing more confusing for a child than to master one set of rules in his or her classroom and then find out that the librarian or gym teacher operates from a totally different set of rules. When a staff can reach consensus on the core rules that must be followed by all children regardless of the setting and can clearly state them, children with ADHD are much more likely to follow those rules. We spent time as a faculty discussing and deciding on which rules were basic to the smooth running of our school. We then had signs printed up for every classroom and hallway. If a child had trouble remembering the rule, it was clearly visible and could be pointed out.

Consistent enforcement. Consequences for breaking the rules must be swiftly and fairly administered to all children. Discipline must be attended to with consistency, firmness, fairness, and expediency. There must be an organized system for dispensing consequences, and this system must work like clockwork. Every staff member must know his or her role and play it well. Administrator backup and support is crucial. Parental support in structuring consequences is very important. Creativity and flexibility are essential.

Order and structure. The school must be well structured with familiar routines. All staff members must be proactive. They must anticipate possible problems and plan for contingencies. Field trips, assemblies, holiday programs, substitute teachers, classroom parties, fire drills, and special events (e.g., a balloon launch, a visit from the zookeeper with live specimens, or a drama presentation by a local play group) are fraught with the possibility of upset for the child with ADHD. During these times, the order, structure, constancy, and predictability of routines can help, and so can an early warning system that lets a child know what is coming.

Motivational activities. The school must believe in positive reinforcement, incentive programs, and motivational activities. Children with ADHD need much more positive reinforcement from teachers and other staff members than children without ADHD. If staff members take the position that it's the responsibility of children to learn and if they don't, "it's not my problem," the culture of the school will not be supportive of changing some of the traditional approaches to help your child. Motivational and incentive programs need to change constantly, and what worked last month may be passé by next month. Staff members must be willing to explore enough options to find out what works with your child.

What Types of Teachers Work Best?

I'm a little embarrassed as a professional educator to be writing about the types of teachers who work best with students who have ADHD, as if it were not important for teachers of all students to have these qualities. All parents want the teachers of their children to be educated, flexible, intelligent, cooperative, open-minded, structured, confident, knowledgeable, and well trained. The difference is that children without ADHD can usually manage to compensate for a year with a less than stellar teacher. It isn't ideal, but they have more coping strategies, higher self-esteem, more intrinsic motivation, and adequate rule-governed behavior. A child with ADHD needs the best every day from the starting bell till dismissal time. A child with ADHD can scarcely cope with his or her own issues. How can this child be expected to compensate for a teacher's lack of skill?

Watching an effective classroom teacher at work is like watching a conductor directing a symphony orchestra. The process looks effortless until you get up and try it for yourself. What kinds of qualities does the effective teacher possess that are so important to the academic success of a child with ADHD?

- informed and educated about the symptoms and treatments of ADHD
- empathetic about the struggles of a child with ADHD
- loving, kind, and supportive
- highly structured and organized
- calm and nonreactive
- active in recognizing, rewarding, and encouraging positive behavior
- articulate about expectations
- flexible and willing to change
- communicative and empathetic with parents
- able to teach a concept using many different approaches
- tenacious about student learning and success

What Types of Educational Practices Work Best?

The Chesapeake Institute, under contract with the Office of Special Education Programs (a division of the U.S. Department of Education) conducted a field study of effective practices for educating children with ADHD. The team visited six public-school districts in five states across the country, observing more than fifty children with ADHD in thirty classrooms in eight elementary schools. They found that successful programs have three key components:

1. The child with ADHD is included in most regular classroom instruction, and academic instruction is individualized where needed.
2. There is a well-developed plan in effect to help the child learn how to manage his or her own behavior in the classroom.
3. Classroom accommodations or changes are made that recognize the special needs of the child with ADHD.

How Can Teachers Provide Effective Instruction?

The following checklist includes many important things that an effective teacher should be doing to maximize learning for your child with ADHD. The items are drawn from scientific research, professional judgment, consultation with effective teachers, and plain common sense. It's unrealistic to think that you'll be able to improve a marginal teacher with this checklist. This information can be of help, however, in discussing why your child should be placed in Mrs. Smith's room, if she is the best teacher for your child and Mr. Jones is not. If you can speak knowledgeably about the elements of good teaching, you will have credibility and be more likely to have your child placed with an effective teacher. Does the teacher . . .

___ 1. Introduce lessons by setting the stage of learning? Some educators call this "getting ready to learn" or "anticipatory set." Your child will be cued that an important lesson is coming and will be more likely to attend.

___ 2. Review how students are expected to behave during the lesson?

___ 3. Let students know what they will be covering and should be learning from the lesson?

___ 4. Review and recall prior learning from earlier lessons?

___ 5. Question the children's understanding of the lesson from time to time?

___ 6. Allow "wait time," which gives a student a chance to think about the answer? Giving cues and probing for correct answers gives every student a chance to be successful, not just those who can quickly come up with the answer.

___ 7. Move about the room during instruction and notice cues that students are having difficulty, without waiting for the student to initiate a request for assistance?

___ 8. Give advance warning that the lesson is about to end and make sure that students clearly understand the assignment for the following day?

___ 9. Instruct students how to begin preparing for the next activity and help them make a smooth transition?

___10. Supplement classroom instruction with direct instruction? Direct instruction is very structured with much repetition of answers from the teacher.

___11. Use techniques like partner reading and peer tutoring to give students special help?

___12. Introduce special strategies, like memory devices, that provide reminders about grammar and punctuation?

___13. Teach basic computation with kinesthetic techniques such as Touch Math, a special procedure for touching and counting touchdowns on the numerals one through nine?

___14. Follow lectures with hands-on activities?

___15. Use programmed materials that require correction before the student proceeds to the next activity?

___16. Anticipate problems and plan ahead to avoid them?

___17. Accept responsibility for ongoing communication with parents? A daily note is sent home for elementary students, and a weekly progress note is used for junior and senior high students.

___18. Provide ongoing cues to help the child with ADHD return to task and avoid becoming overaroused?

How Can Teachers Help My Child Manage Behavior?

The following list of helpful, handy hints includes many important things that an effective teacher ought to be doing to help your child manage his or her behavior in the classroom.

Avoid seating student near distracting stimuli.

- Do not seat student near air conditioner, heater, pencil sharpener, high traffic areas, windows, or noisy classmates.
- Seat student near teacher's desk but as part of regular class seating.

- Seat student up front with his back to the rest of class to keep other students out of view.
- Allow the child to use ear plugs or headphones to block auditory distractors.

Provide appropriate role models.

- Encourage peer tutoring and cooperative learning.
- Seat the student near peers who are positive and seen to be significant others by the student.

Provide alternative areas for study and learning.

- Create a "stimuli reduced study area" to which all students have access.
- Give the student an option to study or learn standing up.

Allow opportunities for controlled movement.

- Permit the student to be of assistance in classroom by distributing materials, running errands, erasing the board, or watering plants.
- Have the student use seat isometrics (push feet down on floor; pull up on bottom of chair).
- Use the "two-seat method," in which the student has two seats and can move back and forth between them.
- Use the "round-table method." Place the student at a round table, and allow him or her to move around it while he or she works.
- Provide regular work breaks.
- Provide time for sitting or lying on the floor.
- Allow some assignments to be done at the chalkboard.
- Allow the child to stand as long as he or she is working on an assignment.

Provide frequent verbal and physical reinforcements.

- Use more praise than reprimands.
- Make direct eye contact to hold attention.
- Use other forms of positive teacher attention, such as a smile, a nod, or a pat on the back as often as appropriate (and in as close proximity to the behavior as possible) to praise specified appropriate behaviors.
- Keep reprimands brief and directed at the unwanted behavior rather than at the child.
- Redirect (verbally instruct the child back to a task) in a calm, insistent, firm, and immediate manner.
- Help the child monitor his or her own behavior with questions like: Do you know what you just did? How do you think you might have done that differently? Never ask, "Why did you do that?"
- Use visual or other clues to assist the child in attending, and reinforce appropriate conduct (reminder notes around the room, a tape recorder tone on a 90- or 120-minute cassette, removal of poker chips from one pocket to another during a specified period of time). Attend to positive rather than to negative behavior.
- Stand near the child with ADHD during a lecture, to increase interaction with the child and to hold his or her attention.

Develop a program of systematic praise and encouragement.

- Avoid embarrassment or put-downs of student.
- Build on strength areas (music, sports, art).
- Have the student tutor a peer in his or her area of strength.
- Help student learn to ask for help.

- Work on building a warm, understanding relationship with the student.
- Provide school counseling, if appropriate.
- Provide a school support group, if appropriate.

Use the behavior management approach that best fits the child and his or her needs.

- Develop a hierarchy of classroom punishment (e.g., head down on desk, response cost fines in token economy, loss of points, time out in corner, loss of recess, after-school time, time out in school office, detention, suspension to go home).
- Use positive reinforcement of appropriate academic and social behavior as the cornerstone of any classroom behavior management system.
- Try contingency management systems, which involve the awarding of points or tokens for desired behavior and are often effective in producing on-task behavior and work completion.
- Use a token economy system to help motivate the child to achieve the goal identified in the behavioral contract. A child might earn points for each homework assignment completed or lose points if an assignment is not turned in on time. After earning a specified number of points, a child can purchase something from the school store or earn a privilege, such as extra recess or computer time. Response cost can be used as a part of a token economy program. It is a penalty technique involving the loss of privileges, rewards, or tokens based on the occurrence of unacceptable behavior.
- Ignore unwanted behavior completely (most appropriate for nondisruptive minor motor and nonattending behaviors used to get the teacher's attention).

- Praise other students who are exhibiting the desired behavior, while ignoring the child with ADHD who is exhibiting undesired behavior.
- Give consequences immediately following a behavior.
- Avoid lengthy reasoning with a child over his or her misbehavior.
- Use a behavioral contract to identify specific academic or behavioral goals for the child.
- Use time out judiciously in the school setting, as it does not always have the desired consequences. A student may enjoy being sent from the classroom to another location. In some cases, the alternative location has more interesting things happening than the classroom (e.g., the principal's or secretary's office).
- Try a home/school incentive program, which can often be very effective. If students are permitted television, video games, or special privileges at home when they complete assignments at school, they may be highly motivated.
- Try giving students a break before a situation gets out of hand.
- Use rewards identified by the student (Nintendo™, Legos™, helping the teacher clean blackboards).
- Enlist assistance of peers in the classroom to ignore disruptive behavior and reinforce positive behaviors.
- Try cognitive-behavioral interventions in which students self-monitor and self-reinforce their own behavior. They must be used regularly in day-to-day interactions and must be adequately praised and reinforced to be successful.
- Avoid ridicule and criticism. Remember that ADHD children have difficulty staying in control.
- Reward more than you punish.
- Change rewards if they are no longer effective in motivating behavioral change.

- Rewards might include one of the following:

  Funny Money—Hand out funny money for desired behavior. At the end of the day have an auction. Auction several small items, like snack size candy bars, bag of chips, peanuts, erasers.

  Good Slips—Cut colored paper into small squares. Give to students for desired behavior. When a slip is given, also provide verbal praise, "I like it when you work quietly; here's a good slip." Tell the student to write his or her name on it. In two days, have an extra recess time for every student who has ten good slips. For those who have more than ten slips, place the extras in a bag and have a drawing.

  Raffle Tickets—Hand out raffle tickets for desired behavior. At the end of a specified time, have the drawing for a "Grand Prize" and several runner-up prizes.

  Party—Have a popcorn party on Friday with students earning points to get popcorn and juice. Give points so they can earn one to three cups of popcorn and one to three small (3 oz.) cups of juice. This will allow everyone to get at least some juice and popcorn.

  Coupons—for computer time, free time, no homework, etc.

  "Good Gram"—Give a telegram written to parents about their child's good behavior.

Teach social skills to the student.

- Encourage the student to interact with younger children if he or she is more comfortable in this setting. Many social skills can be learned from interaction with younger children.

- Include the student in a social skills development group with peer role models.

What Instructional Environment Is Best?

There are many ways that classroom techniques can be modified to better suit the needs of the child with ADHD. Here are some ways:

Modify the way instructions are given to students with ADHD.

- Maintain eye contact during verbal instruction. This is one of the best ways to guarantee attention. For the child with ADHD, eye contact is required at any time a teacher is giving directions.
- Make directions clear and concise.
- Be consistent with daily instructions.
- Simplify complex directions.
- Avoid multiple commands.
- Make sure the student comprehends the task before permitting him or her to begin independent work. This is called "checking for understanding" and is essential to verify that a student is ready to proceed. Some teachers require students with ADHD to repeat the directions, jot down the essential points on paper, or highlight the key directions with a pen or highlighter if a written handout has been provided.
- Repeat directions in a calm, positive manner, if needed.
- Encourage the child to seek assistance.
- Allow the student to have another student repeat directions to him or her.
- Make sure the student has begun the assignment.

Modify guided and independent sessions in the classroom.

- Have more frequent but shorter work periods.
- Emphasize quality of work, not quantity. Increase quantity as the child has success.
- Break assignments into smaller segments, and present only one at a time.

Modify tests.

- Give out only one task or direction at a time.
- Test knowledge and not attention span.
- Test skills, not speed with which they can be completed.
- Give extra time whenever it is needed.
- Measure quality, not quantity.
- Encourage the use of a computer to complete assignments.
- Provide breaks when tedious or uninteresting work has been assigned.
- Get rid of timed tests for the student with ADHD.
- Provide a quiet zone for test taking.
- Test verbally.

Modify homework expectations.

- Make assignments interesting and stimulating.
- Keep homework assignments to no longer than thirty minutes for elementary students and sixty minutes for high school students.
- Focus first on productivity, then on accuracy.
- Permit parents to keep an extra set of books at home.

- Reduce amount of homework to reasonable expectations.
- Don't send unfinished classwork home. If the child is not completing work that should be finished in school, this is a sign that the classroom program needs to be changed.

Systematically teach organizational skills. (Do not assume students will pick them up on their own.)

- Teach students to use highlighting markers to outline the text during reading.
- Teach students the use of graphic organizers like webbing, charting, and outlining.
- Color-code books and notebooks.
- Teach students how to:[7]

  - organize their material
  - organize their workplace
  - record their assignments
  - make lists
  - prioritize activities
  - plan for short-term assignments
  - break down long-term assignments
  - know standards of acceptable work
  - read and use a calendar
  - read a clock and follow a schedule
  - know what to take home and leave home
  - know what to take home and return
  - know when and where to turn in assignments
  - know what to do specifically during seatwork time
  - know what to do when seatwork is completed
  - know what materials are needed and expected

Use technology.

- Provide cassette recordings of books or reading assignments.
- Provide earphones to reduce outside distraction.
- Use a Franklin Speller.
- Use a calculator.
- Use a word processor with spell check.
- Use computer-assisted instruction (CAI) for drill and practice.

Teach children an exercise to monitor their own productivity and behavior.

- Tape a small file card on the student's desk. Divide the card in half with a marker. Place a plus sign (+) or smiley face over the top of the left side, and minus sign (-) or a frowning face over the top of the right side.
- During the work period, play a tape with soft tones, recorded randomly.
- Tell the students that whenever they hear the tone, they can award themselves a check mark in the plus column if they are doing their work. If they were off task and not doing their work, they must place a check mark in the minus column.
- At the sound of the tone, the teacher must scan the room to make sure everyone is following directions.
- The teacher may also post a set of rules which is reviewed just prior to turning the tape on. The rules include, "Stay on task; stay in seat; don't bother others; do your work."

- Self-monitoring can be done with an individual student using a cassette player and headphones. The headphone may also help to limit auditory distractors.

Make curricular adjustments wherever necessary.

- Individualize expectations for spelling.
- Individualize expectations for penmanship and/or neatness.
- Provide after-school study assistance.

Provide structure for all class procedures.

- Post classroom rules in several places in the room.
- Structure all classes with a home-to-school assignment notebook.
- Check to make sure the child with ADHD has written the assignments down correctly and has the needed materials to complete homework assignments before dismissing class for the day.
- Post the daily schedule and homework assignments in the same place.
- Provide boxes for homework assignments for each subject.
- Set aside specific periods for specific tasks. Short time limits will work better than long ones will.
- Provide a time, at the end of the day, for students to organize their desks and homework materials.
- Minimize long-range assignments.
- Give adequate warning and preparation for transition times and changes of schedule (assemblies, field trips, classroom visitors, etc.)

- Set guidelines for formatting homework assignments (placement of headings, spacing, etc.).
- Use buzzers and timers for self-monitoring.
- Provide close supervision of the child with ADHD during unstructured times, like recess, to help avoid conflict with peers and reduce risk taking that could result in injury.

Develop the schedule with variety and brevity in mind.

- Schedule academic subjects during morning hours.
- Intersperse classroom lecture with brief moments of physical exercise.
- Change your teaching style often. Be animated, dramatic, and enthused. Make presentations interesting, novel, and fun.
- Be less rigid. Allow some restlessness.
- Use an active learning approach, in which the child participates in activities.

The Michigan Department of Education has prepared a helpful list of accommodations for dealing with specific behaviors of children with ADHD. A summary of these interventions and accommodations is presented in Appendix D. They may be helpful to you as a parent in working with your child personally, or you may wish to share them with administrators and teachers in your child's school as possible solutions to problems they may be having.

Recently, educators have begun to employ a technique called *functional analysis*. This method of developing interventions to help students with ADHD approaches the child's behavior by asking the question, "What function does the child's behavior serve?" If a child's frequent interruptions and loud "talk-outs" are maintained by positive reinforcement (e.g., adult attention), some other means of gaining positive adult attention must be provided. The child must be taught new behaviors that result in the same product as the inappropriate response. For example, the student could be reinforced with adult attention for raising his hand; he could be taught a secret signal to use to gain teacher attention or feedback, or the teacher could completely ignore talk-outs and reinforce other class members for ignoring them as well. Rather than approaching ADHD interventions using a "cookbook" approach, functional analysis examines the immediate classroom events preceding and following the child's behavior. Educators are finding that this approach, which is based on the specific needs of the child, is more effective.

♦ **Endnotes**

1. Taylor, 157.

2. Michigan Department of Education, *Attention Deficit Hyperactivity Disorder: ADHD Task Force Report* (Lansing, Mich.: Michigan Department of Education, 1993), 62.

3. See Appendix C for a copy of this Policy Memorandum.

4. Public Law 102-119, 20 USC 1401 (a)(1).

5. Public Law 102-119, 20 USC 1401 (a)(1).

6. Arizona Council for Children with Attention Deficit Disorders, *Attention Deficit Disorder: A Parent's Guide* (Tucson, Az.: Arizona Council for Children with Attention Deficit Disorders 1992), 16.

7. Sandra Rief, *How to Reach and Teach ADD/ADHD Children: Practical Techniques, Strategies, and Interventions for Helping Children with Attention Problems and Hyperactivity* (West Nyack, N.Y.: The Center for Applied Research in Educaton, 1993), 45.

6

MANAGING
BEHAVIOR AT HOME

Your sanity depends on it. Your family won't survive without it. And it's absolutely essential for your child's success in the future. What is this magic ingredient? *Consistency.* If you and your child are going to navigate the stormy waters of ADHD and emerge without going aground or altogether drowning, your home (and you) must be predictable, explicit, and, above all, *consistent.* Naturally, none of these conditions are "fun." When compared with their counterparts on the opposite end of the behavioral continuum—spontaneity, flexibility, and freedom—predictability and consistency sound restrictive and boring. And achieving consistency in your home is doubly difficult if you (and/or your husband) have ADHD. But make no mistake about its importance. If you read no other chapter in this book, read this one carefully. And heed well the advice of experienced parents who have weathered the storms.

Research shows that consistency applied early and well in the home life of your child will increase the likelihood that your child will experience success in school and hence, success as an adult. In the chapter ahead, you'll find the help you need to design a home-management plan, suggestions for disciplinary methods that have worked well for other parents, and advice from parents who, like you, are working to meet the needs of their children with ADHD.

Is It All My Fault?

You've no doubt had this experience more than once in the course of parenting your child with ADHD. You've been in a restaurant, grocery store, or shopping center when your child has "gone over the edge." You may get one or two sympathetic glances, but for the most part, you can read the minds (or hear the comments) of those nearby. "Why can't that parent control that child?" or "That child just needs some discipline." Teachers, grandparents, and neighbors have all had their say. They've made you feel guilty and responsible for your child's behavior. You're not alone if you've experienced guilt feelings and major stress over your seeming inability to "control your child." The behavior of any child is the result of a complex interaction of factors—the child's characteristics, the parents' characteristics, situational consequences (i.e., what happens to the child when he or she misbehaves), and family stress. These same factors interact to create the behavior of a child with ADHD, but often with more disastrous outcomes—hence the need for you to fully understand these factors and how they affect your child's behavior. Then you can move from feelings of guilt and blame to a proactive, positive stance.

Russell Barkley and his staff at the University of Massachusetts have developed a training program for parents set forth in his excellent book, *Defiant Children: A Clinician's Manual for Training Parents.* He has developed a model for understanding child misbehavior which incorporates the four major factors mentioned above.[1]

The child's characteristics. If you've parented more than one child, you know that children seem to emerge from the womb with many of their dispositions preset. Many of the parents we interviewed for this book noted differences in activity level, attention span, emotionality, sociability, response to stimulation, and habit regularity in their children who have ADHD. Brian Adams didn't sleep at night even though he was tired, and instead of walking down the hall, he bounced off the walls and did somersaults. From the first night she came home from the hospital, Jennifer Beacon slept no more than twenty minutes at a time. As a toddler, Kevin Corcoran moved constantly, running from room to room, emptying drawers of their contents as he went. Brett Kingman's parents noticed immediately that he was different from his older brother and sister—willful, demanding, and easily overstimulated. John O'Brien was in perpetual motion before he was a year old. Christopher Rollins could crawl out of his crib by eight months and was walking by eleven months. Each of these children came into a home where parents were intelligent, loving, well-adjusted, and committed to doing the right thing. But these children were unpredictable and difficult; they challenged their parents' belief in themselves as competent people, and caused them to totally re-evaluate and realign the family structure. In addition to the qualities of temperament that can affect a child's behavior, physical characteristics such as appearance or motor coordination and developmental abilities such as speech and language, intellect, and visual-motor coordination can predispose a child toward misbehavior.

The parents' characteristics. Parental characteristics also play a role in determining the behavior and or misbehavior of a child. Parents may have some of the same temperamental challenges exhibited in their children, making it doubly difficult for them to manage their off-spring effectively. A family like the Marshalls, where all family members have ADHD symptoms, creates an inter-esting set of challenges for managing behavior and house-hold organization. Donna Marshall laughingly describes their life: "Imagine five people with ADHD. Mornings are a battlefield!"

Situational consequences. The most important factor that can contribute to and exacerbate the behavior of a child with ADHD, however, comes in the form of what Barkley calls "situational consequences."[2] What happens to the child when he or she misbehaves? Does he or she get something positive in the way of rewards or attention through misbehavior? Does the child escape from activities that are boring, difficult, or just plain hard work when he or she misbehaves? Through a complicated set of behaviors, parents of children with ADHD often unknowingly perpetu-ate unwanted behaviors by giving their children exactly what they want. Parents don't cause the behavior, but they're permitting it to grow and flourish, mostly because they don't understand some key principles of human behavior. Hence, the behaviors become well-entrenched habits that are more difficult to eradicate with each passing year.

Family stress. A final factor that can contribute to a child's misbehavior is family stress. Stress can come in the form of marital problems, personal problems, health and financial factors, sibling rivalry, and work-related issues. These stressors can all serve to create uncertainty and instability in a household that absolutely requires struc-ture, organization, and predictability.

If parents are depressed or anxious about work, health, or marital issues, they are often unable to react to their children with consistency and objectivity. A vicious cycle of negative, oppositional behavior on the part of the child will further exacerbate the stress, creating a home environment that is uncertain at best and chaotic at worst. The families interviewed for this book were sensitive to the need for balance and perspective, but they each faced unique challenges in maintaining family normalcy while living with ADHD. The Martinellis, parents of two sons with ADHD, highlight some important characteristics of their family that have helped them cope with the challenges.

> ADHD children add a huge stress to a marriage and home life. Fortunately, we both had a great deal of education behind us before we became parents and have always been quick to recognize when we've needed further education. We are fortunate to be in an income bracket where we can travel (with or without sons) and seek rest and relaxation. We've also been blessed with extended family who help out in emotional emergencies.

Other families who completed the questionnaire are not as blessed. The Scott family is still struggling with the challenges of two sons with ADHD.

> My husband, who has ADHD symptoms himself, doesn't understand why the children act the way they do. He is easily frustrated and has on occasions reacted physically with our children out of his impulsiveness.

The Dixons have a similar problem. Janet shares her frustration.

> My husband yells at Jacob a lot, even when his brothers are causing the problem. I'm guilty of this, too, on occasion.

Then Jacob has hard feelings for his dad and me, and I resent my husband. Jacob's brothers feel bad when he gets blamed; they won't admit to their dad they were at fault, but they do try to make up with Jacob.

The situation is further complicated by the fact that Janet works twelve-hour days on the third shift and her husband refuses to attend counseling. Although Jacob's original behavioral problems were not the result of what was happening in the family, they were clearly aggravated by the interaction of many family variables.

How Can I Help My Child Behave?

In response to the question, "What's he(she) done now?" there are usually three general answers.

- My child doesn't mind. He refuses to do homework. He talks back when he's told to do something. He just won't get with the program.
- My child can't get along with anybody. That includes siblings, neighborhood children, and classmates. The litany of evils includes arguing, hitting, not taking turns, not sharing, interrupting, being bossy, and throwing temper tantrums.
- My child never finishes anything. Schoolwork, chores, and even recreational projects and activities are left undone. The child may be distracted, may start a project and never finish, or may simply not even hear the directions in the first place.

Whatever your child has done in the last twenty-four hours to make you pull out your hair, it probably falls into one of these three categories. Up to this point, if you haven't designed and implemented a workable home management plan for your child, your responses may have been sporadic, unpredictable, and even nonexistent. You've even thought down deep that if you ignored the problem it would go away. Dream on. It won't happen. Your response to any misbehavior on your child's part must be based on the following ten commandments for behavior management. The wording is my own. The concepts and principles have been adapted from Whitman and Smith[3] and John F. Taylor.[4]

First Commandment: Thou shalt have clearly defined lines of authority. Your child needs to know who's in charge, what the rules are, and what happens when the rules are broken. These guidelines will make life safe, predictable, and stable for your child who inwardly is experiencing chaos on a daily basis. Get your collective acts together (as husband and wife), and always present a united front to your child.

Second Commandment: Thou shalt not "go with the flow." Children with ADHD need predictability and routine constantly. The more consistent you can be regarding bedtime, mealtimes, and procedures for getting dressed, leaving for school, and doing homework and chores, the easier your life will be. Spend time getting yourself, your household, and your child organized. Spend time teaching organizational strategies to your child. Then, don't deviate from them. Children with ADHD have a difficult time dealing with any kind of change. If they are expending their energies coping with a fluid lifestyle at home, they will have a very difficult, if not impossible, time accomplishing any of their own tasks.

Third Commandment: Thou shalt always think and plan ahead. As annoying as it is to always be thinking ahead, it's an essential skill for managing life with ADHD. Overplan and you can't go wrong. Think about how your child responds in supermarkets, restaurants, and church. Then decide what props (snacks, coloring books, quiet toys) will be needed. Warn your child of upcoming changes in the schedule or situations that will be different than anything he or she has encountered before. Rehearse and role-play behavior if necessary.

Fourth Commandment: Thou shalt communicate. Effective communication is assertive. Clearly expressing your ideas and requests to your child in a direct and reasonable way sets the stage for a long-term relationship based on trust. Some parents feel guilty when they are direct and assertive with their children. It's easy for this kind of parent to be manipulated by an argumentative or uncooperative child. The permissive parent frequently asks the child whether he or she would like to do something rather than giving a direct command. Just as debilitating to the management system, however, is a punitive, threatening, and harsh approach to communication. Either extreme on the continuum will result in an unfortunate backlash of behavior. Assertive communication exhibits patience, self-control, firmness, and clarity.

Fifth Commandment: Thou shalt not obfuscate. You may not be familiar with this very unusual verb, but it's perfect for this context. Obfuscating means hiding, confusing, or muddling. And that's precisely what many parents do when giving directions to their children or setting forth behavioral expectations. Make sure that whenever you communicate with your child, whether it be regarding cleaning his room or apologizing to her brother, that you give explicit and specific directions. Children with ADHD cannot "fill in the blanks" or "read between the lines." They need to have it spelled out exactly. Put it in writing, explain it verbally, draw some simple pictures, or make a chart. Don't leave it to chance.

Sixth Commandment: Thy consequences shall be constructive and logical. Consequences are what happens to your child after he or she behaves or misbehaves. Consequences that require restitution or contribution always work best. When I was an elementary school principal, I specialized in these kinds of consequences. Always with parental permission, I would frequently assign physical work tasks like cleaning washroom walls or picking up trash on the playground. Sitting in detention hall or writing sentences (typical elementary school consequences) frequently only resulted in further punishments being heaped on the student. They couldn't sit still or stay on task at 3:30 after a long day at school, and repeated writing was doubly painful. Work (although it required a different kind of supervision) kept them active, moving, and productively engaged. I often worked alongside to provide a role model. Marilyn Bryne discovered early on in dealing with her son, Brandon, that work can be a very effective consequence.

> Grounding doesn't work on ADHD kids. I'll go to the mat on that one. All you do is ground yourself, and it doesn't produce any better grades or behavior. It only torments everyone involved. It only further isolates them from normal family life, and what they need is a tremendous amount of acceptance. Giving a child an extra chore not only is a disciplinary step, but gives them something to do to burn off some energy.

Seventh Commandment: Thou shalt be consistent. Consistency means always doing the same thing in the same situation. Children with ADHD will constantly test the limits. They will test them far more persistently than other children will. The more often the child is unsure of what the parental response will be or if there will be any response at all, the more frequently he or she will test the limits. Only by exhibiting consistency can you help your child begin to develop internal controls on impulsivity. He or she will eventually decide that misbehaving is not worth what will happen to him when he does.

Eighth Commandment: Thou shalt continually provide supervision. Children with ADHD cannot be left unsupervised, even when they reach ages where common sense would tell you they could function on their own. It just doesn't work that way, and you'll regret it if you don't follow this commandment. You might find your child swinging from the chandelier or destroying your prize collection of Faberge eggs if you become complacent. Vivian Martinelli has perfected supervision to an art.

> Dustin (almost twelve) is not the kind of child I can leave alone for an afternoon while I run errands or take a nap. Dustin is a real "Ferris Bueller," who never ceases to come up with unusual new schemes. In the same way that I monitor Dustin's free time, I also monitor his homework time. I help him to divide and conquer his work and to pace himself for the evening as he accomplishes harder tasks. For Dustin, idle time means boredom, and boredom means trouble.

Ninth Commandment: Thou shalt not become angry, vindictive, hostile, argumentative, or physically abusive. Although we've all done it—lost our temper, angrily spanked our child, shouted out in frustration—we know it doesn't work. Once we've lost control of ourselves, we've most definitely lost control of our child. Holt and Ketterman have some wonderful advice for us when we've reached the end of our proverbial rope in *When You Feel Like Screaming! Help for Frustrated Mothers* (Harold Shaw, 1988). Pick

up the pieces, apologize, and regroup. Using physical punishment such as spanking is much less effective than any of
the other techniques we have mentioned. Physical punishment rarely has the desired long-term effect and often causes
emotional difficulties such as fear, worry, deep sadness, or
even increased disobedience in children. Modeling physical
aggression when that is often the behavior we are trying to
extinguish just doesn't make sense.

*Tenth Commandment: Thou shalt affirm, support,
redirect, and educate.* Never lose an opportunity to give
your child some positive strokes. The more positive input
your child can receive, the more positive output he will be
able to produce. Learn to empathize verbally with your
child by making statements like "I understand how you
feel," "How can I help you so you'll feel better?" or "Tell me
more about how you feel." Always be ready to step in and
redirect your child to another activity if boredom, fatigue,
loneliness, or irritability are boiling over. Valerie Martinelli
believes it is important for her to "deactivate" her son Dustin
intellectually, physically, and creatively each day.

> Dustin's psyche is on constant overdrive and must be
> "drained" daily, or he can't sleep at night. I complement
> his school curriculum with books, rental movies, trips to
> museums and exhibitions, theater, and even travel. I try
> to keep up with and saturate his ever-racing mind with
> new information and problems to consider. I send him on
> fact-finding missions to CNN News, newspapers, ency-
> clopedias, and the library.

Why Isn't My Discipline Working?

Perhaps you've been reading the chapter thus far with a
sense of disbelief and frustration. "That may work for

them," you're muttering to yourself, "but they don't know my child." If your discipline plan isn't working, sit back and do some troubleshooting with our parental experts.

Avoid the frantic life. Is the pace of your home so hectic and harried that there is little time for reflection and communication? Joan Griswold periodically takes stock of their busy two-career household when things seem to be spinning out of control. She can usually pinpoint that she hasn't been spending time with her daughter and that hugs and positive strokes have been few and far between.

> I often find that simply slowing down long enough to give my children some extra feedback goes a long way towards helping them want to cooperate with me. For a reminder of how effective positive attention can be, I love Ross Campbell's book *How to Really Love Your Child* [Victor Books]. It's a classic.

Karen Beacon echoes Joan's sentiments:

> An atmosphere of peace and stability is important. Routine and regularity of schedules are also. We are constantly reevaluating our priorities.

Streamline and organize your home. Try to keep mealtimes, bedtimes, and other schedules as predictable as possible. Learn to say "no" to those who call with requests for your time. If you have any leftover time, use it for yourself.

Model behaviors you want to see. Although your child may be inattentive, he or she has an uncanny ability to discover the inconsistencies between what you say and what you do. Remember to "walk your talk" as consistently as possible. If you become angry, critical, frustrated, and manipulative in dealing with your child, count on getting the same behaviors back in kind. Children do, indeed, "learn what they live," as that well-known poem so eloquently describes.

"Accentuate the positive" while trying to "eliminate the negative." Encouragement and incentive are the most powerful tools for change. Reward your child externally with attention and concrete external motivators. Don't fall into the trap of thinking your child "should" behave because it's the right thing to do or because behaving will make him or her feel good. Forget that line of thinking altogether. Children, especially those with ADHD, don't think like that, and when you fall into the trap of thinking they do, you'll spend a lot of time being angry at your child for irresponsibility and lack of self-discipline. Responsibility and self-discipline will take years and years of hundreds of positive and successful experiences rewarded by your affirmation and recognition. Marilyn Bryne suggests that you spend some time with parents of "normal" children as well. "It helps to realize that all kids are weird! Not everything is ADHD."

Accept your child. Are you trying to fit your "round child into a square hole"? Rather than accepting your child's limitations, are you trying to turn him or her into a quiet and model child? Relax. Provide lots of outlets for excess energy. Avoid gatherings where your child is bound to get into trouble. Don't let your child get a bad reputation in the family or neighborhood. Protect him or her from sharp-tongued aunts and nosy neighbors.

Remember the basic principles of human behavior. The first and most important principle of human behavior is simply this: Children behave the way they do to get our attention. And they will get what they want regardless of the consequences. The best and most effective classroom teachers use this principle well and wisely. They don't wait for students to misbehave to give them attention; they meet them at the door with a smile, a word of greeting, and a pat on the back. Find ways to give your child positive attention before he or she does something negative and you find it almost impossible to be positive. Your child wants to be loved, accepted, and noticed by you more than anything in the whole world. Even your negative attention is better than nothing. Be certain you are noticing and affirming the right things.

Avoid inconsistency and wishy-washiness in following through. Miriam Montgomery speaks for many parents of ADHD children when she bemoans her lack of consistency in discipline.

> I'm a single parent, and sometimes I feel so exhausted, it's easier to let him do what he wants. Reality discipline and time-outs work well—when I follow through.

Have a few clear, consistent rules. Don't waste your breath on negative comments like "Don't do that," or "Stop that." Enforce the rules with time-outs, loss of privileges, or other consequences that your management plan sets forth.

What Are the Components of a Home-Management Plan?

Your home-management plan should have the following components to be successful:

A. A behavior management plan: comprises a set of rules and expectations for your child, and guidelines for what you will do and what will happen to him or her when the rules are not kept. The plan will govern how you discipline your child and how you respond to misbehavior.

B. A problem-solving model: consists of a several-step process that parents can use with each other and children to identify and solve common problems. The model should be "practiced" and perfected using neutral dilemmas so that when genuine family problems arise, the skills are in place. A model that I have found helpful in my family and professional life is the following:[5]

Step One: Begin to define the problem. Talk it over and write it down.

Step Two: Gather information. Get input from all of the people involved in the problem.

Step Three: Redefine the problem. The problem may be worse than you thought and have several aspects, or you may discover that you really don't have a problem at all.

Step Four: Establish an acceptable outcome. Decide what you want to have happen as a result of solving the problem, and if at all possible, make the outcome measurable.

Step Five: Generate alternative means. Don't just settle for one solution to the problem; your first solution may not work.

Step Six: Establish the plan. Make sure you detail why the plan is being prepared, who is going to participate, what specific actions each individual will take, when these activities will be performed, and where they will occur.

A simpler plan that is more appropriate for younger children consists of the following steps:[6]

Step One: Stop! "What is the problem I am having?"

Step Two: "What are some plans I could use?"

Step Three: "What is the *best* plan I could use?"

Step Four: Do the plan.

Step Five: "Did my plan work?"

Many families post these steps on the refrigerator and refer to them during particularly tense situations, either for the child or the family. When Mary Ellen Corcoran occasionally "blows it" due to sheer weariness, or a particularly incomprehensible action on Kevin's part, she tries to model problem-solving behavior, thinking out loud about the choice she made, how it worked out, and what other choices she could have made. She is never reluctant to apologize to her children when it's needed.

C. Instruction for the child: includes help in developing skills that allow children to develop an internal language of positive self-statements. This type of training is usually offered in clinic settings, where professionals focus on a comprehensive treatment plan for children with ADHD and their families. "Talking to oneself" is something that adults do quite automatically. Children are not usually capable of self-talk until the age of six or seven. Examples of positive self-statements that children might learn are "I think I can do it"; "If I try, I can be successful"; "If I keep working, I'll improve."

D. A family communication model: covers conflict-resolution training, including help in avoiding vague or ambiguous statements, blaming, getting off the topic, dominating conversation, put-downs and destructive verbalizations, interrupting, poor listening and poor eye contact, and incongruent verbal and nonverbal messages. This type of training is most useful when families have older school-aged children or adolescents. Here is an example of one family's plan for their child. Cameron Martinelli, age seven, has been classified as a behavior-disordered student at school. His treatment plan has been multifaceted, including lots of parent training courses, counseling, an IEP (individualized education plan) at school, daily visits from the special education itinerant teacher, a daily progress chart from school, and a reward system for good behavior in school, at church, and at sport events. Special play times and token reward systems have worked well. His mother, Vivian, doesn't just "hope for the best." She has carefully structured her home and Cameron's schedule around his needs.

> I run a very carefully supervised household. I try as much as possible to take proactive measures with Cameron so that I can avoid disciplinary problems. I make sure he gets his medicine (Ritalin™) exactly on time, that he doesn't get overtired, and that he gets adequate nourishment (protein, complex carbohydrates, and very little sugar). I supervise his homework closely. I also direct Cameron into safe, constructive activities and choose just the right friends to invite over. I encourage friendships with active children who usually have big brothers also. In other words, I encourage friends who "speak the same language" as Cameron, literally and metaphorically.
>
> Sometimes I need to send Cameron to his room to "chill out" when things get out of hand. This happens less and less now as he grows older.

I reward Cameron's good behaviors at school (as identified on a daily progress chart that the teacher sends home) with tokens. He can then redeem his tokens for movie or video-game rentals or trips to a favorite restaurant. I change the rewards regularly to keep them novel and interesting. Cameron has trouble playing with a few of the kids on our street. To avoid any more neighborhood problems, I don't allow him to roam freely around the street. I accomplish this by playing with him myself outdoors (a.k.a., our special play time) or by having his own carefully selected friends over. By doing fun and interesting things on our property, Cameron doesn't get into any problems with the neighbors. I'm ready to do whatever it may take to keep Cameron's life running smoothly. It is almost a twenty-four-hour-a-day job, but it's worth it. I never leave things open to chance or leave Cameron to his own desires. His natural instincts are to be extremely reckless, aggressive, rambunctious, and impulsive if he gets overstimulated. To balance these characteristics at home, I hold to very clear limits and low-key activities to keep things in control.

How Can We Develop a Behavioral Plan?

Finding a behavior-management system that works for you and your child may not be easy. Many parents wrestle with this assignment for a long time. Adolescence poses a particular challenge for many parents. The O'Brien family is struggling with John, age fourteen.

There have been *no* strategies or disciplinary programs we have tried that have been successful with John. As an infant, when he was out of control, my husband would hold him to his chest in a tight bear hug lock until he

stopped fighting and relaxed. But I have a special way of
reaching John even in the most nightmarish situations.
We have a deal—either my son or I can request that we
read the book *Love You Forever.* We will not refuse the
other, no matter what. Make sure you let your child
know that you love him, although you hate his behavior
at times.

Other families recognize the need for constant evaluation
and fine-tuning of their behavior management plans as
their children pass through various stages. Vivian Martinelli
explains the plan she uses with her other son, Dustin.

I have used a variety of disciplinary programs at any
given time, and alter them as we pass through different
stages and encounter new difficulties. I most often use
the home token program where I reward specific positive
behaviors with poker chips and take away chips for specific items of misbehavior. At the present time, the reward is a ski trip at a nearby hill with the redemption of
twenty-five chips. This system works well for us with the
least "wear and tear" on me.

Behavior management programs have six basic goals or
activities:

1. Increasing the number of positive parent-child interactions
2. Reinforcing positive behaviors in specific, tangible ways
3. Ignoring negative behaviors
4. Using clear and consistent demands
5. Providing consequences to decrease negative behaviors
6. Overcorrecting to eliminate negative behaviors and
   teach positive behaviors

Increase the number of positive child-parent interactions. Typically, when kids are behaving, we ignore them. The minute they act up, we zoom in with both barrels blazing. The first focus of your behavior management plan will be to become aware of, adept in, and focused on using "differential attention." This means that you're going to work at "catching your child being good" and at those moments give positive attention. There is, however, something deeply ingrained in our psyches that seems to believe it's better to "let well enough alone." The average parent thinks, "Next thing you know, he'll be wanting my attention all the time." It just doesn't work that way. Marilyn Byrne tried hard to catch her now twenty-nine-year-old son, Brandon, being good when he was an adolescent.

> More than noticing what they do wrong, you have to work hard catching them doing something right. That's not an easy task when they can be so disruptive. However, making yourself notice something right—no matter how minimal—also helps you to remember that there's more to this child than bad grades and behavior. It's good for everyone.

Miraculously enough, once you show an interest in your child and approach him or her rather than waiting to be "asked" for attention, the quality of your relationship and time spent together will deepen. There are several ways to have this positive interaction, depending on the situation and the age of the child. One way is to simply provide a commentary or description of what your child is doing. Don't lecture or teach. Simply observe and comment (e.g., "That's a really interesting bridge you're building"). Comment only on positive things the child is doing.

A second way of building positive interactions is by rewarding your child. These "rewards" come in the form of physical affection such a hug, kiss, or pat; a praise statement that is general in nature (e.g., "Very nice work"); or a specific praise statement that describes a particular behavior that you are reinforcing (e.g., "Thank you for sharing your toys with Susie"). Stephen and Marianne Garber, authors of several popular books on managing behavior, suggest six noteworthy rules for using praise with children:[7]

1. *Praise behavior, not personality.* Take care to avoid using words like *good* and *bad.* Rather, describe the specific actions that are eliciting your praise.
2. *Use specific praise.* There's nothing worse than empty praise. "You've done a great job" doesn't motivate and inform me like "You really made me feel a part of the group during that discussion."
3. *Praise progress.* Communicate the concept of lifelong learning to your child. We're never there! We are always growing and changing. Point out the difference between your child's behavior or achievement today in comparison to last week or last month.
4. *Praise appropriately.* Don't overdo praise in public for shy children. And don't praise a child to the skies for a tiny accomplishment. Design the praise to fit the milestone.
5. *Give praise immediately.* Don't save it up for a rainy day. Deliver that compliment on the spot.
6. *Mix praise with unconditional love.* While praise is important, don't ever send the message to your child that your love is conditional upon achievement and accomplishment. Be there with love no matter what!

Reinforce positive behavior in specific, tangible ways. This second step of your behavior management plan includes tangible rewards that your child would like to have.

As an elementary school principal, I frequently inherited the behavior problems that were hard-core. The teacher and parent had tried everything, and nothing worked. My favorite was Dylan. A fourth grader, he simply didn't do his work. Not only did he not turn in any homework assignments; he just didn't bother to work much during the school day either. Dylan was obviously starved for attention. And he'd been getting plenty of it. The teacher was "on his case" from morning till dusk. And then his mother took over from there.

I spent some time talking with Dylan and found out what his favorite restaurant was. It just happened to be mine as well. We both had an obsession with cheeseburgers and french fries from McDonald's. I didn't have a clue as to whether my plan would work, but since all else had failed, I had nothing to lose. Dylan needed immediate feedback, but my budget and schedule did not permit daily lunches at the Golden Arches. So, I proposed to Dylan that if he could complete all of his assignments for three consecutive days, on the fourth day I would take him to lunch at McDonald's™. He brightened at the prospect. But I'd been fooled before. I checked in at the end of the first day. Dylan was on-track. Ditto for day two. I held my breath for day three, but Dylan came through for me. Dylan and I became good friends as he moved through fifth and sixth grade.

Our lunches became more infrequent, but I never stopped going to lunch with him. I discovered many of the challenges that faced him in his home life, and he got to know all about my children and work. I've tried this same system on other students, and it doesn't always work. They didn't find the idea of a one-on-one lunch with an adult all that attractive! To design a management system that works for you, you'll need to determine what your child's preferences may be at any given time. And then be prepared to vary the menu of choices as time passes. Of course, your budget and family values must always be kept in the forefront as you determine what reinforcers will be used. The Garbers suggest the following brief survey to determine your child's preferences.[8] Depending on your child's age, you may need to modify the questions:

- If you could wish for three things, what would they be?
- If you had the following amount of money, how would you spend it? ($.05, .10, .25, .50, 1.00, 5.00, more)
- If you could do something alone with Dad, what would it be?
- If you could do something special with Mom, what would it be?
- What extra privileges would you like to earn (extra TV time, later bedtime, etc.)?
- What would you like to do with a friend (play miniature golf, get ice cream cones, etc.)?

Ignore negative behavior. Common sense tells us that this practice should work, but it's much easier said than done. Most parents try ignoring and then report that it doesn't work. But perhaps you haven't *really* ignored your child. Forehand and MacMahon describe very specific skills that parents need to have in order to ignore.[9]

No eye contact or nonverbal cues. Deliberately turn your body away so that if you inadvertently smile or frown, your response cannot be noted by your child.

No verbal contact. Don't give any explanations or rationales for your behavior. Don't respond to your child when he or she asks why you are ignoring. If you feel the need to explain anything to your child, do it well before using the technique, and use statements such as "I'm going to ignore you when you're doing . . . , and when you stop, I will stop ignoring you." You can then demonstrate the ignoring technique to your child.

Use clear and consistent demands. Whenever you give a command to a child, you should be prepared to follow through to ensure that the child complies. Many parents and teachers spray commands like machine-gun bullets, hoping that one or more will find a mark, but unprepared to follow up if their directives are ignored. There are several other inappropriate ways to give commands that cause confusion and noncompliance from children. Chaining together several unrelated commands will cause an information overload and virtually ensure that nothing will happen. Typical of a chain command is "Turn off the TV; put away your toys; and finish your homework."

Vague and ambiguous commands are almost sure to be ignored by children with ADHD as well. "Be a good girl at the grocery store" is a perfect example of a vague command. While Mom may know perfectly well what the definition of a "good girl at the grocery store" is (no tantrums; sit in the cart the whole time), she has not communicated that concept to the child at all.

My favorite type of command that is sure to be ignored is the oxymoronic "question command." "Would you like to have dinner now?" The parent is well-meaning and feels he or she is being polite, but to the child there is clearly a choice involved. And odds are, the reply will be no. Requests in and of themselves are okay, but make sure you don't use the request format when what you really want is immediate compliance.

Another confusion: when commands are phrased in the "Let's . . ." mode, you are sending the message that you will be involved in the activity (e.g., "Let's pick up your toys"). If you don't intend to share the responsibility, then don't use those words. Your child may feel tricked and used. He or she then has a genuine excuse for noncompliance if you don't help. Many parents feel compelled to give lengthy explanations and rationales in conjunction with their commands. But these can also leave a child wondering. If you must give an explanation, then give it first, before you give the command. The last thing your child hears should be the clear and explicit directive. All other words will be lost. Here are a few simple rules for giving appropriate commands:

☐ Be specific and direct. Make sure you have your child's attention and establish eye contact.

☐ Give only one command at a time.

☐ Wait for five seconds for compliance before giving any additional instructions.

Provide consequences to decrease negative behaviors. Some authors use the word *punishment* to describe what happens when a child misbehaves. I prefer the phrase *negative consequences*. If your child doesn't perceive the consequence as negative, then he or she won't be successful in decreasing the inappropriate behavior. Some children delight in being sent to their rooms. They have TVs, VCRs, computers, and hand-held video games. Where's the punishment? The same principle applies when teachers send students to the principal's office for disciplinary reasons. Many students found this excursion to be a welcome respite from classwork. While in the office they visited with the secretary and caught up on school gossip. Unless I was there at exactly the right moment to apply (figuratively, not literally) the appropriate consequences, students missed the message entirely. In order for negative consequences to be effective, remember these helpful rules:

☐ Make sure that both you and your child know exactly what behavior you are trying to eliminate (e.g., interrupting, fighting with sister, talking back to parent).

☐ Make sure that the consequence follows immediately on the heels of the offending behavior.

☐ Make sure that the consequence follows after each and every occurrence of the offending behavior.

☐ Make sure that you are calm and matter-of-fact when you administer the consequence. If your child suspects that you are frenzied and frantic, kiss compliance goodbye.

☐ Make sure that when your child exhibits the desired behavior, he or she is positively reinforced.

Overcorrect to diminish inappropriate behaviors. Overcorrection was first suggested by Dr. Nathan Azrin, a psychologist, and consists of having a child practice and practice and practice the "right" way to behave or do a task. The consequence of repetition is designed to eradicate the unwanted behavior. I've used this procedure with great success on students who persisted in running in the halls. After they practiced walking up and down the halls (with parental permission, of course) for thirty minutes after school, they were more inclined to think twice before racing headlong toward the gymnasium or washrooms.

Token Reinforcers and Time-outs

Reward systems based on tokens or points and time-outs are the two most common behavior-management techniques.

What is a token economy? One common system involves some kind of token economy based on points or an
object of some sort (some families use poker chips, but if
you find this objectionable, find another kind of token in
the toy or hobby shop, like tiddly winks or bingo chips). The
token economy system is very similar to the monetary system on which our society operates, only much smaller. Children will earn tokens or points for their "work," which is
compliance with rules. They will then be able to exchange
their tokens or points for a variety of rewards. Use of the
token economy with children younger than three is not
practical, since their ability to comprehend symbols and
numbers is not developed. There are a number of accepted and well-researched advantages to a token economy program:

☐ Token systems permit parents to manage child behavior
by drawing on rewards that are more powerful than mere
praise and attention. Hence, greater and more rapid improvements in compliance can often be achieved.

☐ Token systems are highly convenient reward systems.
Chips and points can be taken anywhere, dispensed anywhere, dispensed anytime, and used to earn virtually
any form of privilege or tangible incentive.

☐ Token rewards are likely to retain their value or effectiveness throughout the day and across numerous situations. In contrast, children often satiate quickly with
food rewards, stickers, or other similar reinforcers. Because tokens can be exchanged for an almost limitless
variety of rewards, their effectiveness as reinforcers is
less likely to fluctuate than that of a specific reward.

☐ Token systems permit a more organized, systematic, and fair approach to managing children's behavior. The system makes it very clear what children earn for particular behaviors and what number of points or chips is required for each privilege or reward. This avoids the arbitrariness often seen when a child may be granted a reward or privilege on the spur of the moment because the parent is in a good mood rather than because the child has earned it. Similarly, it prevents parents from denying earned rewards simply because the child misbehaved once during the day.

☐ Token systems result in increased parental attention to appropriate child behavior and compliance. Because parents must dispense the tokens, they must attend and respond more often to behaviors that they might otherwise have overlooked. The children also make parents more aware of their successes or accomplishments in order to earn the tokens.

☐ Token systems teach a fundamental concept of society: that privileges and rewards as well as most of the things we desire in life must be earned by the way we behave. This is the work ethic that parents naturally wish to instill in their children: that the harder they work and the more they apply themselves to handling responsibilities, the greater will be their rewards.[10]

Is reinforcement really that important? You may encounter critics along the way or even be skeptical yourself of the importance of reinforcement in helping your child learn appropriate behaviors and skills. But without rewards, children with ADHD are easily pulled toward activities that promise far more rewards. Make no mistake that along with heavy doses of reinforcement, you also must provide education and encouragement for your child to appreciate and reward himself or herself. Being able to take personal pride and satisfaction in one's accomplishments helps to increase self-esteem and give the child a feeling that he or she has some control over life. Shelley and Bob Burns turned to massive doses of positive reinforcement for their son, Daniel, reasoning that he had taken "more hits on his self-esteem than a typical child." They were pleasantly surprised to find that it worked!

It helped us break a cycle of constant negative reinforcement. We chose a few behaviors to target that were really causing major conflict: not waking up Mom and Dad in the morning, getting dressed, brushing teeth, going to the bathroom in the morning (yes, we needed to work on this), and carrying his plate to the sink. We gave Daniel two tokens if he did it without being asked, one token for being asked, and no tokens if asked more than once. When the token jar was full, he could choose an activity to do with Mom or Dad. The activity got to last as long as he wanted, since he was in charge. This helped bring a lot of smiles to our family.

What are some good reinforcers? Your child will no doubt have plenty of ideas for reinforcers that appeal to him or her, but here are some suggestions to get you started. Some short-term or daily rewards might include video-game privileges, videos, TV, CDs, use of the telephone, staying up an extra half hour, playing a game with a parent, having a friend over to play, choosing a special dessert, visiting a friend, or working on a craft project. Some longer-term rewards might include going out to a fast-food restaurant, going out to a more expensive restaurant, going out for a hot fudge sundae, going to a movie, going on a picnic, buying a cassette, or visiting grandparents for the weekend.

What is time-out, and how can I use it effectively? Time-out is a very effective disciplinary methodology. Used properly, it means removing a child, for a specific and relatively short period of time, from a situation that is enjoyable and full of positive reinforcement to a much less pleasant situation. Time-out is a wonderful alternative to spanking younger children and an excellent way to remove an older child from a potentially explosive situation. There are several important rules to remember:

☐ The time-out location must be safe (in case your child becomes upset or agitated), uninteresting, and away from mainstream activity. The child must prefer to be elsewhere.

☐ The time-out rules must be carefully explained to your child ahead of time. Be sure to tell your child that every time he or she engages in a certain behavior, a time-out will result. If your child refrains from that behavior, no time-out will occur.

☐ Set a reasonable time limit based on the child's age. One minute per year of age is reasonable. If your child resists, add minutes for noncompliance. Lead your child back to the time-out area, but do not exceed more than three one-minute add-ons. You'll probably need to try another consequence if the penalties don't work.

☐ Brief periods of grounding function as "time-out" for older children (over twelve), but beware of anything longer than a few days.

☐ Never apologize or discuss the time-out after it's over. And don't require your child to apologize for being in time-out. Once the time-out is over, repeat your command if you were asking your child to do something. Be consistent and mean business.

☐ As soon as possible after a time-out, catch your child being good and give him or her some praise. This will let your child know that you aren't holding a grudge and that you will always give positive attention when he or she behaves appropriately.

What Are the Special Concerns for Parents of an Infant with a Difficult Temperament?

While diagnosing ADHD in infancy is not possible, Stella Chess and Alexander Thomas identified certain temperamental qualities of children that made them more "difficult" to parent. Dr. Stanley Turecki wrote a book about such children, entitled *The Difficult Child*. Difficult children do not respond well to changes in their environment, have greater negative moods, and may also have intense reactions to minor events in their environment. As infants, difficult children have a very high activity level, are restless and overactive in their sleep patterns, and are a challenge during routine care activities, such as changing and bathing. Difficult infants may be picky eaters and often have an unexplained higher occurrence of allergy to formula. While there are assuredly no treatments or programs for difficult infants, experienced caregivers know that certain responses may be more effective in calming difficult infants:

☐ Daily schedules for feeding and sleeping should be consistent and adapted to the child's needs.

☐ When the child cries excessively, swaddling in a tight, warm blanket may be soothing. Help the child calm down by placing your warm hands and fingertips over the forehead and eyes. Keep the head in midline by gently cupping the chin with one hand.

☐ Guide the infant to suck on a thumb or pacifier to gain self-control through sucking.

☐ Avoid dynamic, loud activity within the infant's sight and hearing.

☐ Feed the infant in a quiet, darkened room. A rocking chair provides consistency and soothing motion for feeding and quiet times. Use the same chair, type of bottle, and procedure consistently for feeding.

☐ Be aware of physical distractions within the child's environment, and avoid sensory overstimulation. Examples of sensory stimuli to avoid are a loud radio or television, a fan moving in front of a light source, a computer printer running, flashing lights, or defective fluorescent lighting.

☐ Gradually provide the child with more opportunities to observe people or activities. If the child becomes stressed, swaddle it tightly and give gentle verbal reassurance together with soft strokes.

☐ Avoid sudden changes in environmental conditions. For example, avoid taking the infant directly from air conditioning to hot outside air.[11]

How Do I Manage My Preschooler if I Suspect ADHD?

Children are not usually diagnosed with ADHD until after they enter formal schooling. Kindergarten and first grade are the most common identification points. However, with more and more preschoolers involved in formal school settings and day-care arrangements, the demands for "fitting in" and "behaving" come earlier and earlier. Teachers and caregivers may suggest that your child exhibits ADHD-like characteristics. When a preschooler is exhibiting behaviors that point to ADHD, the following important questions should be kept in mind:

- Is your child just immature? One way to determine this is to consider whether his or her behaviors have improved and are improving over time.
- Is the situation too demanding? Some school settings are inappropriate for preschoolers. They may be expected to sit still too long or to complete tasks that are too difficult for them.
- Is the teacher's classroom management effective? Are the rules clearly stated? Is the child oppositional and defiant toward even the simplest of rules?

Whether a child is formally diagnosed with ADHD as a preschooler makes little difference. Severe behavior problems must be addressed consistently and immediately, regardless. When in doubt, attend the preschool screening in your local school district. The school psychologist along with other professionals will evaluate your child in comparison to the norms for his or her age level. He or she may be eligible for special public school services at the preschool level if he or she is experiencing significant delays or problems in private preschool.

How Can I Keep My Elementary-Age Child with ADHD on Track?

We probably know more about and are more successful in dealing with the elementary-school child with ADHD than any other age group. Teachers at this level are trained to be child-centered rather than subject-centered. Elementary-age children are beginning to develop cognitive skills that enable them to reason more readily than they could as toddlers and preschoolers. They have not yet entered the frustration and confusion of adolescence. This is the time to consolidate your gains in terms of building a relationship with your child. This is the time to build habits, solidify positive behaviors, and gain a strong academic foundation. Parents of elementary-age students can look forward to working with a team of professionals at the school level who are experienced in developing behavior-management programs for children.

Will Our Family Survive an Adolescent with ADHD?

Parenting any adolescent takes uncommon amounts of patience and wisdom. Parenting an adolescent with ADHD must surely qualify you for sainthood. But it can be done. Here are some helpful hints from an expert who has followed many young people with ADHD into adulthood.

☐ Intervene with the outside world on behalf of the child with ADHD as much as needed when the child is young, but begin to slow down each year as he or she gets older.

☐ Give your child increasing responsibility with each year, and let her know you believe she can handle it.

☐ Let go of your dreams for your child's potential. Instead, seek to uncover his dreams. Then support them. Just because he shows natural ability with numbers, that doesn't mean he can or would want to become an accountant. Quit pushing, and let him use those number skills to become a top-notch salesman, or whatever he wants to become.

☐ Let your ADHD young adult follow a creative path toward adulthood. Just because everyone else in the family has a college degree doesn't mean your ADHD child has to have one too. Let go. I'm not saying persons with ADHD can't make it in college, but that decision needs to fit his or her goals.

☐ Give your child your belief in her ability to do well by and for herself. Not only is such belief a precious gift; it also sets up a greater likelihood of success.[12]

Parenting a child with ADHD takes as much self-discipline for parents as it does for your offspring. It's tempting to develop worst-case scenarios by the dozen in your mind as you contemplate your child's future. One must discipline one's self to live one day at a time. One must concentrate on celebrating and rejoicing in the small steps of success. The future will arrive, but only one day at a time.

♦ Endnotes

1. Russell Barkley, *Defiant Children: A Clinician's Manual for Training Parents* (New York: The Guilford Press, 1987).

2. Barkley, 66.

3. Barbara Y. Whitman and Carla Smith, "Living with a Hyperactive Child: Principles of Families, Family Therapy, and Behavior Management," in *Attention Deficit Disorders and Hyperactivity in Children*, ed. by P. J. Accardo, T. A. Blondis, and B. Y. Whitman (New York: Marcel Dekker, Inc., 1991), 187–211.

4. John F. Taylor, *Helping Your Hyperactive/Attention Deficit Child* (Rocklin, Calif.: Prima Publishing and Communications, 1994), 324–352.

5. Elaine K. McEwan, *Solving School Problems: Kindergarten through Middle School* (Wheaton, Ill.: Harold Shaw Publishers, 1992), 13.

6. Lauren Braswell and Michael Blomquist, *Cognitive Behavioral Therapy with ADHD Children: Child, Family and School Interventions* (New York: The Guilford Press, 1991), 192.

7. Stephen Garber, Marianne Daniels Garber, and Robyn Freeman Spizman, *Good Behavior: Over 1200 Solutions to Your Child's Problems from Birth to Age Twelve* (New York: Villard Books, 1987), 9–13.

8. Garber et al., 18.

9. Rex L. Forehand and Robert J. MacMahon, *Helping the Noncompliant Child: A Clinician's Guide to Parent Training* (New York: The Guilford Press, 1981), 68–70.

10. Barkley, 99–100.

11. Clare B. Jones, *Sourcebook for Children with Attention Deficit Disorder: A Management Guide for Early Childhood Professionals and Parents.* (Tucson, Ariz.: Communication Skill Builders, 1991), 30.

12. Lynn Weiss, *Attention Deficit Disorder in Adults* (Dallas: Taylor Publishing, 1992), 102–103.

7

SURVIVAL SKILLS
Commonly Asked
Questions

Surviving at home takes more than good intentions. Just wishing things were better will never result in positive change. You must be proactive and you must have a plan. In parenting a child with ADHD, you will need to break down even seemingly simple tasks and concepts into logical and sequential steps as you teach your child how to survive in a world that most often seems confusing and illogical to him or her.

The families whose experiences have been included in this book are a rich source of helpful ideas and strategies. I have included their advice here along with research-based information from a variety of professional experts.

How Can I Teach My Child a Task?

The mistake that many of us make when asking a child to do a task is we assume too much. We assume, because we've given the directions within earshot of the child, that he or she was listening and understood the directions. We assume, because the child headed off to do the task, that he or she will follow through and complete the task. When teaching your child to do simple tasks, use the following guidelines:

☐ First of all, be sure that your child won't be overwhelmed by the size and complexity of the task. Cleaning one's room is a task that is unmanageable for a child with ADHD. The task needs to be broken down into many small tasks (e.g., cleaning out one drawer, putting all of the games away, or dusting the tops of the furniture).

☐ Make sure that the task is within your child's capabilities to complete. As he or she gains confidence with simple tasks, add one or two more difficult ones to the repertoire.

☐ When explaining the task to the child, make sure that you have eye contact. Never shout instructions in the general direction of the child from another room.

☐ Speak quietly and slowly to the child, using simple words and short sentences. Patiently repeat the instructions if necessary. Some children with ADHD have an auditory problem and will need several repetitions of instructions before processing them adequately.

☐ Supplement verbal instructions with picture cues or actual demonstrations. When demonstrating, proceed through each step slowly.

☐ If the task contains multiple steps, break it down into its parts. Be sure your child understands one part before moving on to the next one.

☐ When your child has completed the task, give affirmation and praise.

How Can I Help My Child Control Anger?

If your child consistently loses his or her temper, it's time to use the following checklist to evaluate your home environment to see what might be changed to help your child gain control.

1. Do you or other members of your family have outbursts of temper? "Children learn what they live" with, so if you can't control your temper, don't expect your child to act any differently.

2. Is your child more likely to be angry when she is hungry, tired, or has been confined to one space or activity for a period of time? Make sure that you adhere to set mealtimes and bedtimes. Carry healthy snacks with you whenever you're on the road, and provide lots of opportunities for physical exercise. Keep track of when and where temper tantrums occur. You may be able to gain insight into what triggers a tantrum and treat the problem.

3. Does your child always or usually get what he wants from a temper tantrum? If you cave in and buy the toy at the supermarket or give him the sweet before dinner, you are teaching your child to use temper tantrums. These tantrums will escalate as the child gets older and the stakes get higher.

4. Are there warning signals that your child is headed toward a tantrum? With concern and empathy, help your child talk out her feelings.

5. Do you give your child praise and positive reinforcement when you see him handling a frustrating situation well?

6. Have you taught your child some skills to use when he's feeling "ready to blow"? Self-talk (referred to earlier) and assertive statements may help (e.g., "I'm mad about the way you treated me"; "I'm upset about something. Can we talk about it right away?"). Give your child a phrase or warning indicator that he can use with you if he's feeling upset and frustrated. You should attend to this key phrase with no questions asked. Role-play some typical situations where he loses his temper. Practice responses that might work in place of a tantrum. Does your child know the value of physical exercise in defusing explosive feelings? Run laps or do push-ups with your child if he needs a release from building emotional pressure.

7. Have you learned how to ignore a temper tantrum? Ignoring is an effective way to diminish unwanted behaviors like tantrums. If physical harm or property damage are likely, this won't be practical. Having a safe time-out place is ideal.

How Can I Get and Keep My Child's Attention?

Getting and keeping your child's attention is crucial to successful communication. You can never assume, just because your child is in the same room with you, that he or she will be attending to what you say. Educators are particularly good at inventing and experimenting with "attention-getters," and parents can definitely benefit from borrowing some of them:

☐ Agree on a special signal with your child (e.g., turning off the lights, flashing the lights, ringing a bell, playing a bar of music on the harmonica). When that signal occurs, it means your child should stop what he is doing and look at you for instructions.

☐ Vary the tone of your voice. If you are always speaking loudly, try following your loud command with a whisper.

☐ Make eye contact. Proximity is also helpful. Even though your child may be looking at you, if she is across the room, the possibility for "losing her" is strong.

☐ Use silliness, humor, mystery, and a few theatrics when appropriate. Just remember your child's penchant for "going off the deep end," and don't overdo it.

☐ Use multisensory approaches. Draw pictures, use color, and employ demonstrations when explaining something new to your child.

☐ Explain the purpose and relevance of what you are telling your child.

☐ Build connections for your child between what you are saying and something he already knows or has done.

☐ Use physical contact (e.g., hands on shoulders or side of head).

☐ Take time to praise your child when she's focused and attending.

☐ Agree on a private signal that can be used when you're in public (e.g., pointing to eyes or ears, meaning you want your child to look and listen; or tapping your chin, meaning, "Watch my face and pay attention").

☐ When your child is able to write, encourage him to take notes about what you are saying. Or, make a list of notes while you are giving the explanation, and give it to your child to keep. You can draw simple pictures for children who don't yet read.[1]

There are a number of games and activities that can help to improve your child's attentional skills. They include:

Simon Says. Start with one or two instructions, and gradually add more as the child's skills improve.

Concentration™ Game by Milton Bradley.

Treasure Hunt. Give a map with a series of locations marked. Have the child find each location with instructions on what to do at each location (e.g., go to the pantry and find a can of tomato soup. The message will be taped on the bottom). Make sure you provide a treasure at the end of the hunt. Alter the clues and length of the hunt according to your child's age and abilities.

Flashcards. This simple and inexpensive learning aid will improve visual memory for words and train attention. The content of the cards can change (e.g., math facts, common sight words, colors, reading vocabulary), but always give positive reinforcement and rewards for goals accomplished. And don't overdo it—a short time on a set of cards is enough.

Rhymes and poetry. Memorize poetry, nursery rhymes, and Bible verses to improve listening skills, attention, and memory.

Jokes and riddles. Use jokes and riddles to improve listening and thinking skills.

Games. Games with cards, dice, or Dominoes can help develop counting skills and concentration.

Computer games. These can improve concentration and eye-hand coordination. Use with good judgment and sparingly, however.

What Are Techniques for Channeling My Child's Energy?

Bob and Shelley Burns recommend getting a mini-trampoline for your home. Whenever Daniel, age six, gets a little wild, he has the option of using his excess energy in an acceptable way. Other parents recommend sports activities, especially those that are very active but not highly competitive (e.g., gymnastics, dance, soccer, swimming). Discuss your child's needs with the coach, and make sure that he or she has the right qualities to work with your child. Avoid sports like baseball or golf, where the demands for concentration are very high. I highly recommend martial arts training as a vehicle for developing self-confidence, concentration, and self-control. The right instructor (one who emphasizes self-control and calmness, not violence and aggressiveness) can teach your child much about sportsmanship, cooperative learning, respect, and discipline.

Social and church organizations, particularly those that combine physical activities with learning, are excellent. Earning Awana or Scout badges can help your child learn to tackle a small task as part of reaching a larger goal.

The Martinellis have their son Dustin, who is extremely hyperactive, involved in a variety of sports.

A great deal of Dustin's treatment revolves around "deactivating" him constantly. We channel his physical energies into year-round sports to eat up the top layer of activity: hockey, football, skiing, and swimming. He also played soccer, baseball and basketball for three years each before moving on to the aforementioned sports. In addition to organized sports, I make a very deliberate effort to "deactivate" Dustin with bike riding, roller blading, sledding, and other seasonal outdoor play. I strive for two hours of physical activity a day . . . just to take out that *top* layer of energy!

How Can I Help My Child Control Impulsiveness?

Impulsiveness is a hallmark of children with ADHD. It's the attribute that gets them into trouble more often than not. Even when your child can tell you what the rules are and what the reasons are for the rules, impulsiveness will overcome all rationality, and he or she will do it anyway. Your child is oblivious to consequences and may even totally deny being the perpetrator when caught in the act. Here are several methods that may help you reduce impulsivity in your child.

Delay of gratification. Stand firm that she cannot always have what she wants when she wants it, but keep a positive or neutral mood, so that waiting is seen as a normal part of growing up.

Self-talk. We have used this term before, and it is an important one as you work with your child. Teach your child to give himself quiet directions when feeling an impulse coming on: "I can wait"; "It's not a good idea to throw snowballs when it's against the rules"; "Calm down"; "Ask Mom first before I take the last piece of pie." When your child is able to talk to himself effectively to moderate impulsiveness, be sure you give him reinforcement and praise. Rewards that are given unpredictably at intervals are very powerful in encouraging your child to repeat a behavior.

Thinking about the reward. Teach your child to delay gratification through picturing the benefit that will result. She can see herself receiving praise and a hug, playing with a new toy, or enjoying lunch at McDonald's. Another tactic is to have the child distract herself by thinking of something else.

Role-playing. Act out scenarios involving patience and consideration for others. Practice taking turns, sharing toys, carrying on a conversation without interrupting. By telling stories, role playing, and drawing pictures with a child, you can model numerous self-control behaviors.

Bibliotherapy. Find books in which fictional boys and girls have the same types of problems as your child. Use the book as a springboard for discussion. *How to Help Children with Common Problems* suggests read-alouds for dozens of the common problems of childhood, and there are new books being written all the time.[2]

Group reward. Help your child realize the impact of his actions on others. Impatience causes problems and annoyance to others. Rewarding the group when the child can be patient may be helpful for some children, and will provide a degree of peer pressure for them to maintain control. Use this technique judiciously in the family group. You will want to build rapport and cohesiveness first.

Problem solving. We have already mentioned this important technique, and teaching your child to use it to reduce impulsiveness is important. Ask your child to evaluate her thinking: Was that a good idea? Preschoolers especially should be shown alternate solutions. Rather than getting angry because a friend won't play the child's favorite game, teach your child some alternatives. "If you'll play my favorite game now, then I'll play your game next." Parents should always be ready to jump in with possible solutions and alternatives to show the child that there's more than one way to get what she wants. Whenever you see a good decision being made, be sure to praise it. Above all, don't launch into comparisons (verbal or mental) of your child with a more well-behaved friend or sibling.

Working off frustrations. Some parents find great success with periods of exercise. Having a child perform useful household tasks as "work" for which he is "paid" can often be helpful. Be flexible, and see what helps your child.

Motor inhibition. Teach the child to do slowly some purposeful activity, such as stringing beads, snapping together blocks, or assembling models that require glue. This activity may help to develop slowness and accuracy. Choose the activity or model with care so that it is not beyond your child's capabilities.[3]

How Can I Teach Responsibility and Independence?

One of the major reasons that children are often not responsible is that parents have always done everything for them. This is an easy trap to fall into when you believe your child is not capable of making wise choices and good decisions. Frequently children with ADHD give their parents plenty of reason to feel this way. It's a vicious cycle that you will need to break out of if you want to raise a child who is independent and responsible. You must stop thinking of your child as incompetent and unreliable (even though the school may reinforce this feeling for you) and start thinking of his or her future. Your child's feelings of self-worth and the ability to get along in "real life" are more important than academic skills.

Find areas in which you can teach responsibility to children, and gradually increase those responsibilities as they demonstrate competence—including caring for a pet, caring for personal belongings, looking out for a younger child, and performing household chores. Involve family members in a discussion of responsibility and what it means. List the responsibilities of each family member on a large piece of paper. These lists can include the mundane tasks of life (earning money, buying food, cooking, and cleaning) as well as attitudes and feelings (being good-natured, helping others). Teach your child as many "real world" skills as you can. Teach your child some basic survival skills for social situations. Help your child learn to use leisure time productively. Organize social experiences for your child that will help him or her to be responsible and independent in interactions with others.

How Can I Get My Child to Keep His or Her Room Clean?

Neatness and organization pose real challenges to children with ADHD. The child with ADHD lacks the organizational skills that are needed to complete the many steps

that go into cleaning up a room. Here are some hints to
help you get started.

☐ Start early with continuous training and expectations.
  Hold a small child accountable for picking up toys. Provide
  baskets, boxes, and containers so toys can be organized.
  Without appropriate storage or organizational structure
  provided by the parents, children with ADHD will be at a
  real disadvantage.

☐ Assign cleaning tasks that are simple and age appropriate. The toddler can put dirty laundry in the hamper.
  The five-year-old can empty waste baskets and take out
  the garbage. The key is regularity and expectations.

☐ Reward neatness. Hold your child accountable, and give
  rewards for goals that are met.

☐ Do a task analysis of a clean room, and develop a chart
  showing the various jobs that must be completed to qualify (e.g., clear the floor, dust the tops of furniture, put all
  dirty clothing in the hamper, vacuum the carpet, put all
  games and toys in the closet, throw away things that are
  no longer used).

☐ Model neat behavior, and be willing to construct a chart for
  cleaning your room (or some area of the house that needs
  it—like the garage or basement). Your child will be motivated by the fact that you are participating in the project.

How Can Our Home Support Learning?

There are many things you can do to communicate to your
child that learning is important.

In the family:

- Be aware of what is being studied at school, and try to apply what is learned in school to activities of daily living. This will help build connections for your child.
- Encourage reading at home. Visit the library at least once a week, and read aloud on a daily basis. Read the comics together. Read a current event from the newspaper every day and discuss it. During long car rides, listen to books on tape.
- Schedule parent-teacher conferences regularly to discuss your child's progress at school. Don't wait for the teacher to call you.
- If your budget permits and your child needs help, hire a tutor once or twice a week. This tutoring should continue throughout the summer to consolidate gains.
- Develop a behavior plan that incorporates behavior both at home and at school. Correspond daily with the teacher if needed.
- Arrange a quiet study area.
- Play games that use numbers. Use math daily.
- Develop a list of activities that you can draw from when boredom and misbehavior hang heavy over your household. The following suggestions were provided by many parents of ADHD children. Gather your own family council together to brainstorm your own list.

Outdoor or good weather play with others:

- Have a popcorn and fruit drink stand
- Camp in the backyard in sleeping bags or tents
- Go for a walk or a hike
- Swim, run, or play ball
- Water play with hose and plastic slide cloth

Indoor or inclement weather play with others:

- Play jacks
- Make a tent with a sheet and a card table
- Telephone a friend
- Gather shoes from around the house and play shoe store
- Using a comb, brush, cup with water, and towel, play barber shop or hairdresser
- Put things in a mystery sack, allowing another child (sibling or playmate) to reach into the sack and feel the object as the last clue
- Play card games
- Play table games
- Make up a pretend radio or television interview, and talk into a recorder

Outdoor or good weather solitary play:

- Watch the stars through a telescope
- Look through binoculars
- Work on gardening
- Line up pop cans and throw pebbles at them
- Feed pets
- Practice jump-rope
- Draw pictures of your yard to show the seasons of the year
- Water some flowers with a sprinkling can
- Make a collection of leaves from the yard
- Swat flies
- Feed spiders
- Volunteer to sweep a neighbor's sidewalk without pay (or shovel if it's snowy)
- Draw a portrait of a house, tree, flower, or other outdoor scene on an art pad

- Play on a climbing structure or swing set
- Play in a sandbox
- Roller skate
- Ride a bike
- Use a skateboard
- Go jogging, ice skating, swimming, fishing, horseback riding
- Build something for the backyard (bird house, bird feeder)
- Feed bread to birds
- Train and groom pets
- Select, clean, and label objects for a garage sale
- Earn money by washing cars or mowing lawns
- Feed ducks, pigeons, songbirds, or squirrels
- Collect interesting rocks
- Write or draw on the sidewalk with chalk.

Indoor or inclement weather solitary play:

- Listen to music
- Try out an electronics kit
- Punch a punching bag
- Make muffins
- Hum
- Pop popcorn
- Make an item for a model railroad or toy car set out of frozen fruit sucker sticks, toy logs, or building toys
- Plan a day trip for the family to take
- Write letters to relatives, friends, or pen pals
- Color in a coloring book
- Make a crossword puzzle for family members to solve
- Organize a home slide show
- Dance
- Work on a large jigsaw puzzle

- Play with building toys and construction kits
- Draw with colored pencils
- Sing
- Using liquid glue, make a collage out of pictures from old magazines
- Practice a musical instrument
- Start or work on a collection (stamps, butterflies, bottle caps, coins, trading cards)
- Play with a flashlight
- Make shadow pictures on the wall
- Make new greeting cards using pictures and words from old ones and drawing additional designs
- Make things with modeling dough
- Draw a picture of something you would like to do
- Invent a machine that would help you in some way, and draw a picture of it
- Draw a picture of your house or apartment
- Draw pictures of inventions we could use in our family
- Put one letter of the alphabet on each of twenty-six cards, shuffle them, and try to put them in order faster each time
- Cut shapes from construction paper and paste them on a large piece of colorful cardboard to make an attractive design
- Paste a pretty picture on cardboard, then cut it into pieces to create your own jigsaw puzzle.

Family activities:

- Have a backward dinner (dessert first)
- Watch home videos
- Play word games and trivia games
- Have a story-in-the-round, in which each member adds the next page to the story

- Tell fill-in-the-blank stories, in which each member adds a word when invited to do so by the storyteller
- Read aloud from a favorite book, and act it out
- Go to a show, sports event, museum, or zoo
- Do a benevolent project anonymously for a needy person or family
- Play instruments and sing
- Go window shopping
- Drive to a nearby interesting place[4]

How Can I Avoid Homework Hassles?

Homework is the dreaded "*H*-word." Just at the time when everyone is exhausted and your child's medication is wearing off, it's time to do homework. Many parents dread this time of day because of the potential for frayed tempers and short fuses. Joanna Griswold, age ten, is exhausted when she comes home from school. Her mother reports that evenings are a challenge.

> It seems that the mental energy required to perform all day at school just totally wears her out. By the end of the day she has a very low tolerance for frustration, has great difficulty doing schoolwork legibly, and gets into fights with her sister. She is not physically tired, and will not be able to sleep if I put her to bed early, but she is mentally fatigued.

Monica Kingston says that when Danny comes home from school, his medication has pretty much worn off, and if his homework isn't done by dinner, he is shot for the day. The Scotts experience a similar situation with Billy and Phillip: "When the Ritalin™ wears off around 5:00 p.m. and can't be repeated, we have real problems with homework." Here are some hints that may help you ease the homework hassles:

☐ Establish a routine and set goals. Designate a specific location and a specific time, and try not to vary from it.

☐ Divide and conquer. Don't consider the entire assignment at once. Divide it into small parts, and work on only one at a time.

☐ Make lists of tasks and sub-tasks, and cross them off as you go. Give plenty of praise for each small item accomplished.

☐ Start with the easiest assignments first.

☐ Don't try to teach remedial reading along with homework. If there's an assignment that requires reading a passage or a lengthy set of directions, read them aloud to your child so he can move quickly to accomplish the task.

☐ Don't be shy about going to bat for your child if you believe the homework assignments are excessive and beyond her reasonable capabilities. Ask for modifications.

☐ Do keep the responsibility focused on the child.

☐ Make sure that your child knows exactly what has to be done and when it is due. Make sure he has an assignment notebook, and if necessary, send it back and forth every day with signatures from teachers and parents until habits are well formed. Develop a large monthly calendar for the wall or refrigerator that contains all of the activities and assignments that are due.

☐ Be a silent partner in the completion of homework. Be around and available to encourage and reinforce his attention to the task. Try not to interfere or be coercive.

☐ Be prepared and willing to answer questions. Read her textbooks if you have to in order to ensure that you understand the assignment and can answer questions quickly and keep her on task.

☐ Get to know each of your child's teachers and find out how willing they are to receive telephone calls regarding homework assignments. Some teachers readily provide their phone numbers. Some schools have homework hotlines.

☐ Make sure you have an ample supply of glue, poster board, note cards, colored pencils, folders, construction paper, and (if available) extra copies of textbooks at home. This will save last-minute trips to the store for materials that are needed to complete an assignment your child just remembered.

☐ Invest in a good dictionary, atlas, thesaurus, and perhaps a reasonably priced encyclopedia. If you have a computer, consider purchasing one of the major encyclopedias on CD-Rom. This will save those frantic last-minute trips to the library (if it's even open when you need it).

☐ Consider investing in a computer so your child can learn to type assignments on the computer. This will save hours of recopying rough drafts and will make all assignments look neater.

☐ Teach your child how to use the library and find information. If you don't have the skills, find and hire someone who does. A bright high-school student may be within your budget and could provide an excellent role model for your child.

☐ Minimize the frustration of math homework by using graph paper to align numbers in math problems. Before beginning a page of mixed problems, have your child circle the sign in each problem to make sure he or she uses the correct operation (+,-,x).

☐ Make sure the completed homework is returned. Supervise your child while he places the completed assignment in his book bag, which is placed in a strategic location near the door through which he will exit in the morning. If your child has a problem remembering to take the assignment out of the bag and turn it in, perhaps you'll want to have his teacher sign his assignment notebook at the end of the day to indicate that he turned in everything.

☐ Model doing homework for your child. While your child is doing homework, pay bills, write letters, or organize your schedule. Take a class yourself so that you have papers and assignments to complete.

☐ Use background music for variation. Some children find that this reduces distraction. Experiment.

☐ Introduce your child to graphic organizers like webs and mind maps.[5]

☐ Permit your child to change positions when studying to find the most efficient one. Some students work better lying stomach-down on the bed with the book on the floor.

☐ Give special assistance to your child before a test.[6]

☐ Break up homework periods into two or three smaller sessions with a snack or physical exercise in between.

☐ Be sensitive to your child's frustration level (and yours). Don't try to do too much at once.

☐ Agree on which parent will be the "homework buddy." Too many cooks will spoil this "homework brew."

How Can I Reduce Sibling Rivalry?

The parents whom I interviewed find that keeping harmony among family takes creativity, energy, and perseverance. Vivian Martinelli describes her family:

> Dustin has a "normal" brother who is two years older than he and another brother who is four years younger with very obvious ADHD. As my eldest son is now going through adolescence, not one of my three sons could be called easy or effortless to deal with. I pour all of my energies into effectively raising my children with every bit of education, counseling, and support that I can get hold of—I leave nothing to chance.

Brett Kingman has two older siblings, and his parents, Kay and John, feel sorry for the other children because they often don't get a fair share of their parents' time and attention. The siblings see Brett as a pest and often don't want to play with him, which exacerbates an already unfortunate situation.

Joan Griswold is very sensitive to the effects of ADHD on the household.

> Because the ADHD child is more difficult, I am aware that she tends to demand more of our attention. Her sister tends to play the "perfect" child and the clown to get attention. I am working on giving this sister more attention so she doesn't feel cheated. Also, the ADHD child tends to be impulsive, so she can haul off and hit her sister with very little provocation. I try to make them solve their problems, and while I discipline them for hitting each other, I try to avoid just blaming the ADHD child for the fights because I know that her sister is very good at (silently) egging her on and picking a fight to get her into trouble.

Siblings accuse children with ADHD of interrupting them, pestering them, borrowing things and breaking or losing them, and intruding on their space. Siblings also are aware of the amount of time and energy required to parent a child with ADHD and can be resentful and impatient. Your non-ADHD children need some basic information and understanding of what ADHD is. Jeffrey Tyrone's eighteen-year-old sister did a research paper for one of her college classes on ADHD, and her mother reports that she is much more understanding of her brother's behavior now. Siblings of children with ADHD also need to be taught some appropriate responses to use when their hyperactive and impulsive siblings act inappropriately. Here is one recommended technique that can be taught to siblings when inappropriate behaviors are used:

1. Stop whatever your are doing, and look directly into the eyes of the child with ADHD.

2. Ask him what he wants.
3. If possible, make a deal in which you let him have his way, to some extent, in exchange for no longer bothering and interrupting you.
4. End the conversation with a firm statement of exactly what you want (e.g., "Stop pestering me"; "Let me finish watching this TV program"; "Be quiet so I can finish my homework").[7]

Another alternative to verbally confronting the child with ADHD as illustrated above is to simply leave the scene so that a full-blown conflict does not arise. Telling the sibling to ignore the child with ADHD isn't good advice. Sometimes the best way to handle the situation is for the bothered sibling to stop what he or she is doing for a minute or two to give the child with ADHD some attention and then to let that child know, "Now I need to get back to my homework (or model building, or computer game)."

Maintaining consistency in the treatment and discipline of all children in the family when one or more of the children has ADHD is difficult. Some parents, in their attempts to avoid favoritism, fall into arbitrary traps of consistency, which in reality cause more stress and disharmony than an honest appraisal of the situation and a little truth. You can't possibly treat your child with ADHD and your non-ADHD children the same. They handle responsibilities differently; they are different ages; they are developmentally different. And you will be different in your approach to parenting at different points in your life. More important than artificial consistency are congruence and contemporaneous treatment.

Congruence means matching your feelings and your actions—giving your children honest appraisals of how their behavior has made you feel and what the impact will be.

We are human beings, and our sleep, nutrition, stress levels, and work demands vary greatly. It's okay to "lose it" once in a while if you respond to your child with honesty and clarity. "I'm sorry I was cross with you. We're not going out for ice cream right now. I feel the way I do because you said some nasty things to me. I'm going to sit in my time-out chair for a while and catch my breath. Maybe we'll go for ice cream in a little while."

Contemporaneous treatment is treatment according to the readiness and developmental level of your child. Treat your child according to his or her readiness to engage in an activity or handle a responsibility—regardless of what you would do with another child. It's okay to tell a second child, "When you're ready to handle this kind of responsibility, I'll let you do the same thing." Penalizing one child for the inability of another child to handle something is not fair. Families that are able to use the problem-solving processes mentioned earlier and talk out conflicts in family meetings will handle sibling rivalry with a minimum of problems. If your children can learn to express their feelings in calm but assertive ways rather than screaming, whining, hitting, grabbing, and teasing, your family climate will be much less stressful. Ignoring the problem, however, will not make it go away!

How Can I Teach My Child Social Skills?

Children with ADHD will not gradually learn social skills in the same way that other children learn them. Unfortunately, children with ADHD are often rated as the person least liked in the classroom. The child is completely unaware of the impact that his or her noisiness (clicks, whistles, sounds), curiosity, impatience, grabbiness (touching, poking, feeling), constant movement (fidgeting, drumming, chewing, bouncing), and talkativeness (interrupting, not taking turns, not listening to others) have on peers. Younger children (those in preschool and possibly even kindergarten or first grade) are much more forgiving of their classmates. But as children get older, they can be cruel and heartless in their responses to inappropriate social behavior. Set about to systematically teach your child social skills in five basic areas (conversational skills, adult interactions, peer interactions, handling emotions, and survival skills). You can't teach them all at once, of course. Don't even try, or you will be totally frustrated. Choose only one skill, and work on it in a variety of settings until you feel your child is showing the skills at least 50 to 60 percent of the time before you start a new skill. Your child's age and/or developmental level will dictate your level of expectation. An appropriate skill for a three-year-old is waiting his or her turn in a conversation, rather than making introductions or giving positive feedback. These social skills will be taught and learned over a period of many years.

Conversational skills

- Introduces self to others
- Introduces two people who don't know one another
- Starts a conversation
- Keeps a conversation going
- Interrupts a conversation
- Ends a conversation
- Gives positive feedback
- Gives critical or negative feedback
- Receives positive feedback
- Receives critical feedback
- Waits turn in conversation

- Demonstrates listening skills in conversation
- Uses telephone for conversation

Adult interactions

- Follows directions
- Accepts responsibility for own actions
- Offers help to adults
- Asks for help
- Accepts no for an answer
- Accepts help from adults

Peer interactions

- Shares
- Compromises
- Handles being teased
- Joins a group
- Offers to help
- Asserts own opinion
- Participates in group activities and games
- Handles peer pressure
- Handles being left out
- Leaves a group

Handling emotions

- Identifies own emotions
- Expresses own emotions
- Handles other people's anger
- Handles own anger
- Handles others' failure
- Handles own failure

- Handles others' success
- Handles own success

Basic skills

- Makes eye contact with other person
- Keeps pleasant face when conversing
- Maintains physical distance between self and others
- Speaks in a pleasant voice
- Keeps a still and relaxed body
- Speaks at an appropriate rate[8]

The first step in teaching a specific social skill is under-standing the basic components of the skill. In order to teach it to your child, you will have to break it down, explain what it looks like, tell your child the situations in which he should or shouldn't use the skill, give him some con-crete examples, and then model and role play the skill. That's all before your child can practice and use it in the "real world."

How Can I Help My Child's Self-Esteem?

Kermit the Frog of *Sesame Street* sings a song called "It's Not Easy Being Green." Children with ADHD could well sing their own version—"It's Not Easy Having ADHD." And it's not. The child with ADHD is a simmering pot of feelings that can boil over at a moment's notice. The child with ADHD has feelings of being a brat, being rejected, and being attacked. Brett Kingman is a particularly gifted six-year-old who was recently diagnosed with ADHD. He ar-ticulated his feelings to his parents so eloquently that they immediately made an appointment with a child psychologist to find out what was going on. He said:

> Everybody thinks I'm a brat. My teacher, my brother and sister, and even you. Nobody likes me. I can't do anything right. When I get bigger, I'm going to kill myself because I'm not good for anything.

Although every child with ADHD won't be able to put their feelings into words like Brett did, they are nonetheless very real. As Kay shared this experience with me, she was shaken.

> The terrible thing about what he was saying is that it was all true. He drives his siblings crazy. His teacher is on him all the time. And even my husband and I weren't totally in control of our feelings. I couldn't even tell him it was all in his imagination—because it wasn't. That's when I knew we needed help.

Parents of children with ADHD often feel depressed, frustrated, tired, trapped, exasperated, discouraged, intimidated, controlled, angry, overwhelmed, embarrassed, ashamed, and powerless. With feelings like this, it's no wonder that their children are feeling angry, criticized, attacked, abused, rejected, and annoyed. This vicious cycle must be interrupted and redirected to build self-esteem and develop pride. Your child's self-esteem is either nurtured and increased or torn down and destroyed by the messages he gets from you (and the rest of the people in his life). These messages are verbal and nonverbal, and unless the messages change drastically, your child's perception of himself will spiral downward.

Check yourself against the list below to find out whether you're sending the right messages.

1. Am I sending the message to my child that he is deliberately being "bad"?
2. Have I told my child either verbally or through my actions that "she could do better if she just tried"?
3. Do I make more negative than positive comments to my child?
4. Do I avoid spending time with my child because he is difficult?
5. Do I unfavorably compare my child to her peers or siblings?
6. Do I fail to listen to my child's concerns and fears?
7. Do I overprotect or do everything for my child?
8. Am I more often than not annoyed, impatient, and frustrated in my interactions with my child?
9. Do I blame my child (either verbally or nonverbally) for family stress and marital problems?
10. Do I criticize my child in front of other family members?
11. Do I pity my child?
12. Do I reject my child?

If you are guilty of even one of these self-esteem sins, begin now (with the help of professionals) to change your attitudes and the way you interact with your child. Dorothy Corkille Briggs' classic work, *Your Child's Self-Esteem,* on building self-esteem in children is worth reading from cover to cover if this is an area that is a problem for you. She says, "Children survive on acceptance, but they do not blossom on it. They need something stronger. They need cherishing. They must feel valued and precious and special just because they exist. Then, deep down they can like who they are."[9] Use the following guidelines and principles to begin building (or rebuilding) your child's self-esteem.

☐ Show faith in your child's ability.

☐ View your child as having special needs that you will help him to overcome rather than viewing your child as someone who is deliberately making life difficult for you.

☐ Emphasize your child's strengths (Karate, baseball, violin, drawing, picking up trash by the roadside, vaccuuming). Find an area in which your child can excel.

☐ Structure the environment to build successful experiences.

☐ Try to maintain a ratio of four positive comments to each negative comment.

☐ Keep a good behavior diary. Record everything your child does right. At the end of a day or two, sit down with your child and review the list together.

☐ Make a "Things I Like About Me" list. Make it a regular part of your interactions. Ask the question often (e.g., "What's one thing you like about how you acted at school today?")

☐ Teach your child to respond to unjustified criticism in nonaggressive ways.

☐ Use role playing to overcome the negative effects of teasing.

☐ Explain ADHD to your child in an age-appropriate, simple and honest way. Help him to understand that it is difficult for him to sit still, stifle interruptions, pay attention, and control his temper. Let him know that you understand him and will help him every day to learn better ways of responding. Reassure him that it isn't his fault that he's that way, but that he has to learn to change and grow.

☐ Make a list of what you like about your child, and share it with her often.

☐ Provide structure and organization for your child so he can feel successful and in control. Children need to feel that you are strong enough to protect them against their impulsive behavior. From her perspective as the mother of a grown son who is "successful," Marilyn Bryne has this advice for parents:

> Understand that there is more to your children than what is wrong. There are many things right. Look for them. Concentrate on them. Remember that your children are children of God. Don't miss what's right about them because you're too busy being mad about what's wrong with their behavior. Talk to people like me who have grown children who have turned out to be wonderfully accountable and self-sufficient adults.

That just about says it all.

♦ Endnotes

1. Adapted from materials in Sandra R. Rief, *How to Reach and Teach ADD/ADHD Children: Practical Techniques, Strategies, and Interventions for Helping Children with Attention Problems and Hyperactivity* (West Nyack, N.Y.: The Center for Applied Research in Education, 1993), 37–38.

2. Charles E. Schaefer and Howard L. Millman, *How to Help Children with Common Problems* (New York: Van Nostand Reinhold, 1981), 417–20.

3. Adapted from materials in Guy D. Ogan, *Can Anyone Help My Child: Therapies and Treatment for Attention Deficit and Other Learning and Behavioral Disorders in Children, Adolescents, and Adults* (Abilene, Tex.: Faith Publishing, 1994), 113–15.

4. John F. Taylor, *Helping Your Hyperactive/Attention Deficit Child* (Rocklin, Calif.: Prima Publishing and Communication, 1994), 417–20.

5. McEwan, *Solving School Problems,* 260–66.

6. McEwan, 143–48.

7. Adapted from Jack L. Fadley and Virginia N. Hosler, *Helping Your Hyperactive/ADD Child* (Springfield, Ill.: Charles C. Thomas Publisher, 1992), 173.

8. "Social Skills Checklist" developed by Dr. Jimmy L. Middlebrook and Dr. Rena B. Zweben, as cited in Garber et al., *Good Behavior.*

9. Dorothy Corkille Briggs, *Your Child's Self-Esteem* (New York: Dolphin Books, 1975), 89.

8

KEEPING MARRIAGE AND FAMILY ALIVE

The votes are in, and the results are almost unanimous. Having a child with ADHD can frequently result in depression, guilt, and family and marital discord. Please notice the phrase "can frequently result in." The culprit is not the ADHD, but the way in which the family handles it. I agree with the statement made by Robin Simons in *After the Tears:* "Having a handicapped child doesn't make a marriage fall apart. Not dealing with your feelings does."[1] The key to survival in your family and marital life is your ability to confront your feelings honestly, talk about the critical issues, and then brainstorm and solve problems creatively. In this chapter, we will explore some ways that families have tried to cope with ADHD.

How Can ADHD Affect Family and Marital Life?

The families I interviewed were eloquent on the topic. Rosemary and Walter Tyrone are attempting to deal with fourteen-year-old Jeffrey's rocky passage through adolescence on their own without counseling or support groups, and Rosemary confesses it hasn't been easy.

> I feel last year before Jeff was diagnosed I almost lost my family and my marriage. The problem is the grounds for all of our fighting. The problem is, nothing is ever accomplished.

Rosemary sometimes feels like she would like to quit being a parent, because there's a new hassle every day. But then she comes to her senses and realizes how very much she loves her child. Her salvation is a good friend whose son also has ADHD. They share funny stories and pray together.

There's no doubt in Laura Adams's mind that ADHD has affected her marriage and the atmosphere in her home:

> You're always dealing with a "problem" child. We can't go places or do things because Brian can't control himself in a new situation. My stomach is always in a knot whenever we try to go anywhere. It's no fun for anyone. It's always been a problem to get and keep baby-sitters.

When mothers and fathers don't agree, the problems are often more stressful. Helen Brown has to work at keeping her resentment and disappointment under control.

> Perry has added a certain stress in that he has to be monitored and disciplined a lot. That's not how we wanted

to spend our lives. It seems much more peaceful when he's not at home. My husband isn't much of a disciplinarian, and he isn't a Christian either. I have an extra burden.

The Kingstons are an inspiration to those families who are struggling with discord and division. Monica shares their secret:

I feel our marriage would be just as stable with or without the problem of ADHD. Greg and I have a deep love and commitment for each other that surpasses many of the problems that would otherwise become hazards in a marriage. We often balance each other out when it comes to dealing with Danny, as well as other issues. When I think I'm going to lose it, Greg steps in and can objectively handle a problem on a less emotional plane. By the same token, I am often able to speak for Danny when Greg puts too many restrictions on him. The general atmosphere in our home is not exactly peaceful. Danny loves to talk and demands much attention. It's hard to have any "quiet time" unless he's sleeping or outside playing.

How Can Counseling Help?

Those families who have used counseling as part of their treatment plan generally find it very helpful. Joan Griswold summarizes the issues very nicely:

We find it very helpful. When my ADHD daughter gets older, I may get her into some therapy to help with self-esteem issues if she is interested. I think that therapy has helped me a lot to identify what the issues are and open up new options for handling them. I realized that we have a tendency to let the ADHD child run the household, spending all of our energies on her and not setting enough limits. Therapy helped remind me who's in charge and helped me set better limits without feeling guilty about that. Therapists also have a broad range of ideas for discipline problems, reward systems, chores, etc. It's the practical advice that really helps, along with getting some encouragement that "You're doing okay. You're not a failure as a mother."

Counseling can be expensive, especially if your medical insurance doesn't pay, and it's often difficult to find just the right therapist. A counselor who specializes in the treatment of ADHD may provide the best services.

What about a Support Group?

Reviews are mixed regarding support groups. Some moms couldn't live without them. Vivian Martinelli has received both individual and family counseling, but she believes her CHADD support group is far more helpful:

The feeling of being part of a group facing the same challenges gives me an enormous boost, which carried me through longer than a counseling session.

Others do not find what they need. Diane and Robert Marshall attended two meetings of a support group together. Bob made this humorous observation before he dropped out: "We can help them. I need someone who will help us."

Diane gave the group another chance but eventually dropped out as well. She observes:

> There are two mothers who monopolize the group with whining about their children whom they can't take anywhere with them. When others try to give advice or ask questions to help them figure out their own problem, they always say, "I tried that, and it didn't work." I found this to be very frustrating and not at all helpful.

In this case, the local support group needed leadership to refocus the group when these two parents monopolized it and kept it focused on negative issues. The area of support groups is one in which your personality, preferences, and local resources will determine the usefulness of meeting with others on a weekly or monthly basis.

Destructive Family Patterns Often Associated with ADHD

A child's problems often threaten the family's stability. There are twelve common patterns that, while certainly not causing ADHD, can exacerbate the management and discipline problems associated with the disorder.[2] These patterns will not disappear if they are left untreated. Perhaps you will recognize your family pattern among them. If you do, please seek professional advice and counseling immediately. The patterns involve a number of combinations and permutations:

☐ *Partial denial.* One spouse denies the hyperactivity, while the other recognizes and correctly labels it.

☐ *Joint denial.* The second parent joins the first in denying the existence of the problem, and both parents are left with inadequate and self-defeating explanations for the child's behavior.

☐ *Partial abuse.* One parent becomes abusive. The abusing parent may blackmail the other parent by threatening to cease all parental functions if the nonabusive parent complains. The nonabusive parent begins to hide things the child has done and protect him against the abusive parent.

☐ *Joint abuse.* Both parents become abusive to the child. This abuse could take a verbal, emotional, or physical form.

☐ *Partial overinvolvement.* One parent becomes overinvolved—running interference to the point of overprotection, spoiling, infantilizing, nagging, or pitying the child. The parent who is not overinvolved often wants to correct the situation, and the resulting conflict puts additional strain on the marriage. This parent may react by overcompensating in the opposite direction and therefore becoming somewhat abusive toward the child.

☐ *Joint overinvolvement.* Both parents overprotect, spoil, nag, infantilize, or pity. The result is a demanding child who is unprepared to meet the challenges of life and who is catered to continually by two exhausted and guilt-ridden parents.

☐ *Partial emotional bankruptcy.* One parent declares emotional bankruptcy, forcing the other parent to assume the total burden of parental responsibility.

☐ *Joint emotional bankruptcy.* The second parent responds to the first parent's behavior by joining in an attempt to unload the problem child onto an external source. They may give the child away, neglect or abandon the child, or move in and out of the child's life on an irregular basis.

☐ *One-upmanship.* The second parent criticizes the first. The first parent feels misunderstood and senses a lack of empathy from the second parent. The second parent seems not to understand the stress that the first parent is experiencing. Both parents allow the primary burden of child rearing to remain with the first parent, who suffers not only from the burden of dealing with the child but also from the critical task of dealing with the second parent.

☐ *Mutual one-upmanship.* Each parent considers the other to be weak, incompetent, abusive, and unfit. Both assert that everything would be all right if only the other parent would change.

☐ *Divide and conquer.* Through lack of communication, the parents are deceived by the child's manipulations. As a result, the situation deteriorates to the point where the child needs to deal with only one parent, rather than both. The parents are thus first divided, then conquered by the child.

☐ *Deceit.* One parent is the softy, and the child uses this parental condition to pester, bulldoze, bully, and blackmail the parent.

☐ *Overcompensation.* The excess of one parental trait in the first parent is responded to by the second parent, who develops too much of the opposite trait.

If you recognize one or more of these common destructive marital patterns, seek help at once. Your child is depending on you for a unified, collaborative, and cooperative approach. Your child needs you! Begin now to cultivate positive patterns.

Building Positive Habits

You can counteract the stresses of ADHD on family life by initiating and encouraging positive ways of relating. Here are some suggestions:

1. *Don't permit ADHD to dominate your family.* Take time for each other, for other family members, and for your family unit as a whole.
2. *Recognize your child's manipulations.* Look at your child's behavior objectively, and if you can't, get help from outsiders. Don't become the victim of blackmail and manipulation.
3. *Accept the differences in approach* between you and your spouse. Complement and strengthen each other. Don't criticize and carp.
4. *Spend time alone together.* Find a way to have a "date" once in a while. It's essential for your mental health.
5. *Use the co-parenting technique.* Never give your child a quick answer. Always check with your spouse before giving the child an answer to a request. The answer must always be an agreed-upon solution. Negotiation between parents should always take place in private, away from the child.
6. *Have regular family meetings.*
7. *Cultivate a spirit of love,* excitement, and unity in your family by doing some of the following:

- Work and play as a family unit with the common goal of cooperation and companionship (clean the house, do a service project, plant a garden).
- Exchange small gifts either planned or spontaneous. Our family always did a Secret Santa each year at Christmas, but the same activity could take place for Valentine's Day as well. Family members draw each other's names and buy special gifts for several days in a row. Younger children can be assisted by another family member.
- Pair off one-to-one with different children in the family to do something special alone.
- Put special surprises in lunch boxes.

Unproductive Attitudes

There are three highly unproductive attitudes that almost every parent of a child with ADHD has fallen into at one time or another: *guilt, anger, and defeat.* These feelings frequently result in nagging, spoiling, pitying, and babying, behaviors that will further debilitate and disenfranchise your child. The source of anger, defeat, and guilt is not your child, but you. Don't let yourself fall into those traps. You can't control your child; you can only control your own reactions to your child.

The families I interviewed experienced many of these feelings, so you are not alone. Here are some of their remarks:

"It often feels like you can't win, because even when positive programming works, you get snide comments about bribery."

"I feel guilty about setting limits."

"It takes so much energy to be on top of my feelings all of the time."

"Sometimes I wish he were an only child; other times I wish he weren't my child at all."

"There is no ignoring this situation for even one second of the day."

"Her tantrums leave all of us on edge and 'at' each other. She sure knows how to stir things up."

"I feel guilty that they have to deal with this problem at school."

"The general atmosphere in our house is tense."

"I struggle with favoritism towards my ADHD child because of his disability. I tend to want to make things easier for him."

"She saps our energy. The atmosphere is chaotic at times. We are irritable far too often and are constantly having to regroup and calm down."

In order to meet your child's needs in a productive way, you must move beyond these feelings to a proactive, problem-solving mode.

How Can I Be More Positive?

In spite of the stresses of parenting a child with ADHD, many of the families I interviewed were positive and up-beat in their advice to other parents. The families that were willing to "bare their souls" and share their experiences are intelligent, resourceful, and energetic individuals who have wasted very little time agonizing over injustice and unfairness of parenting a child with ADHD. Rather, they have found opportunities for spiritual and psychological growth, discovered nurturing and parenting skills they didn't know they had, and developed problem-solving abilities that astound them.

Here are some of the insights they wanted to share:

"Don't expect understanding from those who have not walked down your path. Then when you don't get it, you won't be bitter. When you do find acceptance and understanding, it will be a special blessing."

"I'm currently in individual counseling to help me with the general organization and discipline of my home."

"Above all, don't fall into the trap of thinking that your child is 'stupid' or 'bad.'"

"Be aware of your child's strengths (as well as his weaknesses). Help your child be objective about himself. Realize he will be a success."

"Don't worry about next week, next month, or next year. It'll be overwhelming. God only gives you enough resources to deal with today."

"Don't give up. Pray and seek God's guidance."

"If parents and teachers would work with all children the way they work with ADHD kids, we would have a much

more responsible society and people would have higher
self-esteem."

"Each day is filled with frustration and things that could
push us over the edge, but my three are the most loving
children around."

"Realize that eventually children with ADHD will be the
movers and the shakers of this world."

"Learn to laugh at yourself."

"Having a child with ADHD can help you become a very
compassionate and understanding person. Look at it as a
great opportunity for personal growth."

Insights from the Children

It wasn't easy to get children with ADHD to complete questionnaires. They didn't want to stop long enough to write
out answers. But in many cases, they applied self-discipline
and did. Or they dictated the answers to their moms and
dads. But they showed remarkable insight into their problems. Ten-year-old Brian Adams had this to say:

> I wish my parents wouldn't get so upset. But I do get
> wild and crazy when they forget to give me my pills. It's
> hard for me to concentrate, especially on math. I think
> about my favorite animals and stuff like that. The kids in
> my class pick on me. People tell on me because I think
> out loud and start singing or tapping my feet. My sister
> always says, "Brian, be quiet!" I get embarrassed when I
> get in trouble.

Daniel Burns, the six-year-old son of Shelley and Bob, hasn't been told formally that he has ADHD. His parents have talked to him about his "wildness" and trouble concentrating. Daniel shows remarkable perceptiveness about his problem, however. One of his favorite songs is "There's a Wiggle in My Toe" by Joe Scruggs. Daniel has penned his own verse.

> I've got a wiggle in my brain
> And I think I'll go insane.
> Cause I just can't stop
> The wiggle in my brain,
> Or in my knees,
> Or in my feet,
> Or in my toe,
> Oh no!

Jennifer Beacon is a freshman in high school. She is just beginning to fully understand the implications of ADHD. She feels different from her friends and now understands "that I'm not retarded." She wishes her parents would understand that she is what she is and can't change. She uses a technique she learned in counseling to help her manage her ADHD symptoms:

> You must realize when you're starting to get off track; you have to stop that little guy in your head with ADHD written on his T-shirt. You have to force yourself to get control again and kick the little ADHD guy out. Sometimes when I see my friends not paying attention in class, it makes me mad. They *can* pay attention if they want, whereas with me it's difficult. They're wasting their abilities.

Matt Harris was skeptical when he was first diagnosed with ADHD. His advice for parents is wise beyond his years:

> It seemed like a scapegoat for what I thought was laziness. But when I started taking medication for ADHD, I could see a dramatic difference in how I felt and how I thought. . . . ADHD is a disorder that mainly affects oneself. So, as long as those around you are supportive and helpful, that's all any person can ask. The fact that some have ADHD and some don't seems unfair. But constantly asking "Why me?" won't get you very far. Don't ignore it; learn to overcome it.

◆ Endnotes

1. Robin Simons, *After the Tears: Parents Talk about Raising a Child with a Disability* (New York: Harcourt Brace Jovanich, 1987), 24.

2. John Taylor, *The Hyperactive Child and the Family: The Complete What-to-do Handbook* (New York: Everest House, 1980), 11.

9
WHY ME, LORD?

Because we are spiritual, there is a spiritual side to everything that affects us. ADHD has a spiritual side, too.

Facing the Fact

Everyone receives the diagnosis of ADHD differently. Diane Marshall has three children with ADHD.

> It was so hard to get to Rachel's diagnosis that when I found out she had ADHD, it was a relief. With the other two children I cried the whole drive home. I knew from what I had read that they were [ADHD], but I was secretly hoping the doctor would say they weren't. Time has helped me deal with this fact and we work on it. To have three children with ADHD is not a preferred situation, but it is a livable, doable situation.

Karen Beacon is a strong and devoted Christian with a vital prayer life and witness, but she still feels the burden of ADHD in her family.

A great struggle for me is the sad weariness. ADHD is like a giant monster who has come to reside in my home. As a parent, it would be so easy to react in anger and pain. It takes so much energy to be on top of it and monitoring my own feelings all of the time.

Janet Dixon couldn't believe there was anything wrong with her son.

I would defend Jacob and say he was just being a boy. But deep down in my heart I knew he was different. I just didn't want him on drugs to control his behavior.

It's okay to be angry, depressed, weary, discouraged, or even defensive. Cognitively you may know that the diagnosis of ADHD is not God's punishment visited on you for something you did wrong, but deep down there may be anger and resentment at the unfairness of it all. You may even pass through the stages of grief that affect those mourning the loss of a loved one. You, however, will be mourning for the child you don't have, the child who can pay attention, follow the rules, succeed in school, and be "normal." Karen Beacon put it this way: "I had to give up many of the dreams I had for my daughter." But don't get mired down in these feelings for long. Your child needs 110 percent of your creativity, energy, attention, and problem-solving abilities. Pray for wisdom, courage, acceptance, and energy. And read God's Word.

Take a Spiritual Approach

Christians will be helped by trying to gain a biblical perspective on ADHD and its effects on their families.

You don't have to carry the burden alone. Whatever the problem, help is on the way. God expects, even commands us, to bring our problems, large and small, to him for help. "Let him have all your worries and cares, for he is always thinking about you and watching everything that concerns you" (1 Peter 5:7). "Commit everything you do to the Lord. Trust him to help you do it, and he will" (Psalm 37:5).

Don't be angry, and don't worry. Sometimes our first tendency when faced with a problem as pervasive and monumental as ADHD is to get angry. We get angry either at ourselves, our child, the doctor, or the teacher. Then we begin to worry and fret over the problem. Both approaches are counterproductive. "Stop your anger! Turn off your wrath. Don't fret and worry—it only leads to harm" (Psalm 37:8). Turn your energies to productive solutions and plans.

Forget the past. Another trap we fall into when faced with a problem like ADHD is to focus on past mistakes and failures—ours, our child's, our parents', our spouse's parents'. "I don't mean to say I am perfect. I haven't learned all I should even yet, but I keep working toward that day when I will finally be all that Christ saved me for and wants me to be. No, dear brothers, I am still not all I should be, but I am bringing all my energies to bear on this one thing: Forgetting the past and looking forward to what lies ahead, I strain to reach the end of the race and receive the prize for which God is calling us up to heaven because of what Christ Jesus did for us" (Philippians 3:12-14).

Rearrange your priorities. Dealing with your child's ADHD must be a high priority in your life. It's more important than your job or career, personal hobbies or interests, or even church. Our children are one of our most precious resources. "Children are a gift from God; they are his reward. Children born to a young man are like sharp arrows to defend him. Happy is the man who has his quiver full of them" (Psalm 127:3-5). How we shape and mold their young lives will have an impact on the future for good or evil. "Teach a child to choose the right path, and when he [she] is older, he will remain upon it" (Proverbs 22:6).

Don't be a wimp. Don't be afraid to provide structure and leadership in your home. Your child is powerless to cope with the disability of ADHD without your help. "Don't fail to correct your children; discipline won't hurt them!" (Proverbs 23:13). Have confidence in your role as a parent. Invoke the biblical advice from Proverbs often and loudly in your children's presence: "Young man, obey your father and your mother. Take to heart all of their advice. . . . Every day and all night long their counsel will lead you and save you from harm; when you wake up in the morning, let their instructions guide you into the new day" (Proverbs 6:20-22).

Use resources that are available to you. God knows and understands our weaknesses, and he can help us. This help will come in the form of friends, relatives, professionals, and reading material. God doesn't answer prayer only in miraculous ways. He does it in ordinary, everyday ways through the people he sends into our lives. "For the eyes of the Lord search back and forth across the whole earth, looking for people whose hearts are perfect toward him, so that he can show his great power in helping them" (2 Chronicles 16:9).

Know the real source of confidence. Our true source of confidence is not experts who have written books, but the Lord himself. "But when I am afraid, I will put my confidence in you. Yes, I will trust the promises of God" (Psalm 56:3).

Celebrate uniqueness. We are fearfully and wonderfully made. Your child has unique gifts and strengths. Discover them and celebrate them often. Continually build up your child. Help your child to understand that he or she is God's special creation and that God will help your child to become the best he or she can be. "So God made man like his Maker. Like God did God make man; man and maid did he make them" (Genesis 1:27).

Karen Beacon gives this advice to parents struggling with the issue:

> Find your child's strengths through thorough testing and counseling. Try to understand how his or her [talents] could "flesh out" someday. Give your child that identity and dream early on—"Someday you're going to be our writer or our scientist." Then it's okay if the child doesn't achieve in every other area where he or she is handicapped. Keep priorities in order. The most important thing is the development of the child's character and affirmation of the good things inside the person. Academics may or may not come along.

Be a witness. We want what is best for our children in the context of our values and beliefs. We also want our faith to shine through our relationships and interactions with all of the professionals who diagnose and treat our children.

Recognize your personal limitations. Without help and guidance from the Lord, you can read all of the books published about ADHD, have the best doctors, and still fall flat. Our true strength is in the Lord. "Oh, praise the Lord, for he has listened to my pleadings! He is my strength, my shield from every danger. I trusted in him, and he helped me" (Psalm 28:6-7).

Be willing to grow and change. Model openness and flexibility for your children. Confess mistakes to your spouse, your child, and his or her teacher. "A man [woman] who refuses to admit his mistakes can never be successful. But if he confesses and forsakes them, he gets another chance" (Proverbs 28:13).

Honor and respect your child. Whenever we approach our children to offer them our help (with homework, tutoring, advice about friends) or to give them discipline or directives about their behavior, we must take care that it is done in the spirit of respect and honor for each child as God's unique creation. "And now a word to you parents. Don't keep on scolding and nagging your children, making them angry and resentful. Rather, bring them up with the loving discipline the Lord himself approves, with suggestions and godly advice" (Ephesians 6:4). "Fathers [and mothers], don't scold your children so much that they become discouraged and quit trying" (Colossians 3:21).

Train them up. The Bible provides an excellent process for training and teaching our children. The four steps to this model are 1) teaching, 2) internalizing, 3) correcting, and 4) training. They come from 2 Timothy 3:16. "The whole Bible was given to us by inspiration from God and is useful to teach us what is true [teaching] and to make us realize what is wrong in our lives [internalizing]; it straightens us out [correcting] and helps us do what is right [training]." These four steps need to be present as you work with your child with ADHD. The process is progressive; it has a beginning and an end. We can chart our accomplishments. But it is also cyclical. Once we have reached the end, there is always a new beginning—a new skill to be learned, new knowledge to acquire, and behaviors that exemplify the best in your child. Training children with ADHD takes on additional significance and meaning because they need more of it; they need it more consistently; and they need it for longer periods of time.

APPENDIX A
The Families Who Participated

The privacy of the families described in these pages has been preserved by using pseudonyms throughout the book.

Family Number One

Brian Adams is the ten-year-old son of Laura and Lyle Adams. He was diagnosed with ADHD (combined) at the age of seven. Brian has two siblings, a fourteen-year-old brother and an eight-year-old sister. Neither of Brian's parents nor siblings have ADHD, but his maternal grandfather and uncle both have ADHD symptoms which were undiagnosed. Brian takes imipramine (100 mg.) and Ritalin™ (10 mg.) He is enrolled in a Christian school where his teachers are responsive to his needs and modify the curriculum as needed. His parents struggle with discipline at home because Brian is very oppositional, and he also suffers with social problems at school. Brian's ADHD has definitely affected the family's life; they don't get out much because of problems finding baby sitters who are willing to meet Brian's needs for discipline and structure.

Family Number Two

Jennifer Beacon is the fourteen-year-old daughter of Karen and Sonny. She has one younger sister, twelve. Jennifer was diagnosed with ADHD (with attention deficit only) at the age of ten. Although neither of her parents have ADHD, Jennifer's maternal grandfather and his sisters have very severe cases. Karen reports that the outcome was a tragic, loveless home filled with anger, abuse, and great sadness. Jennifer takes Ritalin™ and Tegretol™ (prescribed to treat a general seizure disorder). Until this year, the Beacons have found "stubborn ignorance and unprofessional attitudes" among the educators in their suburban school system. Now in the high school, they have found knowledgeable administrators and creative and energetic teachers who have put Jennifer's best interests first. Jennifer's grades are marginal but her interactions with teachers and school experiences are definitely more positive. Jennifer is receiving counseling from a successful professional who also has ADHD, and this experience is proving very beneficial for her self-esteem.

Family Number Three

Perry Brown is the eighteen-year-old son of Helen and Shelby Brown. He is an only boy with five sisters, two older and three younger. Perry was diagnosed with ADHD (combined) at the age of twelve. Although his parents do not have ADHD, Helen reports that her forty-nine-year-old brother shows many symptoms of ADHD. Ritalin™ was recommended for Perry. Although his parents supported this, he hated it, saying it made him feel weird. After one month he stopped taking the drug. Perry graduated from high school and completed two college courses, but lied about attending a third. Perry is rebellious, oppositional, and irresponsible. His parents found it necessary to ask him to leave their home because of his problems with the law. They took away his car and he is presently living with an uncle and working a part-time job. He refuses to follow rules and spends most of his time hanging out with friends.

Family Number Four

Daniel Burns is the six-year-old son of Shelley and Bob. He was diagnosed with ADHD (combined) at the age of four and has one sibling, a three-year-old sister. After reading about ADHD and talking with the psychologist who diagnosed Daniel, his father believes he may have ADHD as well. He struggled through school, "feeling out of step with what was going on." Bob's father and maternal grandmother have symptoms similar to both Bob and Daniel. Daniel's parents have decided not to use medication and are trying diet and vitamins. These treatments are difficult to monitor but his parents believe they could be helping. Daniel has severe problems with insomnia, often waking up for two to three hours in the middle of the night. Daniel's behavior is a challenge to manage; they carefully plan where they go to avoid embarrassment at Daniel's behavior. Daniel's current school placement is a frustration for his parents. The teacher believes that "if he just learned to mind" he would be fine. She has felt free to criticize Shelley's parenting skills—"she's too laid back"—and believes that parents use ADHD as an excuse not to discipline their children.

Family Number Five

Brandon Byrne is the twenty-nine-year-old son of Charlene. Charlene and her second husband, Tom, have a second child, twenty-three. Brandon was diagnosed as hyperactive (the only diagnosis used at the time) at the age of seven. He took Ritalin™ until puberty and then stopped taking the drug because of the doctor's recommendation. His grades fell dramatically at that point and his mother believes it would have been beneficial to keep him on the drug longer. Charlene worked hard at catching Brandon doing things right even though he was a disruptive child. Today Brandon is the co-owner of a business, a homeowner, and a responsible and happy adult. His mother reports that he skateboards, snowboards, rides motorcycles, and generally still needs to go fast. He is a sensitive and loving person and has learned to concentrate when he needs to.

Family Number Six

Israel Castro is the ten-year-old son of Miriam Montgomery, a single parent. He was diagnosed with ADHD (combined) at the age of eight, much to his mother's relief. The blame for his behavior had been laid heavily on the shoulders of Miriam by family members and school officials. Miriam believes her ex-husband has ADHD, and her older son, who lives with his father, exhibits many of the same characteristics. Since taking Ritalin™, Israel's behavior has changed drastically. He is more calm. Miriam experienced a great deal of frustration with school personnel until Israel's diagnosis. They sent Israel home from school two days a week or sent him to another classroom. As a result, he was held back a grade. Since the diagnosis, she has been able to insist on more specific instruction for him, and teachers seem more patient now.

Family Number Seven

Kevin Corcoran is the nine-year-old son of Mary Ellen and Kevin. He is the oldest of three boys. Kevin was diagnosed with ADHD (combined) at the age of seven, but was treated for anxiety beginning at age five. Kevin takes both Ritalin™ and imipramine. No other family members have ADHD. Until this year Kevin's school setting was not ideal; gang shootings were commonplace and a sexual assault occurred inside the school. School personnel did not cooperate in the administration of medication, and Kevin was once thrown out of school for his lunchroom behavior. Since moving to a new neighborhood, he is in a structured classroom in a well-run school where everyone works together to meet his needs. His parents are thoughtful and energetic individuals who are constantly working on new interventions and run a "tight ship."

Family Number Eight

Jacob Dixon is the ten-year-old son of Janet and Joe. He is the middle child between two other boys. He was diagnosed (with ADHD combined) at the age of seven and takes Ritalin™. His mother has experimented with eliminating sugar and preservatives in Jacob's diet, but has seen no changes in his behavior at all. No other family members have ADHD. Jacob's schooling experiences have been mixed. He also has a learning disability, and his mother reports that the LD teacher is condescending and demeaning to her and Jacob. However, she is grateful to many school personnel for making her aware of her child's problems and for the work they have done to help Jacob. She believes that Jacob's successes are "due to the 'real teachers'" and that the others "should find a new line of work."

Family Number Nine

Joanna Griswold is the ten-year-old daughter of Joan and Robert. She was diagnosed with ADHD (without hyperactivity) when she was nine years old. Joanna's father has ADHD symptoms. She is one of two daughters and there is a good deal of sibling rivalry and fighting between the girls. Joanna takes Ritalin™, and her mother credits the drug with Joanna's improved ability to follow through and complete projects for school without constant monitoring. Joanna is most fortunate to have a wonderful teacher, receives As and Bs, and loves school. The current teacher works with Joanna each term to set new goals. They have worked on doing assignments more thoroughly and neatly, and now they are working on speaking up in class. The teacher goes way beyond the call of duty, according to Joan, who credits her for the success her daughter is having. Joanna's ability to concentrate, get along with family members, and deal with frustration diminishes in the afternoon hours, so evenings can be a challenge in the Griswold household.

Family Number Ten

Matt Harris is the nineteen-year-old son of Lori and Tom. He is the youngest of three children, and his siblings have graduated from college and married. Matt was diagnosed with ADHD (without hyperactivity) at the age of fifteen. Tom believes he was borderline ADHD but was able to compensate for the symptoms because of his high level of interest and aptitude in both math and science. Matt's older brother was very impulsive, but extremely gifted. His teachers seemed to accept his behavior as part of his giftedness. After his ADHD diagnosis and Ritalin™ treatment, Matt had a successful two years in high school. His parents believed that perhaps he had been "cured." Matt tried a year away at a college of his own choosing, but the unsupervised and unstructured environment was not conducive to success. He then returned home and attended a community college. With that successful experience behind him, he will now attend a college that offers special programs for students with ADHD and learning disabilities. His parents are confident that in this atmosphere he will be successful.

Family Number Eleven

Josh Hunt is the fourteen-year-old son of Bonnie and Laird Walker. He was diagnosed with ADHD (combined) at the age of ten. Josh has two older brothers and, although they do not have ADHD, Bonnie reports they are strong-willed. The oldest has been hard on Josh and very unaccepting of his behavior. Although Josh takes Ritalin™ , he doesn't like it and his parents aren't sold on it either. It does seem to help, though. They twice tried to start a school year without the medication, but then had to begin using it. Josh is a challenging child in the area of discipline, and his mother's passive personality and stressors at home combine to create a less-than-favorable situation. Laird would like Bonnie to be firmer and more consistent with consequences. Josh recently transferred from a large, public, junior high school to a small (100 students), very structured Christian school. He seems to be doing much better in the smaller setting. He was doing very poorly in the public school. Bonnie believes that many teachers pay lip service to understanding ADHD, but are either unwilling or unable to adapt their teaching strategies to meet the child's needs.

Family Number Twelve

Brett Kingman is the six-year-old son of Kay and John. He has recently been diagnosed with ADHD (combined) and has just begun Ritalin™. He is the youngest of three children. Brett is in kindergarten and is learning his academics, but is a discipline problem and has a short attention span. The teacher says she is "on him all the time." Brett creates problems for his family with his demanding and intolerant ways. He constantly talks, makes noises, and finds ways of getting attention. His parents are working to develop a more consistent approach to discipline and family structure.

Family Number Thirteen

Danny Kingston is the eleven-year-old son of Monica and Greg. He was diagnosed with ADHD (without hyperactivity) at the age of ten. Danny has responded extremely well to Ritalin™ during the day, but by the time he comes home from school the "wailing and gnashing of teeth" begins. Danny's fourteen-year-old brother has a "rare love" for him and seldom lacks patience with Danny's antics. Greg definitely feels that he suffers from ADHD. He often expresses empathy toward Danny, reliving the pain he felt in childhood. He continues to have many frustrations today. Monica believes that she may also have a tendency toward ADHD. Her early report cards indicate distractibility and fidgeting. Danny's teachers seem overworked and burdened by several children with ADHD, and they whine about the difficulty of taking time for the needs of each child. Monica feels that she is "just another mom with a problem child" and has requested a reassignment for Danny to a school where children like Danny are accommodated. But she feels fortunate to have an educator-husband who has experience with children like Danny and knows how to interpret district policies, procedures, and "lingo."

Family Number Fourteen

Jameson Kirkpatrick is the six-year-old son of Linda and James. He has just been diagnosed with ADHD (combined). Ritalin™ has been recommended. Jameson is one of five children, having a sister, twenty-five, and three brothers, nineteen, fourteen, and two. Linda believes that she may be ADHD. She had a hard time staying on task and finishing things in school. Since she was adopted, she has no knowledge of her relatives. She is currently in counseling to help her with the general organization and discipline of her home. Linda has found school personnel to be extremely helpful in developing an individualized education plan for Jameson and in providing materials and suggestions for a home discipline program. Linda's biggest challenge with Jameson is that he thinks the living room is an outdoor soccer field and gymnasium. He is always running, jumping, skipping, hopping, and rolling.

Family Number Fifteen

Donna and Ryan Marshall have three children: Matthew, eleven, Rachel, nine, and Sandra, seven. They were all diagnosed with ADHD in the past year. Both Donna and her husband have all the symptoms of ADHD, although they have never been formally diagnosed. There are indications of ADHD on both sides of their families—Donna's brother and father have symptoms; Ryan's brother and cousins also have symptoms. All three children are on Ritalin™ with great success. Donna reports that mornings are the most challenging for the Marshall family. "Imagine five ADHD people with poor memories. No one can remember what they were doing or where they put their shoes. We daydream far too long without getting dressed and hair combed. Rachel can forget she is taking her medicine with it right in front of her. Mornings are a battlefield." But ADHD has strengthened the Marshall family, and their wonderful sense of humor keeps them going. Donna looks for teachers who love children, but school can be a nightmare, she reports. She fights for her kids but becomes exhausted and gives up now and then.

Family Number Sixteen

Dustin and Cameron Martinelli are the eleven-year-old and seven-year-old sons of Vivian and Bob. Dustin was diagnosed with ADHD (combined) at the age of eight and Cameron at the age of four. Vivian's response when Cameron was diagnosed was, "Not again! Why me?" Both boys take Ritalin™, but Vivian believes that a multi-faceted program is very important—parent training courses, counseling, daily progress charts at school, and a reward system for good behavior in school, church, and at sporting events. Dustin's intelligence has given him an edge at school. Also, Vivian volunteers there regularly and so knows the staff well. She credits her heavy involvement with the smooth road that Dustin has experienced in school. Cameron has more severe behavioral problems in school and needs the "ideal" teacher. The principal has been difficult to work with in this regard. This is the first year that Cameron is really experiencing success in the classroom. The Martinellis have been in counseling but have had difficulty finding just the right person. Vivian reports that the therapist must be one who specializes in ADHD, and the search for a good counselor can be costly and emotionally draining.

Family Number Seventeen

John is the fourteen-year-old son of Patricia and Robert O'Brien. He was diagnosed with ADHD (combined) at the age of ten. Patricia can trace several ADHD indicators in her family tree. She reports that on her mother's side "all the men were a little crazy but nothing more specific was ever said." Robert feels that he has ADHD symptoms which were never diagnosed. Although John's parents resisted medication at first, life at home became a nightmare. In desperation Patricia called the pediatrician. She reports that the first week he was on the medicine they were able to attend church and not come home upset. John was able to sit for the entire hour without excessive talking, noises, drumming on the pews, and tapping his feet. She got no stares and looks from the people sitting around her. She believes God was letting her know that giving her son the medicine was the right thing. She still believes this today. Up to this year, freshman year, John had been doing very well in school—As and Bs. But high school has been a different story. Placed in the highest level academic classes, he has encountered teachers who refuse to accept his diagnosis, including one who accused his parents of "drugging him into a zombie." Patricia advises others not to let the school pass the ball back to parents, but to force them with repeated contact to deal with the issue.

Family Number Eighteen

Jeff Reasor is the nine-year-old son of Bruce and Marilyn. He was diagnosed with ADHD (combined) at the age of six. Bruce believes that he may have ADHD, but no other family members exhibit symptoms. Jeff has been taking Ritalin™ since his diagnosis with outstanding success. His parents have structured their home, eliminated as many distractions as possible, and use time-out very effectively. One of three children, Jeff is experiencing a high level of success in school. He is part of the Gifted and Talented Program, and his parents find school personnel very willing to listen and work with them. Teachers are knowledgeable about ADHD and are eager to learn and share information. Bruce and Marilyn agree that a "triple dose of patience" is needed when raising a child with ADHD.

Family Number Nineteen

Christopher and Cindy Rollins are nine and six. Their mother, Kandi, is divorced and lives with her parents. Christopher was diagnosed with ADHD (combined) at the age of six and his sister at the age of five. Christopher has been taking Ritalin™ since kindergarten, and doctors are still experimenting to find the right dosage and combination for Cindy. Many family members on both sides have ADHD symptoms. Both children attend a private Christian school. Christopher is a straight-A student, but Cindy is suspected of having minor learning disabilities in reading and spelling. The family-like atmosphere at the school, the care of the teachers, and the evidence of Christ's love everywhere have contributed to a wonderful school experience for the Rollins.

Family Number Twenty

Billy and Phillip Scott are the twelve- and ten-year-old sons of Jane and Richard. Billy was diagnosed with ADHD (combined) at the age of seven. His original diagnosis was for an anxiety disorder. When treatment with therapy for eight months was not entirely successful, he was diagnosed with ADHD and began treatment with Ritalin™. This caused some side effects, so Billy began taking Cylert™, which did not prove effective either. Now he is taking Adderol™ (a Dexedrine™ derivative which is currently in short supply), and his mother reports "it is working great." Phillip, even though also ADHD, is more compliant and easygoing than Billy, and this causes charges of favoritism from Billy. Both parents have multiple ADHD symptoms. Jane has been officially diagnosed and is taking slow-release Ritalin™ with great success. Although Richard has never been officially diagnosed, Jane reports that he is impulsive, easily distracted, and hyperactive. Denial of his symptoms causes severe marital stress. He is easily frustrated, fails to understand why the children behave as they do, and has on occasion reacted physically toward the children. Jane has stated that if this occurs again, she will seek a separation. Billy receives support services in school. Although he is in accelerated math, he has been close to failing two other subjects. Jane is in constant contact with the school and has encountered her greatest frustration in understanding the assignments given to the boys. The support-services teacher has been the greatest help, keeping assignments updated, working with the regular teachers to complete a daily reporting sheet, and allowing previously missed assignments to be turned in.

Family Number Twenty-One

Raymond is the eight-year-old son of Maxine and Raymond Sullivan. He was diagnosed at one year, which is an unusually early diagnosis. No other family members have ADHD symptoms, but Raymond was decidedly different from his two older siblings in sleep patterns, eating habits, activity level, and concentration level. He began taking Ritalin™ in first grade, and this was successful for about a year until he suddenly developed tics. Now the doctor is trying Wellbutrin™. Raymond is an uncooperative child who is very moody, and his behavior has adversely affected the Sullivans' marriage. Although he has been labeled a special education student, Raymond is "included" in the regular-education classroom with special help. Maxine works closely with school personnel and finds them supportive. She feels a little guilty, however, that they have to deal with Raymond's problems all day every day.

Family Number Twenty-Two

Jeffrey Tyrone is the fourteen-year-old son of Rosemary and Walter. He was diagnosed with ADHD (combined) at the age of thirteen. He has one older sister, eighteen, who is "average." Although he had always had trouble in school with behavior, and his mother suspected there might be something wrong, the combination of an interested teacher and a radio program on ADHD motivated Rosemary to seek professional attention. Before Jeffrey began to take Ritalin™, Rosemary reports that he told her that life wasn't worth living. "He seemed to change right before my eyes." Rosemary believes that she has ADHD. She has the same feelings her child has but thinks that because she is a female she has had an easier time compensating for her disability. She still looks for shortcuts for everything, and she hated school, except for the social life. Jeffrey seems to handle only one challenge at a time. If he's managing school, he's a grouch at home and vice versa. His mother fights to keep from being "pushed through the cracks" at school. Although he has a special-education label, he is mainstreamed (in regular classes), except for math. Rosemary keeps the lines of communication open with the school and goes to them, not as an irate parent, but as a concerned parent interested in her child's welfare. Jeffrey's behavior is a constant strain on the Tyrones' marriage. Before Jeffrey was diagnosed, Rosemary believes she almost lost her family and marriage. Jeffrey seems to be the ground for fighting between husband and wife. However, Walter is starting to understand ADHD, and Rosemary understands all too well, having been there.

Family Number Twenty-Three

Darrell Woods is the seven-year-old grandson of Brian and Kristen Woods. He was diagnosed with ADHD (combined) at the age of six. The Woods have legally adopted Darrell since his mother (the Woods's daughter) has severe mental problems. The Woods have other children, including a son with spina bifida. Darrell takes Ritalin™, which has been effective in helping him attend to tasks. Darrell will start school in the fall, and his grandparents are in a quandary about where to send him. They don't see public education in their area as a positive choice, but private school is financially prohibitive. Although the Woods have sought counseling, insurance pays only for "desperation times." Their budget does not permit additional visits.

APPENDIX B
Organizations and Resources

Organizations for Information, Support, and Advocacy

Attention Deficit Disorder Association (ADDA)
P.O. Box 972
Mentor, OH 44061
800-487-2282

Attention Deficit Information Network (AD-IN)
475 Hillside Avenue
Needham, MA 02194
617-455-9895

C.H.A.D.D. (Children and Adults with Attention Deficit Disorders)
National Headquarters
499 N.W. 70th Avenue
Suite 308
Plantation, FL 33317
305-587-3700
(C.H.A.D.D. has local chapters throughout the United States. Locations, contact names, and phone numbers are available through National Headquarters, or check your local newspaper.)

Council for Exceptional Children
1920 Association Drive
Reston, VA 22091
703-264-9474
800-328-0272
FAX 703-264-9494

Heath Resource Center
(National Clearinghouse for Postsecondary Education for People with Disabilities)
1 DuPont Circle N.W.
Washington, DC 20036

Learning Disabilities Association
4156 Library Road
Pittsburgh, PA 15234
412-341-1515

National Center for Learning Disabilities
381 Park Avenue
New York, NY 10016
212-545-7510

NICCHY (National Information Center for Children and Youth with
Disabilities)
P.O. Box 1492
Washington, DC 20013
800-695-0285

Disability Rights Advocacy Organizations

Bazelon Center for Mental Health Law
1101 15th Street N.W.
Suite 1212
Washington, DC 20005-5002
202-467-5730
202-467-4232 TDD

Center for Law and Education, Inc.
955 Massachusetts Avenue
Cambridge, MA 02139

DREDF (Disabilities Rights Education and Defense Fund, Inc.)
1616 P Street N.W.
Suite 100
Washington, DC 20036

National Council on Disability
800 Independence Avenue S.W.
Suite 814
Washington, DC 20591
202-267-3846
202-267-3232 TDD

NPND (National Parent Network on Disability)
1600 Prince Street
Suite 115
Alexandria, VA 22314
703-684-6763
(NPND has a listing of parent networks throughout the United States.
They will mail or fax it to you upon request.)

United States Government

For questions about IDEA and PL 94-142 call or write to:

U.S. Department of Education
Office of Special Education Programs
400 Maryland Avenue S.W.
Washington, DC 20202
202-205-5507

For questions about Section 504 call or write to:

U.S. Department of Education
Office for Civil Rights
400 Maryland Avenue S.W.
Washington, DC 20202
202-732-1635

For questions about Americans with Disabilities Act (ADA) call or
write to:

EEOC (Equal Employment Opportunity Commission)
1801 L Street N.W.
Washington, DC 20507
800-669-4000
(regarding discrimination)

United States Department of Justice
Civil Rights Division
P.O. Box 66118
Washington, DC 20035-6118
1-800-669-3362
(regarding accommodations)

Department of Education Office for Civil Rights Regional Civil Rights Offices:

Region I: Connecticut, Maine, Massachusetts, New Hampshire, Rhode Island, Vermont

> Regional Civil Rights Director
> Office for Civil Rights, Region I
> U.S. Department of Education
> John W. McCormick Post Office and Court House—Room 222
> Post Office Square
> Boston, MA 02109
> 617-223-1154
> 617-223-1111 TTY

Region II: New Jersey, New York, Puerto Rico, Virgin Islands

> Regional Civil Rights Director
> Office for Civil Rights, Region II
> U.S. Department of Education
> 26 Federal Plaza, R33-130
> New York, NY 10278
> 212-264-5180
> 212-264-9464 TTY

Region III: Delaware, District of Columbia, Maryland, Pennsylvania, Virginia, West Virginia

> Regional Civil Rights Director
> Office for Civil Rights, Region III
> U.S. Department of Education
> Gateway Building, 3535 Market Street
> Post Office Box 13716
> Philadelphia, PA 19101
> 215-596-6772
> 215-596-6794 TTY

Region IV: Alabama, Florida, Georgia, Kentucky, Mississippi, North Carolina, South Carolina, Tennessee

Regional Civil Rights Director
Office for Civil Rights, Region IV
U.S. Department of Education
101 Marietta Tower, Room 2702
Atlanta, GA 30323
404-221-2954
404-221-2010 TTY

Region V: Illinois, Indiana, Minnesota, Michigan, Ohio, Wisconsin

Regional Civil Rights Director
Office for Civil Rights, Region V
U.S. Department of Education
300 South Wacker Drive, 8th Floor
Chicago, IL 60606
312-353-2520
312-353-2520 TTY

Region VI: Arkansas, Louisiana, New Mexico, Oklahoma, Texas

Regional Civil Rights Director
Office for Civil Rights, Region VI
U.S. Department of Education
1200 Main Tower Building, Room 1935
Dallas, TX 75202
214-676-3951
214-767-6599 TTY

Region VII: Iowa, Kansas, Missouri, Nebraska

Regional Civil Rights Director
Office for Civil Rights, Region VII
U.S. Department of Education
324 E. 11th Street, 24th Floor
Kansas City, MO 64106
816-374-2223
816-374-7264 TTY

Region VIII: Colorado, Montana, North Dakota, South Dakota, Utah, Wyoming

Regional Civil Rights Director
Office for Civil Rights, Region VIII
U.S. Department of Education
Federal Office Building
1961 Stout Street, Room 1185
Denver, CO 80294
303-884-5695
303-844-3417 TTY

Region IX: Arizona, California, Hawaii, Nevada, Guam, Trust Territory of the Pacific Islands, American Samoa

Regional Civil Rights Director
Office for Civil Rights, Region IX
U.S. Department of Education
1275 Market Street, 14th Floor
San Francisco, CA 94103
415-556-9894
415-556-1933 TTY

Region X: Alaska, Idaho, Oregon, Washington

Regional Civil Rights Director
Office for Civil Rights, Region X
U.S. Department of Education
2901 3rd Avenue, Mail Stop 106
Seattle, WA 98121
206-442-1636
206-442-4542 TTY

Multimedia Resources

The Council for Exceptional Children offers a kit for parents and educators on Attention Deficit Disorder entitled *Facing the Challenges of ADD: A Kit for Parents and Educators.* Following is the order information:

Order item #5105; $50.00 (plus $5 shipping and handling)

Send purchase orders, checks, VISA or MasterCard to:

CEC Publications, Dept. K504450
P.O. Box 79026
Baltimore, MD 21279-0026
or call 1-800-CEC-READ (232-7323)
FAX: 703-264-1637

The kit contains the following materials:

Videos (from the Widmeyer Group)

Facing the Challenges of ADD is a 30-minute documentary that features interviews with parents, children, educators and health care professionals discussing ADD, and looks at the day-to-day realities of their lives as they cope with the disorder.

One Child in Every Classroom, an hour long program, is a panel discussion among researchers, teachers, and a parent. Panelists offer research-based information on ADD characteristics, diagnosis, and basic treatment strategies that are effective for children with ADD as well as children in the classroom.

Publications (from the Chesapeake Institute)

Attention Deficit Disorder: Adding Up the Facts (ED370334)* Introduces ADD, explaining its definition, characteristics, identification, causes, and treatment; outlines the role of the school and its legal obligations.

Attention Deficit Disorder: Beyond the Myth (ED370335)* Rebuts ten commonly believed myths about ADD and explains the facts.

Attention Deficit Disorder: What Teachers Should Know (ED370036)*. Explains ADD to teachers and their role in its identification; describes how they can help identify children with ADD, listing some simple strategies they can use to help students focus more in class and describing some programs adopted by successful schools.

Attention Deficit Disorder: What Parents Should Know
(ED370037)*. Explains ADD to parents to help them determine if
their child shows signs of having ADD; a step-by-step guide to
identification, the role of the school, the laws pertaining to ADD,
and mediation; also describes some simple strategies to help
parents with their child's behavior at home.

*Where Do I Turn? A Resource Directory of Materials About Atten-
tion Deficit Disorder* (ED370333)*. Lists national and state organizations that provide information and help on ADD. It also lists and
describes hundreds of books and other resources on ADD.

*101 Ways to Help Children with ADD Learn: Tips from Successful
Teachers.*

* Items with and ED (ERIC document) number are cited in the
ERIC database. They are available in ERIC microfiche collections
at more than 825 locations worldwide, especially larger municipal
and university libraries. They can also be ordered for a fee
through EDRS (ERIC Document Reproduction Service): 1-800-
443-ERIC. The ERIC database contains more than 400 citations
on ADD. For directions on how to find citations, ask your librarian
or call 1-800-328-0272.

Not available in the kit, but in the ERIC database and worth examining are:

*Promising Classroom Interventions for Students with Attention
Deficit Disorder* (ED374599).* 210 pages.

*Teaching Strategies: Education of Children with Attention Deficit
Disorder* (ED370332).* 43 pages.

You can also access and review abstracts of articles and documents
in the ERIC database as follows:

At a university library or municipal library through CD-ROM
and/or online services. Print or microfiche copies are available
using *Resources in Education (RIE)* and *Current Index* to *Jour-
nals in Education (CIJE).* Call 1-800-LET-ERIC for a provider
near you.

On CD-ROM (compact disc, read-only memory) through:

DIALOG 1-800-334-2564
Silver Platter 1-800-343-0064
EBSCO 1-800-653-2726
National Information Services Corp. (NISC) 410-243-0797

Online via a computer and a modem, through commercial vendors and public networks such as:

DIALOG 1-800-334-2564
CD-PLUS 1-800-950-2035
CompuServe 1-800-848-8199
OCLC 1-800-848-5878
GTE Educational Services
(SpecialNet) 1-800-927-3000
America Online to the Internet 1-800-LET-ERIC
The Internet via university or commercial connection

Order a computer search for a fee from The ERIC Clearinghouse on Disabilities and Gifted Education located at the Council for Exceptional Children by calling 1-800-328-0272.

Internet Listservs

To subscribe (be added) to a listserv:

Send an e-mail message to the listserv address. Leave the subject line blank. In the body of the message, type ONLY the following:

SUBSCRIBE [list name] yourfirstname yourlastname

For example: SUBSCRIBE ADA-LAW Mary Smith

List Name	Subscription Address	Post Messages To
ADD-PARENTS	majordomo@mv.mv.com	add-parents@mv.mv.com
ADDULT	listserv@sjuvm.stjohns.edu	addult@sjuvm.stjohns.edu
LD-LIST	ld-list-request@east.pima.edu	ld-list@east.pima.edu

Other Internet Resources

FTP Sites:

ftp://com13.netcom.com/pub/lds/add/add.faq
ftp://mcs.com:/mcsnet.users/falcon/add
ftp.netcom:/pub/lds/add
Newsgroups: alt.support.attn-deficit

If you subscribe to America Online (AOL), there are several weekly ADD conferences in the Issues in Mental Health Forum (use the keyword IMH). The schedule (listed in EASTERN time):

ADDults Only:	Tuesday, midnight
ADD Partners:	Saturday, 8 PM
Parents of ADD Kids:	Wednesday, 8 PM
ADD Support:	Tuesday, 7 PM
ADD Support:	Wednesday, 2 PM
ADD Parents:	Thursday, 2 PM

If you subscribe to CompuServe, there is an ADD Forum (GO ADD), a DISABILITIES Forum (GO DISABILITIES), and an EDUCATION Forum (GO EDFORUM) that address special needs.

NEWSLETTERS

ADDult Support Network
2620 Ivy Place
Toledo, OH 43613
ADDult News (newsletter, $12/year/4 issues)

ADDendum (for and by ADD adults)
c/o CPS 5041 A Backlick Rd.
Annaldale, VA 22003
$25/year for 4 issues

ADD-ONS (a "paper" support group for those living with ADD)
6 bimonthly issues, $15
ADD-ONS
PO Box 675
Frankfort, IL 60423

CHADDER Box and CHADDER and ATTENTION
CHADD National Headquarters
499 NW 70th Avenue, Suite 308
Plantation, FL 33317
305-587-3700

Challenge
PO Box 448
West Newbury, MA 01985

Educational Vendors

ADD Warehouse
300 NW 70th Avenue, Suite 102
Plantation, FL 33317
1-800-ADD-WARE

APPENDIX C
Department of Education Policy on ADD

UNITED STATES DEPARTMENT OF EDUCATION REHABILITA-
TIVE SERVICES

MEMORANDUM: THE ASSISTANT SECRETARY
DATE: Sept. 16, 1991

TO: Chief State School Officers

FROM: Robert R. Davila
        Assistant Secretary
        Office of Special Education and Rehabilitative Services

        Michael L. Williams
        Assistant Secretary
        Office for Civil Rights

        John T. MacDonald
        Assistant Secretary
        Office of Elementary and Secondary Education

SUBJECT: Clarification of Policy to Address the Needs of Children with
Attention Deficit Disorders within General and/or Special Education

I. *Introduction*
   There is a growing awareness in the education community that
   attention deficit disorder (ADD) and attention deficit hyperactive
   disorder (ADHD) can result in significant learning problems for
   children with these conditions.[1] While estimates of the prevalence
   of ADD vary widely, we believe that three to five percent of
   school-aged children may have significant educational problems
   related to this disorder. Because ADD has broad implications for
   education as a whole, the Department believes it should clarify
   State and local responsibility under Federal law for addressing
   the needs of children with ADD in the schools. Ensuring that

these students are able to reach their fullest potential is an inherent part of the National education goals and AMERICA 2000. The National goals, and the strategy for achieving them, are based on the assumptions that: (1) all children can learn and benefit from their education; and (2) the educational community must work to improve the learning opportunities for all children.

This memorandum clarifies the circumstances under which children with ADD are eligible for special education services under Part B of the Individuals with Disabilities Act (Part B), as well as the Part B requirements for evaluation of such children's unique educational needs. This memorandum will also clarify the responsibility of State and local educational agencies (SEAs and LEAs) to provide special education and related services to eligible children with ADD under Part B. Finally, this memorandum clarifies the responsibilities of LEAs to provide regular or special education and related aids and services to those children with ADD who are not eligible under Part B, but who fall within the definition of "handicapped person" under Section 504 of the Rehabilitation Act of 1973. Because of the overall educational responsibility to provide services for these children, it is important that general and special education coordinate their efforts.

II. *Eligibility for Special Education and Related Services under Part B*
Last year during the reauthorization of the Education of the Handicapped Act (now the Individuals with Disabilities Education Act), Congress gave serious consideration to including ADD in the definition of "children with disabilities" in the statute. The Department took the position that ADD does not need to be added as a separate disability category in the statutory definition since children with ADD who require special education and related services can meet the eligibility criteria for services under Part B. This continues to be the Department's position.

No change with respect to ADD was made by Congress in the statutory definition of "children with disabilities"; however, language was included in Section 102(a) of the Education of the Handicapped Act Amendments of 1990 that required the Secretary to issue a Notice of Inquiry (NOI) soliciting public comment on special education for children with ADD under Part B. In response to the NOI (published November 29, 1990 in the *Federal Register),* the Department received over 2000 written comments, which have been transmitted to the Congress. Our review of these written comments indicates that there is confusion in the field regarding the extent to which children with ADD may be served in a special education program conducted under Part B.

A. *Description of Part B*

Part B requires SEAs and LEAs to make a free appropriate public education (FAPE) available to all eligible children with disabilities and to ensure that the rights and protections of Part B are extended to those children and their parents. 20 U.S.C. 1412 (2); 34 CFR 300.121 and 300.2. Under Part B, FAPE, among other elements includes the provision of special education and related services, at no cost to parents, in conformity with an individualized education program (IEP). 34 CFR 300.4

In order to be eligible under Part B, the child must be evaluated in accordance with 34 CFR 300.530-300.534 as having one or more specified physical or mental impairments, and must be found to require special education and related services by reason of one or more of these impairments.[2] 20 U. S. C. 1401(a)(1); 34 DFR 300.5 SEAs and LEAs must ensure that children with ADD who are determined eligible for services under Part B receive special education and related services needs arising from the ADD. A full continuum of placement alternatives, including the regular classroom, must be available for providing special education and related services required in the IEP.

B. *Eligibility for Part B services under the "Other Health Impaired" Category*

The list of chronic or acute health problems included within the definition of "other health impaired" in the Part B regulations is not exhaustive. The term "other health impaired" includes chronic or acute impairments that result in limited alertness, which adversely affects educational performance. Thus, children with ADD should be classified as eligible for services under the "other health impaired" category in instances where the ADD is a chronic or acute health problem that results in limited alertness, which adversely affects educational performance. In other words, children with ADD, where the ADD is a chronic or acute health problem resulting in limited alertness, may be considered disabled under Part B solely on the basis of this disorder within the "other health impaired" category in situations where special education and related services are needed because of the ADD.

C. *Eligibility for Part B services under Other Disability Categories*
Children with ADD are also eligible for services under Part B if the children satisfy the criteria applicable to other disability categories. For example, children with ADD are also eligible for services under the "specific learning disability" category of Part B if they meet the criteria stated in 300.5(b)(9) and 300.541 or under the "seriously emotionally disturbed" category of Part B if they meet the criteria stated in 300.5(b)(8).

III. *Evaluations Under Part B*

A. *Requirements*
SEAs and LEAs have an affirmative obligation to evaluate a child who is suspected of having a disability to determine the child's need for special education and related services. Under Part B, SEAs and LEAs are required to have procedures for locating, identifying and evaluating all children who have a disability or are suspected of having a disability and are in need of special education and related services. 34 CFR 300.128 and 300.220. This responsibility, known as "child find," is applicable to all children from birth through 21, regardless of the severity of their disability.

Consistent with this responsibility and the obligation to make FAPE available to all eligible children with disabilities, SEAs and LEAs must ensure that evaluations of children who are suspected of needing special education and related services are conducted without undue delay. 20 U.S.C. 1412(2). Because of its responsibility resulting from the FAPE and child find requirements of Part B, an LEA may not refuse to evaluate the possible need for special education and related services of a child with prior medical diagnosis of ADD solely by reason of that medical diagnosis. However, a medical diagnosis of ADD alone is not sufficient to render a child eligible for services under Part B.

Under Part B, before any action is taken with respect to the initial placement of a child with a disability in a program providing special education and related services, "a full and individual evaluation of the child's educational needs must be conducted in accordance with requirement of 300.532." 34 CFR 300.531. Section 300.532(a) requires that a child's evaluation must be conducted by a multidisciplinary team, including at least one teacher or other specialist with knowledge in the area of suspected disability.

B. *Disagreements Over Evaluations*
Any proposal or refusal of an agency to initiate or change the identification, evaluation, or educational placement of the child, or the provision of FAPE to the child, is subject to the written prior notice requirements of 34 CFR 300.504-300.505.[3] If a parent disagrees with the LEA's refusal to evaluate a child or the LEA's evaluation and determination that a child does not have a disability for which the child is eligible for services under Part B, the parent may request a due process hearing pursuant to 34 CRF 300.504-300.513 of the Part B regulations.

IV. *Obligations Under Section 504 of SEAs and LEAs to Children with ADD Found Not To Require Special Education and Related Services under Part B*
Even if a child with ADD is found not to be eligible for services under Part B, the requirements of Section 504 of the Rehabilitation Act of 1973 (Section 504) and its implementing regulation at 34 CFR Part 104 may be applicable. Section 504 prohibits discrimination on the basis of handicap by recipients of Federal funds. Since Section 504 is a civil rights law, rather than a funding law, its requirements are framed in different terms than those of Part B. While the Section 504 regulation was written with an eye to consistency with Part B, it is more general, and there are some differences arising from the differing natures of the two laws. For instance, the protections of Section 504 extend to some children who do not fall within the disability categories specified in Part B.

A. *Definition*
Section 504 requires every recipient that operates a public elementary or secondary education program to address the needs of children who are considered "handicapped persons" under Section 504 as adequately as the needs of nonhandicapped persons are met. "Handicapped person" is defined in the Section 504 regulation as any person who has a physical or mental impairment which substantially limits a major life activity (e.g., learning). 34 CFR 104.3(j). Thus, depending on the severity of their condition, children with ADD *may* fit within that definition.

B. *Programs and Services Under Section 504*
Under Section 504, an LEA must provide a free appropriate public education to each qualified handicapped child. A free

appropriate public education, under Section 504, consists of regular or special education and related aids and services that are designed to meet the individual student's needs and based on adherence to the regulatory requirements on educational setting, evaluation, placement, and procedural safeguards. 34 CFR 104.33, 104.34, 104.35, and 104.36. A student may be handicapped within the meaning of Section 504, and therefore entitled to regular or special education and related aids and services under the Section 504 regulation, even though the student may not be eligible for special education and related services under Part B.

Under Section 504, if parents believe that their child is handicapped by ADD, the LEA must evaluate the child to determine whether he or she is handicapped as defined by Section 504. If an LEA determines that a child is not handicapped under Section 504, the parent has the right to contest that determination. If the child is determined to be handicapped under Section 504, the LEA must make an individualized determination of the child's educational needs for regular or special education or related aids and services. 34 CFR 104.35. For children determined to be handicapped under Section 504, implementation of an individualized education program developed in accordance with Part B, although not required, is one means of meeting the free appropriate public education requirements of Section 504.[4] The child's education must be provided in the regular education classroom unless it is demonstrated that education in the regular environment with the use of supplementary aids and services cannot be achieved satisfactorily. 34 CFR 104.34.

Should it be determined that the child with ADD is handicapped for purposes of Section 504 and needs only adjustments in the regular classroom, rather than special education, those adjustments are required by Section 504. A range of strategies is available to meet the educational needs of children with ADD. Regular classroom teachers are important in identifying the appropriate educational adaptations and interventions for many children with ADD.

SEAs and LEAs should take the necessary steps to promote coordination between special and regular education programs. Steps also should be taken to train regular education teachers and other personnel to develop their awareness about ADD and its manifestations and the adaptations that can be implemented in regular education programs to address the instructional needs of these children. Examples of adaptations in regular education programs could include the following:

> following a structure learning environment; repeating and simplifying instructions about in-class and homework assignments; supplementing verbal instructions with visual instructions; using behavioral management techniques; adjusting class schedules modifying test delivery; using tape recorders, computer-aided instruction, and other audio-visual equipment; selecting modified textbooks or workbooks; and tailoring homework assignments.

Other provisions range from consultation to special resources and may include reducing class size; use of one-on-one tutorials; classroom aides and note takers; involvement of a "services coordinator" to oversee implementation of special programs and services; and possible modification of nonacademic times such as lunchroom, recess, and physical education.

Through the use of appropriate adaptations and interventions in regular classes, many of which may be required by Section 504, the Department believes that LEAs will be able to effectively address the instructional needs of many children with ADD.

C. *Procedural Safeguards Under Section 504*

Procedural safeguards under the Section 504 regulation are stated more generally than in Part B. The Section 504 regulation requires the LEA to make available a system of procedural safeguards that permits parents to challenge actions regarding the identification, evaluation, or educational placement of their handicapped child whom they believe needs special education or related services. 34 CFR 104.36. The Section 504 regulation requires that the system of procedural safeguards include notice, and opportunity for the parents or guardian to examine relevant records, an impartial hearing with opportunity for participation by the parents or guardian and representation by counsel, and a review procedure. Compliance with procedural safeguards of Part B is one means of fulfilling the Section 504 requirement.[5] However, in an impartial due process hearing raising issues under the Section 504 regulation, the impartial hearing officer must make a determination based upon that regulation.

V. *Conclusion*

Congress and the Department have recognized the need for providing information and assistance to teachers, administrators, parents and other interested persons regarding the identification, evaluation, and instructional needs of children with ADD. The Department has formed a work group to explore strategies across principal offices to address this issue. The work group also plans to identify some ways that the Department can work with the education associations to cooperatively consider the programs and services needed by children with ADD across special and regular education.

In fiscal year 1991, the Congress will appropriate funds for the Department to synthesize and disseminate current knowledge related to ADD. Four centers will be established in Fall, 1991, to analyze and synthesize the current research literature on ADD relating to identification, assessment, and interventions. Research syntheses will be prepared in formats suitable for educators, parents and researchers. Existing clearinghouses and networks, as well as Federal, State and local organizations will be utilized to disseminate these research syntheses to parents, educators and administrators, and other interested persons.

In addition, the Federal Resource Center will work with SEAs and the six regional resource centers authorized under the Individuals with Disabilities Education Act to identify effective identification and assessment procedures, as well as intervention strategies being implemented across the country for children with ADD. A document describing current practice will be developed and disseminated to parents, educators and administrators, and interested persons through the regional resource centers network, as well as by parent training centers, other parent and consumer organizations, and professional organizations. Also, the Office for Civil Rights' ten regional offices stand ready to provide technical assistance to parents and educators.

It is our hope that the above information will be of assistance to your State as you plan for the needs of children with ADD who require special education and related services under Part B, as well as for the needs of the broader group of children with ADD who do not qualify for special education and related services under Part B, but for whom special education or adaptations in regular education programs are needed.

◆ Notes

1. While we recognize that the disorders ADD and ADHD vary, the term ADD is being used to encompass children with both disorders.

2. The Part B regulations define 11 specified disabilities. 34 CFR 300.5 (b) (1)-(11). The Education of the Handicapped Act Amendments of 1990 amended the Individuals with Disabilities Education Act (formerly the Education of the Handicapped Act) to specify that autism and traumatic brain injury are separate disability categories. *See* section 602(a)(1) of the Act, to be modified at 20 U.S.C. 1401 (a)(1).

3. Section 300.505 of the Part B regulations sets out the elements that must be contained in the prior written notice to parents:

(1) A full explanation of all of the procedural safeguards available to the parents under Subpart E;

(2) A description of the action proposed or refused by the agency, an explanation of why the agency proposes or refuses to take action and a description of any options the agency considered and the reasons why those options were rejected;

(3) A description of each evaluation procedure, test, record, or report the agency uses as a basis for the proposal or refusal; and

(4) A description of any other factors which are relevant to the agency's proposal or refusal. 34 CFR 300.505(a)(1)-(4).

4. Many LEAs use the same process for determining the needs of students under Section 504 that they use for implementing Part B.

5. Again, many LEAs and some SEAs are conserving time and resources by using the same due process procedures for resolving disputes under both laws.

APPENDIX D
Strategies for Dealing with Troublesome ADHD Behaviors

Following are specific strategies for parents/teachers to use in developing a plan to address students' needs. The specific behavior is followed by various suggested strategies for dealing with it.

Poor Organizational and Planning Skills

- Require that the student have daily, weekly, and/or monthly assignment sheets and lists of materials needed.
- Require that the student have a notebook or folders for each subject. Assist the student in indexing it.
- Assign projects within specified time frames. Assign easy tasks which can be completed in a short time in the beginning. Gradually assign tasks requiring more time.
- Break the task into workable and manageable steps.
- Provide examples and specific steps to accomplish the task.

Losing Things Necessary for Activities

This includes items for activities at school and at home; for example, pencils, books, and assignments lost before, during, or after completion.

- Help the student organize materials so they are kept in a specific place (e.g. pens and pencils in a pouch). Provide boxes, bins, bags, etc., to help the student organize his or her work.
- Frequently monitor notebook and dividers, pencil pouch, locker, book bag, and desk. Emphasize that there is a place for everything and everything should be in its place.

Lack of Follow-Through in Finishing or Bringing Back Homework

- Help the student to prioritize assignments and activities by providing examples of prioritizing. Post the model and refer to it often.
- Increase the frequency of positive reinforcements. Catch the student doing right and let him or her know it.
- Make frequent checks for work/assignment completion.
- Assign a peer to help the student with homework.
- Allow the student to keep an extra set of books at home.
- Send homework assignments and materials home with someone other than the student (e.g. brother or sister, neighbor, etc.).
- Provide written schedules or checklists, possibly broken down by tasks. Have the student cross off items when completed to promote a sense of accomplishment.

Interrupting and Being Disruptive

- Seat the student in close proximity to the teacher so that the teacher can visually and physically monitor student behavior.
- Describe the desired behavior in explicit terms and make expectations clear.
- Establish rules for class participation and conduct. Explain the rationale for the rules and consequences for violation.
- Insist that the student listen to a complete explanation before asking questions, commenting, or beginning work.
- Establish and maintain eye contact.
- Shorten instruction times between discussion periods.
- Help the student identify alternative words or actions to use in times of stress.
- Do not encourage this behavior by tolerating it. Address the problem immediately.
- Draw up a behavior contract with the student who is having difficulty. Establish amounts of time, starting small and gradually increasing, in which the student must control behavior. Be sure to follow up on this both with rewards and punishments.
- Isolate the student who is having repeated difficulty.

Frequent Involvement in Risky Behaviors

- Anticipate dangerous situations and plan for them in advance.

- Pair the student with a more responsible peer. Rotate responsible students so they do not become intolerant and impatient.
- Reinforce critical safety rules as often as possible.
- Explain direct and indirect consequences of risky behavior (such as establishing a bad reputation, invoking limited privileges, developing poor peer relations, getting poor grades, or having problems getting and holding a job).
- Relate circumstances where an accident or near catastrophe took place due to someone's lack of awareness.

Noncompliance with Rules in Unstructured Settings

This applies in settings such as the playground, lunchroom, and bus.

- Encourage organized clubs or planned playground activities during lunchtime.
- Seat the student in close proximity to an authority figure (e.g. lunch monitor, bus driver).
- Assign the student a special responsibility after he or she finishes lunch.
- Seat the student next to a positive role model.
- Discuss any problem in private with the student.
- Avoid direct confrontation with the student in front of classmates.

Tendencies toward Overly Dependent Behaviors

Attempt to reduce the desirability of teacher attention by stressing the value of independent work habits.

- Remember to reinforce students for not seeking attention by providing attention when it is not demanded. This is easy to forget when the student is working alone, but it is very effective.
- Ignore demands for attention that are dependency-related, explaining that you will get back to the student after the work is completed.
- Establish a nonverbal cue with students to tell them that you recognize them—nod, smile, make eye contact, walk towards them. Reduce nonverbal cues as the need decreases.
- Arrange out-of-class time for personal attention.
- Have students work through a task once with a peer and then redo it independently.

- Express belief that the student can successfully work independently.

Inattentiveness

- Draw a student's attention during instruction by writing on the board, using charts, or otherwise providing a visual stimulus.
- Provide personal cues such as maintaining eye contact, touching the student's shoulder, etc., to keep the student's attention.
- Give short rather than long instruction periods and intersperse hands-on activities between instructional sequences.
- Vary instructional techniques: presentations, assignments with a buddy, cooperative educational groups, puppetry, experiments, visual aides, etc.
- Do not deviate from the subject matter; reword main concepts frequently.

Difficulty Staying in Seat or Study Area—Antsiness

- Outline the study area with chalk or masking tape if necessary.
- Make sure the student knows the teacher's expectations for time spent in the study area and appropriate reasons for leaving.
- If possible, place the student in a study area free of distractions.
- Move around the room to be physically close to the student, and answer questions as they arise.
- Build in appropriate opportunities for movement; provide structured breaks.
- Develop a nonverbal cue to let the student know he or she is off task.
- Restructure tasks that are beyond the student's independent work level.
- Limit (as much as possible) extraneous noise in the classroom. Reduce distractions. Isolate the student if necessary.
- For the student's personal awareness, identify the frequency of distracting behaviors. Work with him or her to decrease the amount of off-task behavior.

Dishonesty

- Avoid accusing the student in front of the class. Do not allow other students to publicly accuse the student.

- Clearly identify the consequences for cheating and be consistent with follow-through.
- Prevent the need or the opportunity for cheating by requiring original work only under circumstances you can control.
- Give alternative types of tests which are less competitive or stressful, such as open-book tests, take-home exams, or projects.
- Look objectively at the criteria for success and failure in your program to assure that they are fair and reasonable.

Poor Self-Concept

- Find out the student's strengths and build on those; ask questions; attend an extra-curricular activity in which the student is involved; demonstrate a level of interest in the student.
- Voice your approval of good work habits, positive growth in any area, and work well done. Recognize small changes.
- Encourage the student to talk about himself or herself. Make note of comments you can turn to positive actions in the classroom.
- Recognize the student regularly by greeting him or her daily, asking about weekends or holidays, etc.
- Establish a climate of fairness and support for the student.

Poor Medication Compliance

- Assign a staff member (e.g. secretary, health aide) to remind the student to take medication (if this is not already required by district or state policy).
- Provide the teacher with the child's medication schedule.
- Give verbal praise.
- Have the school nurse educate the student on the benefits of taking a particular medication.
- Have the child wear a digital watch with an alarm as a reminder.
- Use a school/home reward system for complying with medication.

These materials were adapted from the "ADD Teacher Resource Guide" prepared by the Kenosha Unified School District No. 1, Kenosha, Wisconsin.

APPENDIX E

Techniques to Enhance High School Instruction

(Reprinted by permission of the Michigan Department of Education, Office of Special Education, 608 W. Allegan, Lansing, MI 48909, from the public document "Attention Deficit Disorder: ADHD Task Force Report," 1993.)

English Literature

1. Try listening to taped or recorded stories while following in the text.
2. Use a small group of class members to be the readers (by parts or sections to the rest of the class), Reader's Theater technique.
3. Pair readers for reading assignments—put a good or average reader with a poor reader. Use cooperative learning groups to enhance students' strengths.
4. Have the teacher or an excellent reader read orally to the class and let students follow along in the text.
5. Use comic books, student or simplified (version) synopses, films, and filmstrips with classics to encourage attention to the task.
6. For severe reading problems, obtain the Talking Books for the Blind.
7. If parents are cooperative, try to enlist a family member to read to their youngsters with a reading problem.
8. Utilize tutors outside of class—volunteers from school, community, senior citizens' groups, etc.
9. Review lessons frequently to build the sequence for students having some difficulty following the story line.

Written Language

The highest form of language competence is expressive writing. It is a complex process requiring the integration of memory, sequencing, organization, vocabulary, grammar, handwriting, spelling, ideation, and conceptualization. Skills in this area must be taught with careful planning, deliberate step-by-step instruction, and evaluation and feedback.

1. Encourage students to report experiences, share feelings, describe pictures, and participate in interviews and dramatic presentations.
2. Provide a variety of experiences to talk about words and develop an understanding of connotative as well as denotative meanings. Additional activities include: organizing, classifying, reordering a set of sentences to tell a story in a logical order, and reporting events of a story in sequence.
3. Assist the transition from oral to written language. Experiences are reported to the teacher, who writes them in the students' own words. Once the story is written down, it is read out loud to the student. Students begin to understand the written language process.
4. Help the students use a "process cycle" of prewriting, drafting, editing, and sharing.
5. Consider separating the content from the mechanics. The two can be evaluated separately.
6. Consider requiring and evaluating, but not grading the rough draft. Teachers can make positive comments, note errors, and make suggestions for further improvement. This encourages students to continue to strive to do their best.
7. Provide instruction in outlining. Although this is a prewriting skill, many students are unable to outline prior to writing. Outlining helps students complete a thinking process that facilitates organization.
8. Give students a partial, small assignment and then encourage them to try a longer piece of writing.

Math

Many of the problems with math encountered by students with ADHD stem from fear, awe of too much material, or lack of organization in how to attack the material. To help:

1. Assign fewer problems. If pressured by other students, assign all students varying amounts of work (alternate problems, 1–15, another group 15–30, etc., random numbered problems, etc.)
2. Have students fold paper into lines, quarters or halves, and just work the problems on the part of the paper that shows until the whole page is done.
3. Use a tutor who prepares a sheet with wider spacing and fewer problems per page.
4. Have student work a problem out and use a calculator to check it. If student didn't get it right, he/she can ask for help. The emphasis

is on the process because he/she knows the calculator will give the right answer. This is motivating for student.

5. A student often can tell what kind of day he/she is having if asked. When giving an assignment or sheet of problems, have the student write at the top, how many can be done correctly. Then let the student work them, correct them, and see if he/she has met the goal. Proceed gradually to greater numbers.

6. For story problems, have the student read the problem and underline key words and phrases. Or, have someone read story problems aloud to the student with ADHD.

7. If problems are mixed up (e.g. addition, subtraction, etc., on one page), point this out by underlining, circling, or using highlighter on the operational sign to forewarn students. Gradually phase out the use of clues.

8. Set up a system (checklist, if you will) of how to attack a math problem. Put up a chart to which students can refer.

Reading/Study Skills

1. Always introduce new words by going over their dictionary meanings and explaining how the words are related to what students will be reading.

2. Review words occasionally. Do not expect mastery after one introduction.

3. Determine the reading level of your text. If it is too high for some of your students, assign portions of assignments, reading pairs, or something which is near students' reading level. Never expect a student to read and comprehend something very much above his/her reading level.

4. Guide students' reading with meaningful questions.

5. Teach the SQ3R method as a study technique.

S—scan or survey the section to be read.
Q—turn all bold face type into questions, then ask that question.
R—read the passage, answering the question at the end,
R—review what you have read; use the questions at the end of the passage and review the chapter by:
R—reciting them out loud and reciting the answers. (If there are no questions at the end, make up your own from the bold type and recite the answers to those for your review.)

6. Encourage the student to take a sheet of paper before reading or studying and write down everything on his/her mind and place

that at the end of what he/she needs to study. This clears the mind for studying/reading.

Reports

To allow for some individual differences:

1. Let some students do oral reports—this can be done face-to-face, such as one person to others in small groups with each student rating the speaker to a checklist (need to use caution that the checklist is fully understood).
2. Let groups discuss topics and select a reporter to give feedback to the large group.
3. Let a student tape an oral report (which may or may not require a brief written outline).
4. Submit written reports; allow for variations such as illustrations with the report or a series of illustrations with captions which can be substituted for a written report.
5. Write or prepare a report for a younger group of children and go to their class at a prearranged time to give it.

Science

1. Form lab groups with a mixture of students who have varying abilities and talents. (One student may be a skilled reader while another may be good at setting up complicated lab apparatus.)
2. Make science a living thing rather than emphasizing textbook material. Take science out of the classroom.

Social Science

1. Obtain a variety of books covering the various topics that are being studied and individualize poorer readers' assignments to something within their reading ability.
2. Extend the social sciences into the community. Relate history to older people in the area who have community history to tell. In studying the wars, bring in community members who can relate their war experiences (both those who stayed at home and veterans who went abroad).
3. Make social sciences as realistic as possible. If studying the old West, obtain a collection of antiques or artifacts to bring in.

Tests/Evaluations

1. Avoid true-false tests. They emphasize reading and trick reading at that.
2. If possible, change the emphasis in your teaching to learning rather than testing. If a student can do work in class but freezes on tests, find more informal ways to get an accurate assessment of the student's knowledge.
3. Teach what is important and test what is important. Trivia is not the real meaning of education, especially not for students with ADHD.
4. Try not to test too much material at one time. This tends to "overload the circuits." So, shorter more frequent tests are better than infrequent, lengthy exams.
5. Teach and test what your objectives say you will teach and test. A straightforward, no-curves approach will be much easier for students with ADHD to handle.
6. Curb any appetite for pop quizzes as a punishment to make students study. Rather, if you want quizzes, use them with warning and as a means of diagnosing how your students are learning and how you are teaching.
7. If you have presented something new or something difficult, get students' reactions to whether they understood by asking a few simple questions.
8. Use a pictorial test for a change.
9. Interview the student to determine what he/she knows. Grading and evaluation should be open, not a surprise. Try to test according to individual abilities.
10. Give tests orally if students need that type of assistance. This can be done with a teacher, a volunteer, or any other available adult. You can use student assistants, but select carefully and do not use a peer.
11. Tape a test and have a student use a headset in the classroom or just the tape recorder in another room. Responses can either be written or given orally with enough time allowed on tape.

General

1. When working on outlining, instead of two or three pages of a chapter, have the student outline only the two or three paragraphs which are most difficult for him/her.

2. Spelling techniques differ widely, but the most common is writing the word spelled correctly for a specified number of times. In spelling, generally the student is lacking in good memory skills. The extra practice is necessary, but shorten the list of words. Then have students really concentrate on that shorter list. Let them practice both oral and written spelling to see which way they learn best.

3. Correct grammar is difficult to master if a student is accustomed to hearing poor grammar. Do not work on too many changes at one time. Use grammar in games for additional practice. Use spelling and grammar rules. Concentrate on a single grammar rule until it is understood. Allow for lots of practice on each rule.

4. Try making contracts with students regarding work completion. A contract implies input from both parties. A fair contract does not mean that the teacher demands something and the student delivers for some type of reward. The teacher must be willing to hear the student's side of the issue also.

APPENDIX F
Classroom Intervention Checklist

Environmental Adaptations

1. Avoid assigning student to "open classroom" or "split classroom" settings.
2. Seat student where most visual distractions are behind him or her.
3. Seat student away from auditory distractions such as heaters, air conditioners, etc.
4. Seat student near teacher and appropriate role models, but still as part of the group.
5. Surround student by model peers.
6. Create a structured environment with predictable routines.
7. Post class rules in prominent place.
8. Prepare a stimuli-reduced area that all students may use.
9. Allow student to stand at times while working.
10. Provide opportunity for "seat breaks," i.e. run errand, etc.
11. Provide short break between assignments.

Educational/Academic Adaptations

1. Eliminate unnecessary words on tests; use a variety of formats.
2. Capitalize and underline words such as *always, never, not* on test. Avoid negatively stated questions, especially in true and false.
3. Break down lessons into several short segments.
4. Provide student with outlines or class notes.
5. Provide written instructions for lessons.
6. Give more "wait time" (the amount of time you wait for an answer).
7. Permit breaks during tests.
8. When impulsivity on multiple choice tests means the student will not read all choices, have the student eliminate all incorrect responses, rather than choose one correct answer.
9. Allow student to take tests in less distracting environments.

10. Allow student to highlight main ideas in textbooks and jot notes in margins.
11. Encourage computer use.
12. Use checklists that outline directions, steps, or procedures to be followed.
13. Have a more organized student take notes on carbon paper or duplicate their notes.
14. Schedule more demanding classes earlier in the day.
15. Shorten assignments.
16. Ask student to repeat instructions before beginning assignments.
17. Use previewing strategies for reading.
18. If written language is weak, accept nonwritten form for reports (displays, oral projects, etc.).
19. Accept use of typewriter, word processor, tape recorder.
20. Use multiple choice or fill-in questions on tests.
21. Allow use of calculator in math; use graph paper to space numbers; provide immediate feedback.
22. Give specific feedback emphasizing what was done correctly and specific goals for improvement.

Lesson Presentation Adaptations

1. Alternate lessons or classes that require greater auditory attention with those that are more visual or active.
2. Use an interactive teaching approach: introduce information through auditory, visual, and tactile sensory modalities.
3. Use teaching techniques that involve active student participation as opposed to passive listening.
4. Provide advance organizers such as maps, charts, outlines, etc. Use methods that cue students as to the structure of the lesson and expected learning outcomes.
5. Change your teaching style often. Be animated, dramatic, and enthused. Make presentations interesting, novel, and fun.
6. Be less rigid. Allow some restlessness. (ADHD children often attend better if they don't have to focus so much of their energy on sitting still).
7. Provide periodic exercise breaks in longer presentations.
8. Use an active learning approach where the child participates in activities.
9. Use computer-based drills and instructions to supplement your lessons. (ADHD children respond well to computers because they provide frequent, immediate feedback).

10. Don't reinforce speed of responding, but reward the thoughtful "think aloud" approach.
11. Stand near the ADHD child during a lecture to increase interaction with the child, and to hold the child's attention.
12. Make direct eye contact to hold attention.
13. Present more difficult subjects or tasks in the morning when the ADHD child's performance is better.
14. Increase the novelty and interest level of an assignment with the use of color, shape, and texture.
15. Be aware of the time medication is at its peak effectiveness, and have the child do his most difficult work at that time (usually two hours after medication has been given).
16. Teach memory techniques as study strategies (mnemonics, visualization, oral rehearsal, numerous repetitions).
17. Develop classroom routines to facilitate learning and organization.

Organization Adaptions

1. Allow student five minutes at the end of each class to organize books, papers, etc., before beginning next class.
2. Give student extra set of books if he/she has difficulty getting them between home and school for homework.
3. Color code student's materials to help the student keep organized.
4. Use daily or weekly assignment sheets or notebook (with teacher verifying accuracy of assignments recorded).
5. Use calendar to plan long-term assignments.
6. Notify parents immediately at the first sign of missing or incomplete assignments.
7. Use individual assignment charts or books.
8. Develop a reward and consequence system for both in-school work as well as homework completion.
9. Help student develop a system to keep track of completed, incomplete, and corrected work.
10. Provide due dates of assignments each day.
11. Divide longer assignments into sections and provide due dates or times for the completion of each section.
12. Outline steps in checklist form for following directions or procedures. This list should be taped to the desk or kept in a notebook where it is easily accessible.
13. Establish and post a daily classroom routine and schedule.

14. Provide study guides or outlines of the content for which the student needs to be responsible.
15. Have the students organize their desks or lockers on a regular basis. It may help to have them draw a map showing where their items belong. It may also be helpful to have them use a desk or locker organizer. Notebooks and folders also need to be checked regularly.
16. Write the class schedule and assignments for the day on the blackboard (i.e., "in reading we will do small group reading, group practice and partner assignment").
17. Provide a time, at the end of the day, for students to organize their desks and homework materials.
18. Shorten assignments or work periods to coincide with span of attention; use timer.
19. Break long assignments into smaller parts so students can see an end to work.
20. Assist students in setting short-term goals.

Homework

1. Whenever possible, shorten homework assignments. For example, in math, assign one-half of the problems to do at home. This will be less overwhelming and the work has a better chance of being completed.
2. Go over assignments that will be going home. Use both auditory and visual presentations whenever possible (chalkboard, overhead projector, or ditto sheets).
3. Give plenty of time to copy assignments.
4. Institute a homework buddy system where the buddies check each other to make sure the assignments are understood and all necessary materials go home.
5. Set up an assignment sheet or notebook with the student. You might want to include columns for assignment, date due, and corrections turned in. This notebook should be reviewed with the student on a regular basis.
6. Provide study guides or vocabulary lists each week or with each unit so the students know what will be expected, and so they can keep up with the work and not become overwhelmed before exams.
7. Ask for periodic status reports on long-term assignments, such as book reports and research reports.
8. Provide a sequential list of tasks when giving your student an independent assignment.

9. Review successful homework strategies in large group or in cooperative groups.
10. Supervise writing down of homework assignments.
11. Send daily/weekly progress reports home.
12. Giving lesser amount than the rest of the class; i.e., fewer math problems, fewer pages to read, etc.
13. Put only one or two math problems or study questions on a page if necessary.
14. Include in assignments only that material which is absolutely necessary to learn.
15. Check or underline textbook passages which contain the most important facts.
16. Use markers to tell where to start or stop an assignment.
17. Use highlighted textbooks.
18. Give specific questions to guide reading.
19. Show the exact paragraph where information can be found.
20. Establish only a few modest goals.
21. Develop specific strategies to reach goals.
22. Make certain the student's desk is free from all material except what he/she is working on.
23. Accept the student's work as soon as it's completed.
24. Give immediate feedback on tasks or work completed.
25. Keep the number of practice times on any skill to a minimum.
26. Change activities frequently.
27. Have on hand alternate and supplementary materials for optional projects.
28. Give students several alternatives in both obtaining and reporting information: tapes, interviews, reading, experiences, projects, etc.
29. Have frequent, even if short, one-to-one conferences with students.
30. Help students restate what they are responsible for.
31. Help students assess their progress towards completion of work.
32. Assign a peer to help the student with homework.
33. Allow the student additional time to turn in homework assignments.
34. Send homework assignments and materials home with someone other than the student (e.g., brother or sister, neighbor, etc.).
35. Assign small amounts of homework initially, gradually increasing the amount over time.
36. Work a few problems with the student on the given homework assignments(s) in order to serve as a model.

Behavior Adaptations

1. State a specific, one-step command to the child; i.e., "You need to stop talking to Billy." If the child has not complied, give him/her one warning; i.e., "If you don't stop talking to Billy, then you will take a five-minute time-out." Say it exactly like this: "If you don't (do specific command), then you will (have specific consequence)."

   If the child has not complied with the warning within five seconds (count to yourself), implement the consequences. Once the child complies, provide praise or some positive attention to the desired behavior; i.e., "I like it when you follow directions. You did a good job of doing what you were told. I like how you are working quietly by yourself."

2. Implement an individual behavior program and consistently chart progress. You might want to reward with points or privileges for on-task time.

3. Use a kitchen timer to help students stay on task. They can be rewarded when they beat the timer with quality performance as well.

4. Provide short exercise periods after longer work sessions.

5. Establish a secret signal to remind students to return to task. Be sure to praise them when they're on task.

6. Implement a self-monitoring approach to help the student stay on task.

7. Have student chart own instances of appropriate behavior and inappropriate behavior.

8. Develop contracts with the student, parents and teachers to reinforce specific behavior.

9. Implement a social skills program. Many ADHD students are socially imperceptive.

10. Give students choices when possible. They may choose to work on either their math assignment or reading.

11. Praise specific behaviors, avoiding general and vague praise statements.

12. Define classroom rules and expectations regularly.

13. Be as consistent as possible in following through on classroom and individual behavioral programs.

14. Set hourly, daily, weekly, or monthly goals with the student and provide frequent feedback on the student's progress.

15. Use behavior evaluation sheet for students to make a plan of appropriate behavior after repeated instances of inappropriate behavior.

Social Adaptations

1. Use positive practice (vs. punishment) to reinforce desired skills.
2. Praise appropriate behavior.
3. Monitor social interactions.
4. Set up social behavior goals with student and implement a reward program.
5. Prompt appropriate social behavior either verbally or with private signal.
6. Encourage cooperative learning tasks with other students (assure them that group as well as individual rewards are available).
7. Teach prerequisite skills for co-op learning (listening, accepting feedback, praising, giving feedback).
8. Provide classroom group social skills training for skills that are not demonstrated.
9. Reinforce social skills training in natural settings (playground, lunchroom, etc.).
10. Assign special responsibilities to students in presence of peer group so others observe student in a positive light.
11. Use group rewards as an incentive (hero technique).
12. Seat student next to appropriate models.
13. Use study buddies—activities with partners.

APPENDIX G
Case Study Flow Chart

Parent, Teacher, Principal, Psychologist,
SocialWorker, Counselor Notes Attentional Concerns

Consulation Request Made to Building Level Team
(Consultation Form Filled Out)

Discuss Interventions Attempted/Additional
Interventions and Timelines

More Intervention Needed   Intervention Successful

Secure Parent Permission   Continue
ADHD Screening

Building Team Remeets

No Case Study   Case Study

Parent Conference   Multidisciplinary Staffing
Discuss Program Options Not Eligible Eligible

Determine Case Manager
and 504 Plan As Needed   Write   Possible IEP
Set Review Date   504 Plan   *Annual Review*
Yearly Review   *Yearly Review*

          No Services
          Needed

BIBLIOGRAPHY

Abramowitz, A.J., and O'Leary, S.G. "Behavioral Interventions for the Classroom: Implications for Students with ADHD." *School Psychology Review* 20:220–234.

American Psychiatric Association. *Diagnostic and Statistical Manual of Mental Disorders.* 4th ed. Washington, D.C.: American Psychiatric Association, 1994.

Anderson, Winifred., Chitwood, Stephen, and Hayden, Deidre. *Negotiating the Special Education Maze: A Guide for Parents and Teachers.* 2nd ed. Rockville, Md.: Woodbine House, 1990.

Arizona Council for Children with Attention Deficit Disorders. *Attention Deficit Disorder: A Parent's Guide.* Tucson, Ariz.: Council for Children with Attention Deficit Disorders, 1992.

Armstrong, Thomas. *In Their Own Way: Discovering and Encouraging Your Child's Personal Learning Style.* Los Angeles: Jeremy P. Tarcher, 1987.

Barkley, Russell A. *Attention Deficit Hyperactivity Disorder: A Handbook for Diagnosis and Treatment.* New York: Guilford Press, 1990.

———. *ADHD: What Do We Know?* (36-minute video, leader's guide, and manual). New York: Guilford Press, n.d.

———. *ADHD: What Can We Do?* (36-minute video, leader's guide, and manual). New York: Guilford Press, n.d.

———. *ADHD in the Classroom* (36-minute video, leader's guide, and manual). New York: Guilford Press, n.d.

————. *Defiant Children: A Clinicians' Manual for Parent Training.* New York: Guilford Press, 1987.

Bateman, Lawrence, with Riche, Robert. *The Nine Most Troublesome Teenage Problems and How to Solve Them.* New York: Ballantine, 1986.

Becker, W.C. *Parents Are Teachers: A Child Management Program.* Champaign, Ill.: Research Press, 1971.

Briggs, Dorothy Corkville. *Your Child's Self-Esteem.* New York: Dolphin Books, 1975.

Braswell, Lauren, and Bloomquist, Michael. *Cognitive Behavioral Therapy with ADHD Children: Child, Family, and School Interventions.* New York: Guilford Press, 1991.

Camp, Bonnie W., and Bash, Mary Ann S. *Think Aloud: Increasing Social and Cognitive Skills: A Problem Solving Program for Children.* Champaign, Ill.: Research Press, 1981.

Cartledge, Gwendolyn, and Milburn, Joanne Fellows, eds. *Teaching Social Skills to Children and Youth.* 3rd ed. New York: Allyn and Bacon, 1995.

Clabby, John F., and Elias, Maurice J. *Teach Your Child Decision Making.* New York: Doubleday, 1987.

Coons, H. W.; Klorman, R.; and Borgstedt, A. D. "Effects of Methylphenidate on Adolescents with a Childhood History of Attention Deficit Disorder," parts 1 and 2. *Journal of the American Academy of Child and Adolescent Psychiatry,* 26(1987): 363–74.

Copeland, Edna D., and Love, Valerie L. *Attention without Tension: A Teacher's Handbook on Attention Disorders (ADHD and ADD).* Atlanta: 3 C's of Childhood, 1992.

————. *Attention Disorders: The School's Vital Role* (video). Atlanta: Resurgens Press, 1990.

————. *Diverse Teaching for Diverse Learners: A Handbook for Teachers and Parents.* Atlanta: Resurgens Press, 1994.

————. *Medications for Attention Disorders and Related Medical Problems*. Atlanta: Resurgens Press, 1994.

————, and Love, Valerie. *Attention Please: A Comprehensive Guide for Successfully Parenting Children with Attention Disorders and Hyperactivity*. Atlanta: SPI Press, 1991.

Dobson, James. *Hide or Seek: Self-Esteem for the Child and His Family*. Old Tappen, N.J.: Revell, 1974.

DuPaul, George J., and Stoner, Gary. *ADHD in the Schools: Assessment and Intervention Strategies*. New York: Guilford Press, 1994.

Fadely, Jack L., and Hosler, Virginia N. *Attentional Deficit Disorder in Children and Adolescents*. Springfield, Ill.: Charles C. Thomas, 1992.

Fine, Marvin J. *Principles and Techniques of Intervention with Hyperactive Children*. Springfield, Ill.: Charles C. Thomas, 1977.

Forehand, Rex L., and McMahon, Robert J. *Helping the Noncompliant Child: A Clinician's Guide to Parent Training*. New York: Guilford Press, 1981.

Fowler, Mary. *Maybe You Know My Kid: A Parent's Guide to Identifying, Understanding, and Helping Your Child with Attention-Deficit Hyperactivity Disorder*. Secaucus, N.J.: Birch Lane Press, 1990.

Garber, Stephen W.; Garber, Marianne Daniels; and Spizman, Robyn Freedman. *If Your Child Is Hyperactive, Inattentive, Impulsive, Distractible: Helping the ADD Hyperactive Child*. New York: Villard Books, 1990.

————. *Good Behavior: Over 1200 Solutions to Your Child's Problems from Birth to Age Twelve*. New York: Villard Books, 1987.

Galvin, M. *Otto Learns about His Medicine*. New York: Magination Press, 1988.

Gittelman, Martin. *Strategic Interventions for Hyperactive Children*. Armonk, N.Y.: M.E. Sharpe, 1981.

Goldfarb, Lori A.; Brotherson, Mary Jean; Summers, Jean Ann; and Turnbull, Ann P. *Meeting the Challenge of Disability or Chronic Illness—A Family Guide.* Baltimore: Paul H. Brookes, 1986.

Goldstein, Sam, and Goldstein, Michael. *Hyperactivity: Why Won't My Child Pay Attention?* New York: John Wiley and Sons, 1992.

————. *Managing Attention Disorders in Children: A Guide for Practitioners.* New York: John Wiley and Sons, 1990.

Gordon, Michael. *Jumpin' Johnny Get Back to Work: A Child's Guide to ADHD/Hyperactivity.* DeWitt, N.Y.: GSI Publications, 1991.

Gordon, Michael. *My Brother's a World-Class Pain: A Sibling's Guide to ADHD/Hyperactivity.* DeWitt, N.Y.: GSI Publications, 1992.

Greenberg, G.S., and Horn, W.F. *Attention Deficit Hyperactivity Disorder: Questions and Answers for Parents.* Champaign Ill.: Research Press, 1991.

Greenhill, Laurence L., and Shopsin, Baron, eds. *The Psychobiology of Childhood: A Profile of Current Issues.* New York: SP Medical & Scientific Books, 1984.

Hall, R. Vance, and Hall, Marilyn C. *How to Select Reinforcers.* Lawrence, Kans.: H & H Enterprises, 1980.

————. *How to Use Planned Ignoring.* Lawrence, Kans.: H & H Enterprises, 1980.

————. *How to Use Systematic Attention and Approval.* Lawrence, Kans.: H & H Enterprises, 1980.

————. *How to Use Time Out.* Austin: Pro-Ed, 1980.

Hall, R. Vance. *Managing Behavior Part 2: Behavior Modification: Basic Principles.* Austin, Texas: Pro-Ed, 1971.

Hartmann, Thom. *Attention Deficit Disorder: A Different Perception.* Novato, Calif.: Underwood-Miller, 1993.

Ilg, Frances; Ames, Louise Bates; and Baker, Sidney M. *Child Behavior: Specific Advice on Problems of Child Behavior.* New York: Harper & Row, 1992.

Ingersoll, B. *Your Hyperactive Child: A Parent's Guide to Coping with Attention Deficit Disorder.* New York: Doubleday, 1988.

Johnston, Robert B. *Attention Deficits, Learning Disabilities, and Ritalin™.* San Diego, Calif.: Singular Publishing Group, 1991.

Jones, Clare B. *Sourcebook for Children with Attention Deficit Disorder: A Management Guide for Early Childhood Professionals and Parents.* Tucson, Ariz.: Communication Skill Builders, 1991.

Kavanaugh, J., et al., eds. *Learning Disabilities: Proceedings of the National Conference on Learning Disabilities 1987.* Parkton, MD: York Press, 1988.

Kelly, K., and Ramundo, P. *You Mean I'm Not Lazy, Stupid or Crazy?! A Self-help Book for Adults with Attention Deficit Disorder.* Cincinnati, Ohio: Tyrell & Jerem Press, 1993.

Kendall, Philip, and Braswell, Lauren. *Cognitive-Behavioral Therapy for Impulsive Children.* New York: Guilford Press, 1985.

Kennedy, Patricia; Terdal, Leif; and Fusetti, Lydia. *The Hyperactive Child Book.* New York: St. Martin's Press, 1993.

Kirby, Edward A., and Grimley, Liam K. *Understanding and Treating Attention Deficit Disorder.* New York: Pergamon Press, 1986.

Krupp, Judy-Arin, and Parker, Robert. *When Parents Face the Schools.* Manchester, Conn.: Adult Development and Learning, 1984.

Lahey, Benjamin. *Behavior Therapy with Hyperactive and Learning Disabled Children.* New York: Oxford Univ. Press, 1979.

Lavin, Paul. *Parenting the Overactive Child: Alternatives to Drug Therapy.* Lanham, Md.: Madison Books, 1989.

Levine, M.D. *Developmental Variation and Learning Disorders*. Cambridge, Massachusetts: Educators Publishing Service, 1987.

―――. *Keeping Ahead in School: A Student's Book about Learning Abilities and Learning Disorders*. Cambridge, Mass.: Educators Publishing Service, 1987.

McWhirter, J. Jeffries. *The Learning Disabled Child: A School and Family Concern*. Champaign, Ill.: Research Press, 1977.

Mash, Eric J., and Barkley, Russell A.*Treatment of Childhood Disorders*. New York: Guilford Press, 1989.

Moss, D.M. Shelley, *The Hyperactive Turtle*. Kensington, Md.: Woodbine House, 1989.

Moss, Robert A., and Dunlap, Helen H. *Why Johnny Can't Concentrate*. New York: Bantam Books, 1990.

Novick, Barbara A., and Arnold, Maureen M. *Why is My Child Having Trouble at School?* New York: Villard Books, 1991.

Nussbaum, Nancy, and Bigler, Erin. *Identification and Treatment of Attention Deficit Disorder*. Austin, Tex.: Pro-Ed, 1990.

Ogan, Guy D. *Can Anyone Help My Child: Therapies and Treatment for Attention Deficit and Other Learning and Behavioral Disorders in Children, Adolescents, and Adults*. Abilene, Tex.: Faith Publishing, 1994.

O'Leary, Daniel K. *Mommy, I Can't Sit Still: Coping with Hyperactive and Aggressive Children*. Far Hills, N.J.: New Horizon Press, 1984.

Osman, Betty B., with Blinder, Henriette. *No One to Play With*. New York: Warner Books, 1982.

Parker, Harvey C. *The ADD Hyperactivity Workbook for Parents, Teachers, and Kids*. Plantation, Fla.: Impact Publications, 1992.

Parker, Harvey C. *The ADD Hyperactivity Handbook for Schools*. Plantation, Fla.: Impact Publications, 1992.

Patterson, Gerald R., and Gullion, M. Elizabeth. *Living with Children*. Champaign, Ill.: Research Press, 1976.

Pelham, W. E. "What Do We Know about the Use and Effects of CNS Stimulants in the Treatment of ADD?" In *The Young Hyperactive Child: Answers to Questions about Diagnosis, Prognosis, and Treatment.* New York: Haworth Press, 1987.

Pelham, W. E., Bender, M.E., Caddell, J., Booth, S., and Moorer, S. H. "Methylphenidate and Children with Attention Deficit Disorder." *Archives of General Psychiatry,* 42(1985): 948–52.

Phelan, Thomas. *All About Attention Deficit Disorder.* Glen Ellyn, Ill.: Child Management, 1993.

———. *All About Attention Deficit Disorder.* (Video). Glen Ellyn, Ill.: Child Management, 1993.

———. *1-2-3: Magic! Training Your Preschoolers and Preteens to Do What You Want.* Glen Ellyn, Ill.: Child Management, 1984.

———. *1-2-3: Magic! Training Your Preschoolers and Preteens to Do What You Want.* (Video.) Glen Ellyn, Ill.: Child Management, 1990.

Phelan, Thomas, and Bloomberg, Jonathan. *Medication for Attention Deficit Disorder.* Glen Ellyn, Ill.: Child Mangement, 1993.

Phillips, Debora. *How to Give Your Child a Great Self-Image.* New York: Random House, 1989.

Quinn, Patricia O., and Stern, Judith M. *Putting on the Brakes: Young People's Guide to Understanding Attention Deficit Hyperactivity Disorder (ADHD).* New York: Magination Press, 1991.

Rief, Sandra R. *How to Reach and Teach ADD/ADHD Children: Practical Techniques, Strategies, and Interventions for Helping Children with Attention Problems and Hyperactivity.* West Nyack, N.Y.: Center for Applied Research in Education, 1993.

Safer, Daniel J., and Allen, Richard P. *Hyperactive Children: Diagnosis and Management.* Baltimore: Univ. Park Press, 1976.

Schaefer, Charles E., and Millman, Howard L., *How to Help Children with Common Problems.* New York: Van Nostrand Reinhold, New American Library, 1981.

Scott, Sharon. *Peer Pressure Reversal.* Amherst, Mass.: Human Resource Development Press, 1985.

Sheppard, William C.; Shank, Steven B.; and Wilson, Darla. *Teaching Social Behavior to Young Children.* Champaign, Ill.: Research Press, 1973.

Silver, Larry B. *Attention Deficit Hyperactivity Disorder: A Clinical Guide to Diagnosis and Treatment.* Washington, D.C.: American Psychiatric Press, Inc., 1991.

Silver, Larry B. *The Misunderstood Child: A Guide for Parents of Learning Disabled Children.* 2nd ed. Blue Ridge Summit, Pa.: TAB Books, 1992.

Simons, Robin. *After the Tears: Parents Talk about Raising a Child with a Disability.* New York: Harcourt Brace Jovanich, 1987.

Spizman, Robyn Freedman. *Lollipop Grapes and Clothespin Critters: Quick, On-the-Spot Remedies for Restless Children 2–10.* Reading, Mass.: Addison-Wesley, 1985.

Stewart, M., and Olds, S. *Raising a Hyperactive Child.* New York: Harper & Row, 1975.

Taylor, John F. *Helping Your Hyperactive/Attention Deficit Child.* Rocklin, Calif.: Prima Publishing and Communications, 1994.

Taylor, John F. *The Hyperactive Child and the Family: The Complete What-to-do Handbook.* New York: Everest House, 1980.

Teeter, P.A. "Attention-Deficit Hyperactivity Disorder: A Psychoeducational Paradigm." *School Psychology Review* 20(1991): 266–280.

Turecki, Stanley, and Tonner, Leslie. *The Difficult Child.* New York: Bantam Books, 1985.

Watson, Luke S., Jr. *Child Behavior Modification: A Manual for Teachers, Nurses and Parents.* Elmsford, N.Y.: Pergamon Press, 1973.

Weisberg, L.W., and Greenberg, R. *When Acting Out Isn't Acting: Conduct Disorders and ADD.* Washington: PIA Press, 1988.

Weiss, Gabrielle, and Hechtman, Lily Trokenberg. *Hyperactive Children Grown Up*. 2nd ed. New York: Guilford Press, 1993.

Weiss, Lynn. *Attention Deficit Disorder in Adults*. Dallas: Taylor Publishing, 1992.

Wender, Paul H. *The Hyperactive Child, Adolescent, and Adult: Attention Deficit Disorder through the Lifespan*. New York: Oxford University Press, 1987.

Wodrich, David L. *Attention Deficit Hyperactivity Disorder: What Every Parent Wants to Know*. Baltimore, Md.: Paul H. Brookes Publishing Co., 1994.

Wodrich, D.L., and Kush, S.A. *Children's Psychological Testing: A Guide for Nonpsychologists*. 2nd ed. Baltimore: Paul H. Brookes Publishing, 1990.

Zametkin, A.J., and Borcherding, B.G. "The Neuropharmacology of Attention-Deficit Hyperactivity Disorder." *Annual Review of Medicine* 40:447–451.

Zametkin, A.J., and Rapoport, J.L. "Neurobiology of Attention Deficit Disorder with Hyperactivity: Where Have We Come in 50 Years?" *Journal of American Academy of Child and Adolescent Psychiatry* 26:676–686.

INDEX